I0849274

AT THE MERCY
of the
SEA

IYRU

IYRU/WORLD SAILING SPEED RECORD COUNCIL

WORLD RECORD

This is to Certify that:

LISA CLAYTON

In the Yacht:

SPIRIT OF BIRMINGHAM

*Sailed Round the World Single-Handed
Non-Stop*

In an elapsed time of:

285 days 00 hours 26 minutes 27 seconds

Chairman of the Council

*Secretary to
the Council*

5 September 1995

AT THE MERCY
of the
SEA

Lisa Clayton

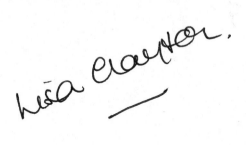

ORION

The right of Lisa Clayton to be identified as the author of this work
has been asserted by her in accordance with the
Copyright, Designs and Patents Act 1988

First published in Great Britain in 1996 by
Orion
An imprint of Orion Books Ltd
Orion House, 5 Upper St Martin's Lane, London WC2H 9EA

A CIP catalogue record for this book is available
from the British Library

ISBN 0 75280 208 9

Filmset by Selwood Systems, Midsomer Norton
Printed in Great Britain by
Butler & Tanner Ltd, Frome and London

For my mother and father
with all my love

Contents

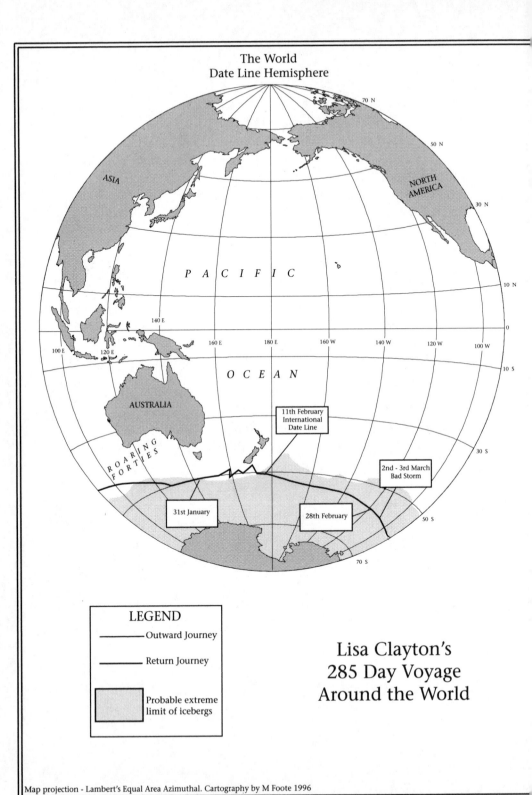

The World
Date Line Hemisphere

70 N

50 N

ASIA

NORTH
AMERICA

30 N

P A C I F I C

10 N

0

140 E

160 E   180 E   160 W   140 W   120 W   100 W

10 S

100 E   120 E

O C E A N

AUSTRALIA

11th February
International
Date Line

30 S

R O A R I N G
F O R T I E S

2nd - 3rd March
Bad Storm

31st January

28th February

50 S

70 S

LEGEND

—————— Outward Journey

————— Return Journey

Probable extreme
limit of icebergs

Lisa Clayton's
285 Day Voyage
Around the World

Map projection - Lambert's Equal Area Azimuthal. Cartography by M Foote 1996

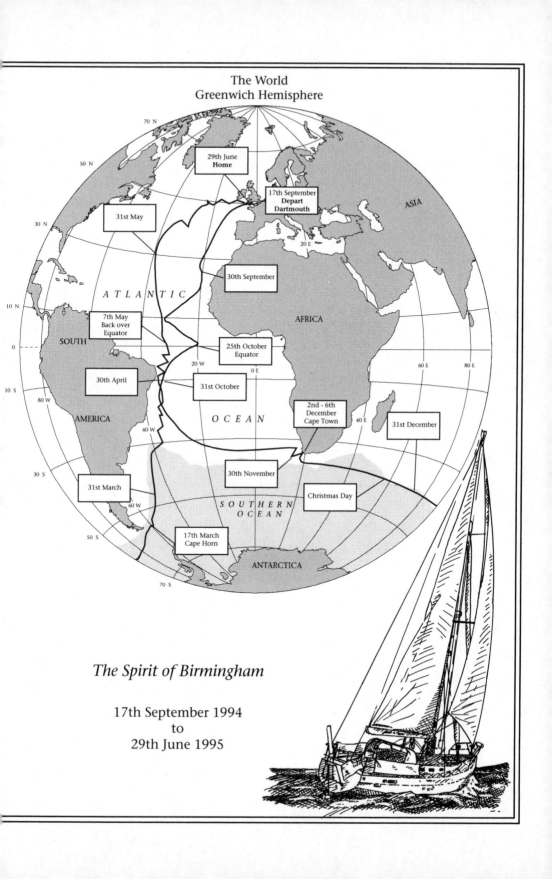

The World
Greenwich Hemisphere

29th June
Home

17th September
**Depart
Dartmouth**

31st May

30th September

7th May
Back over
Equator

25th October
Equator

30th April

31st October

2nd - 6th
December
Cape Town

31st December

30th November

31st March

Christmas Day

17th March
Cape Horn

The Spirit of Birmingham

17th September 1994
to
29th June 1995

Acknowledgements

My whole venture was made possible by the tremendous support I received from many, many people. It would take another book to thank everyone individually, but include....

'The Team'
My parents, Dan and Gwen Clayton, my brother Paul, sister Sara and also David Stone.

A very special thank you goes to Peter Harding for his tremendous contribution to making the project a success.

Carl Hingley and Jason Pinder.

Sponsors and Supporters who include:

The University of Birmingham – who played such a key part – and also:–

Alexander Engineering Co. Limited
Ampair
Doug Angell
Ansell Jones Limited
Arden Timber
Armac
Barber Bros
Peter Barwell JP (Past Lord Mayor of
   Birmingham)
The Very Rev. Peter Berry
Bespoke Picture Framing Service
Birmingham City Council
Birmingham College of Food
Birmingham Evening Mail
Blakes Paints
Bloomer Heaven

Brass Fittings Limited
British Airways
British Broadcasting Corporation –
   Television and Radio
British Telecom
Britool Limited
Dick Bruff
Burts of Birmingham
Butcher & Baker Foods Limited
John Butlin Transport Limited
Bracknell Met Office
CBC
Calor Gas Limited
Canon UK Limited
Richard Cariss
Castle Communications

Charrington's Marine
Charter Heaven
Geoff Chester
Chillington Marine
Climbers Shop Limited
Coffeepoint
Copthorne Hotel
Cosalt
CPC (UK) Limited
Darthaven Marina
Dogwatch
ETA Circuit Breakers Limited
Edgbaston Church of England College for Girls
Doug Ellis (Chairman of Aston Villa F.C.)
Eurospars Limited
Exchange and Mart
F.G.F. (Aston) Limited
Falmouth Coast Guard
Flavel Leisure
Angela Franklin Associates
Ken Franklin
5th Battalion of the Royal Regiment of Fusiliers
Global Cathodic Protection
Grayston White & Sparrow
Peter Gross
Grundig International Limited
H. K. L. Gas Power Limited
HMS Exploit
Harnessflex Limited
Hayward Sailcloth
Henri-Lloyd Limited
Icom (UK) Limited
Intec Lazer Services
Intercity Mobile Communications Limited
John James

H. E. Jones Limited
Jotron Radio Search W. D.
Joe Jordan
Peter Kemp
Kimble Engineering Limited
John Knight Signs
Latch & Bachelor
Lewmar Marine Limited
Guy Litherland
Gordon Love Trailers
All the 'Land Crew'
M.E.B.
M. L. Lifeguard Equipment Limited
M.T.I.
Marlow Ropes Limited
Joseph Mason plc
Bill and Jean Melling
Mulvihill Mitchell
Munster Simms Engineering Limited
National Westminster Bank
OCE Copiers
Oceanroutes (UK) Limited
Omega Watch Co. Limited
Liz Osborne
Pains Wessex Limited
Pertemps
J. L. Pinder & Son
Plymco Superstore
Portishead Radio
W. H. Price
Prontoprint – Birmingham
Raytheon Marine Europe
Risol Limited
Rotary Printers
Rover Cars
Councillor David Roy (Past Lord Mayor of Birmingham)
Royal Cape Yacht Club
Royal Dart Yacht Club

Ricky and Roundy Rudell
S. F. Protection Limited
Rodney & Mike Salmon
Scanmar Marine Products
Sea-Fresh Watermaker Systems
Sharps Tooling Limited
E. C. Smith & Son (Marine Factor)
Sonnenschein UK
South Birmingham Area Health
   Authority
Sta-Lok Terminals
Sterling Marine Power
Tamed and Framed
Teighbridge Propulsion Group
Councillor Paul Tilsley MBE (Past Lord
   Mayor of Birmingham)
Tony Timberlake
Toomer & Hayter Limited

Torbay Hospital
Travel Trade Gazette
Richard Uridge
VDO Instruments
John Venus
Volvo Cars UK Limited
Volvo Penta UK Limited
Wainwrights (Electricians)
James Walker & Co
Gerald & Lynda Walsh
Webasto Heating Limited
Westaway Sails Limited
Western Marine Power Limited
Whitlock Marine Steering Co. Limited
Robert Wilkinson
John & Amanda Wilmott/Bulls Head –
   Wootton Wawen
Works Bookshop

And many hundreds of individuals in the West Midlands, Kingswear, Devon, and throughout the Country.

Grateful acknowledgement is also made to the UK Hydrographic Office for permission to reproduce material from *Ocean Passages*; to Random House (UK) Ltd for permission to reproduce material from *At One with the Sea* by Naomi James published by Stanley Paul; and to Curtis Brown Ltd London on behalf of Francis Chichester Ltd for their permission to reproduce material from *The Lonely Sea and the Sky*.

Preface

4.30 a.m. and suddenly I'm awake. I can hear whispering voices outside – God, they're here already – oh well, let them wait. I have to get myself organised if I'm going to be ready to leave at 10 a.m. My mind is awash with all that I still have left to do, but as the shower pelts down on to my head, my mind gradually untangles until I have a clear plan of attack. First to the boat, and then back to finish packing my last bits and pieces. It sounds as though I am not the only one in the cottage who can't sleep. That's good, it means the kettle should be hot for a quick drink. Down in the kitchen two surprised faces look at me, then at each other – they didn't expect me down this early. Seeing their embarrassment, I can feel my sense of humour returning. It's too late of course, I've seen what they are up to, but realising no one knows what to do next I ask them if they'd like coffee. A couple of quick 'yes's direct me to reheat the water. Not much is said, meaningful glances pass between the two, and by mutual agreement they give in. How can they hide the fact that they are busily wrapping presents which are obviously for me? Feeling just a little guilty I avert my eyes as I pass by, taking my coffee with me to drink outside and enjoy the sunrise over the river.

As I open the door, it's no surprise to see the BBC film crew but I'm really not feeling in the mood just now, so with a cheeky 'Doesn't look too nice out here today' I immediately shut it again and go back inside. Everyone bursts out laughing as some of the tension slips away. Quite openly now, my sister Sara and Peter Harding, my project director, finish wrapping my 'surprise' presents. Then we all troop outside to have coffee with Ewan and Ian from the BBC and watch other yachts leaving for unknown destinations and the fishing boats coming in after a cold night at sea. The swans are there again – how strange, they seem to have been with me since the boat was launched. Much as we would like to idle the morning away there just isn't time. Mum and Dad are now up and about

1

and the cottage is starting to buzz with a frenzy of activity.

There's still so much to do. It's going to be a difficult day – one I'll never forget – and it will undoubtedly be a strain on all of us.

The morning rushes by. At 7.30 it's time to take *Spirit* to the fuel barge to fill up the tanks before motoring down to the Royal Dart Yacht Club to tie up before anyone arrives.

With the fast-ebbing tide it's a difficult landing at the yacht club but soon she is secure and settled. She seems to be very full of her own importance this morning as she lightly dances on the water and sparkles in the early morning sun.

Content that *Spirit* is ready, it's time to return to the cottage and make sure I am totally organised myself. But as I leave the jetty I am swamped by cameras and journalists, all wanting just a few minutes, just a few words. It seems to take for ever to travel the few yards from the pontoon to the cottage. I hadn't expected this and certainly not so early. I don't feel together enough to be giving beaming smiles and making witty comments.

There are lots of friends and wellwishers already here too, each ready with an encouraging word, but I'm still too preoccupied to do much more than smile and say a passing hello.

Retreating back into the seclusion of the cottage, I find Mum and Sara cooking a healthy-sized English breakfast. I really can't face it though – for that matter nobody seems very hungry.

I finish packing my bag and have a last quick look round – have I forgotten anything? One last interview on the radio then all too soon it's countdown time. Peter is ushering me out the door – what's happening now? And suddenly reality dawns.

As I step outside the bagpiper starts up and to the haunting sound of his music I start the final walk. The throng parts as I slowly make my way towards the pontoon and *Spirit*. The Provost of Birmingham, the Very Reverend Peter Berry, is there, Bible in one hand and holy water in the other. If I hadn't been so anxious I would have laughed. With so many people on the floating pontoon it's sinking and water is washing over the Provost's impeccably shiny shoes as he staunchly blesses the boat, says a prayer for my safe return and hands me a copy of the Scriptures.

I'm feeling wretched and tearful as I hug my sister and brother. Then it's time to say goodbye to my parents. Hardly any words are spoken but the love and caring is there in the tightness of our embrace. Brushing away my tears I turn towards *Spirit*. As I step on board I feel my first real emotion of the day and realise I'm nervous. My hands are shaking and my legs have turned to water.

The sailmaker and his crew help me as my old friend, Peter Lucas, tows *Spirit* away from the pontoon, and into the centre of the River Dart. The mainsail is up, there are boats everywhere, and I can see my family and close friends are now on the bridge of HMS *Exploit* to follow me out to sea.

Well, this is it. Peter is the last to make his difficult farewell, tells me to take care, takes the fenders off (I won't be needing those) and jumps on to the waiting launch.

I'm on my own – surrounded by hundreds of wellwishers.

It's hard work at first making my way under sail to the river entrance with so many boats about and so little wind, but soon I'm at the castle – the cannon goes off and everyone hoots their horns. This is really it. My adventure has started.

Three hours into the 30,000 mile journey and the full impact of what I am doing hits me. How on earth did I get to be here …?

Part one

Beginnings

I came into the world at some ungodly hour on 30 December 1958. Selly Oak Hospital in Birmingham was the first place I laid my eyes on though I can honestly say I remember nothing of it.

I found I already had an elder brother, Paul, and fourteen months after my introduction to the world my sister Sara arrived. Paul was great. Very good looking and clever, he was determined to look after, but never be overshadowed by, his younger sisters.

Sara was a poppet, and with the face of an angel soon had everyone oohing and aahing. She was an absolute sweetie, and whilst I am sure Mum and Dad loved us all equally, there was no doubt between Paul and me that Sara was the little goody two shoes. So whenever trouble loomed on the horizon we gently used to persuade Sara to admit to being the culprit. 'What have you got to lose?' we'd say. 'We'll each give you a penny if you own up and they'll never believe you really did it so you won't get into trouble like we would.' She was also the only one of us three who had enough charm to stand her ground and, balancing on her little tree-stump legs, say 'no' to Mum and Dad and get away with it.

I was always laughing and before the age of three my parents had already decided that I would end up working behind a bar. Never aware of the value of possessions, I was always happy to give away what I had. All three of us got on famously.

To give us the very best start in life Mum and Dad decided to pay for our education and sent us all to Rathvilly to be schooled during our first formative years.

When I was still very young we moved to the Lickey Hills just south of Birmingham to a house with a vast garden and, hiding at the very bottom cloaked from view by the magnificent trees, our prize possession – a swimming pool.

Our parents were great, very young at heart and full of fun. They started the tradition of Sunday swimming parties, providing a great excuse to meet up with everyone and enjoy a few drinks.

As the years passed we three started to grow up and shed a few of our sweeter qualities for the harder edges required to cope with the teenage world. It seemed to us that our parents were going through a difficult phase too as nearly everything we did seemed to cause aggravation. We'd hold pow-wows in Paul's attic room, moaning between ourselves about how awkward and unfair they were becoming, and practised for hours in front of the mirror until we had perfected 'the look' – the glaring eyes, the hurt look on the face – the message of which was clear: 'How could you possibly be so unreasonable!'

Happily, we soon grew out of it and started to realise how fortunate we were. Fancy having parents who gave such great parties and didn't object to us bringing our friends along! But we weren't perfect by any means and I really don't know how they coped with us all fighting for our independence.

In a bid to ensure that we at least held a modicum of ladylike qualities, Sara and I were sent to Edgbaston Church of England College for Girls. I can't say we were the best-behaved young ladies there but we were certainly far from the worst. Well educated and well groomed, we left full of self-confidence for the life ahead.

By then we were living in Barnt Green, and I went on to Bromsgrove College for two years to study for a diploma in Business Studies. What fun it was – I knew a lot of the other students and was soon encouraging them to take more enjoyment from their time. It was a wonderful era. Dressed up in our full-length Laura Ashley dresses and straw hats with flowing ribbons we would frequent each others' houses and the local Barnt Green Inn.

Luckily I am one of those people who is bright enough to pass without trying too hard. Many of the others weren't so fortunate. After my diploma I was all set up to lounge around for the next year or two, but my mother had other plans and before I knew where I was I found myself working as a trainee at a chartered accountant's in Bromsgrove.

With the naivety of youth I was convinced my life was mapped out for me and could easily envisage myself in years to come. I was wrong. Over the next five years my life changed dramatically.

In 1978 at the tender age of nineteen I married Rod. His family were lovely and with Rod's sense of fun to match my own we enjoyed the luxury of our newfound freedom. We earned enough between us to be financially independent and this was topped up with the privilege of being able to use his family's private box at Cheltenham races and their summer home in West Wittering. Life was good and we liked each other a lot, but something seemed to be missing, so after four years we agreed to go our own ways. It was a terrible experience for both of us, but as time went by the hurt lessened and we started to get over the trauma of the split. With hindsight I think we just got married too young, and at least we have remained great friends.

By now I had decided that a life as a chartered accountant wasn't for me and I was working for a holiday company – still on the financial side but it was a move in the right direction. I'd also purchased a small flat close to the office. By the age of twenty-three my whole world revolved around work. I was getting on well in my new career with Horizon Holidays in Birmingham and used to fly off for the odd weekend with my mum or a friend from work. However, I was never tempted to take the four weeks that I was entitled to. What would I do with it?

My limited social life almost totally depended on colleagues at work, although much as I enjoyed their company I wasn't totally enamoured by it. Life seemed to be lacking something – but what? I had a good job in a great company with lots of perks and nice people around, so why was I discontented? I'd been invited to join in with lots of different things – hot-air ballooning, sailing – but I felt a little apathetic about it all. I was bored and couldn't make the effort.

Then one Friday morning when I was just on the verge of again refusing an offer from the managing director, Ken Franklin, to try sailing, I found myself saying 'yes'. Returning to my desk I wondered at my stupidity. Who wanted to spend a weekend sailing, for goodness' sake? It seemed so boring. I wasn't worried that I would be a totally useless piece of baggage on the yacht, as Ken had said it was just a matter of drinking gin and tonics at sea instead of on land, and I knew I could fulfil that requirement! The weather forecast was grim but I had agreed now and I wasn't about to go back on my word.

As I sat there at my desk I couldn't help but smile to myself. Who was I trying to kid? Why didn't I just admit to myself that it was to be with Ken that I was going at all? I admired him tremendously: he was intelligent; he didn't try to impress people but was all the more impressive for it; he had a sparkle in his eye that hinted at a sense of fun, and he packed a lot into his life. He was separated from his wife, *but* he was my boss. Still, there was no harm getting to know him a bit better and becoming friends. So off I went to purchase some wellies and a few warm jumpers.

I had been a passenger in some rather bad car crashes during my teenage years which had put me off learning to drive but that didn't matter as Ken gave me a lift down to his yacht at Dartmouth.

The whole weekend was a revelation. The weather was dreadful – cold and wet. Bashing into the waves we quickly became soaked and everyone soon looked miserable. With the water dribbling down the neck of my borrowed waterproofs I didn't know what to make of this so-called 'sport'. Everything felt strange. The movement of the boat was sort of uncomfortable and nobody seemed to be particularly enjoying themselves. It was obvious we all felt the same degree of weariness when after six hours Ken told us that progress was not good in these conditions and it might still be another ten or so hours before we reached the Channel Islands. Good heavens, it would be time to come back before we even got there. In fact conditions were so bad that we eventually gave up and instead went just up the coast to Brixham. Despite all of this it definitely wasn't boring and soon a perverted sense of fun saw me starting to enjoy myself.

Having been once, I couldn't wait to get to sea again and soon I became an absolute fanatic. I still loved work, but now I worked even longer days so that I could take more time off for sailing.

The next four years turned me into a regular seadog, and I became Ken's regular sailing companion. Ken commissioned a new larger yacht which he named *Zany Lady* after me, and I felt ridiculously privileged. At every opportunity we hotfooted it down to Dartmouth and set sail for the Channel Islands, Brittany, northern Spain, Portugal or Ireland. Whatever the weather, I was out there enjoying myself. Whether in the height of summer or the depths of winter, light winds or gale force, my enthusiasm never waned. I was enamoured with my newfound pursuit and sailing companion. I loved the sense of excitement, uncertainty, danger, and the feeling of sheer freedom once out on the ocean waves. For the first time in my life I was having to cope with practical problems rather than just business ones – if something goes wrong at sea, a solution has to be found there and then. I found I reacted well to these challenges. I never panicked but surprised myself again and again with the logical way I approached and helped remedy our dilemmas, and it gave me a new confidence in myself.

However, I still used to look at my life and wonder if this was it. Was there nothing more? I compared my life to many others and I could see I was lucky, but somehow that didn't seem enough – I still wanted something more. But what? Did I need more excitement, or did I want Ken to be more than a sailing companion? Well, if I wanted the latter I would have to forget it. When Ken wasn't sailing he was often abroad on business, and he was still my boss. I didn't really know what I wanted.

Then one morning in March 1985 at 6.30 when I was getting ready for an early start to the office the phone rang.

'Hello.'

'Hi, Lisa, it's Ken. I was wondering if you are free this evening – I have a proposition I want to put to you.'

'Mmmm, sounds interesting, any clues?'

'No, I'll discuss it this evening. I'll pick you up at about 7.30 tonight.'

'Great, see you later, then.'

Replacing the receiver my mind was racing – what on earth could this proposition be? Stop it, don't get excited, you know it's the quickest way to disappointment. And if you don't hurry up you won't be able to get that report finished for the meeting at 9 o'clock.

I made the short journey by taxi to the office, which was still quiet so early in the morning, and got out my half-finished report. Desperately trying to concentrate, I tried to focus on the task in hand but my imagination was dreaming up all sorts of things. Well, it couldn't be to do with work, that was for sure. Whatever most people might think, being friends with the managing director had proved to be a hindrance rather than anything else, and there was only one friend at Horizon who was even aware that I knew how to sail, let alone sailed with the MD. Ken was so keen not to show favouritism that I had been having to push much harder to get anywhere. And anyway, if it was to do with work surely he would have discussed it at the office. Could it be something to do with sailing? But what? Although my mind whirled round searching for the answer, I just couldn't think of anything feasible. Maybe I would get some feeling for what it could be at this morning's business meeting, although it was rather unlikely, but Ken was as brisk as ever and I was none the wiser.

The rest of the day flew by in a rush of work and soon I was winging my way back to my flat. I'd still got a good hour to get ready so I would relax and spoil myself a little. Yes, a glass of chilled white wine whilst luxuriating in a nicely scented bath was well deserved – it would also help me momentarily to forget the feeling of unwelcome I experienced every time I walked into the flat.

I really would have to make up my mind if I was going to stay here or not. I'd bought it purely on its merits of closeness to the office and the security system which kept out those who weren't actually invited inside. Yes, being only five minutes from the office was undoubtedly a big bonus, and so far I'd treated the flat just as a convenience. I closed my eyes and tried to imagine whether all the effort in the world could transform this rather dreary base into a place I could be happy in – would it ever really be home? Oh well, time enough to think about that. Now, I had to hurry up or I wouldn't be ready when Ken arrived.

Ken duly picked me up and took me back to his rather lovely house just round the corner. As we went in I was once again hit by the sheer size of the place – my entire flat would fit in this one room alone. Ken was considerably older than me and had made a success of his life, but would I ever own a place like this?

Ken's voice cut through my thoughts as he started to chat about the forthcoming travel conventions. With more than a slight feeling of envy I listened to all the places that he would be visiting: Cuba, Bora Bora, Australia, Bangkok, Bali, Singapore. Oh why did I have to be working on the administrative side – why hadn't I gone into marketing, then I might be one of the team off on a jolly jaunt?

Ken expanded more and more about everything till I was positively drooling. Because this year he was Chairman of the Tour Operator's Council, part of ABTA, he would be getting VIP treatment all the way. Imagine that – first class around the world! I'd done a fair bit of travelling but it was all fading into insignificance as I listened to his proposed itinerary – beautiful hotels; white sandy beaches; the use of a yacht for two weeks courtesy of the Queensland Tourist Board; trips on the Premier's yacht to see the Americas Cup in Fremantle; private planes to visit vineyards, and all to be enjoyed in style. There would also be a heavily packed business schedule. It sounded fantastic.

He's going to ask me to keep an eye on the house for two months during his absence. Perhaps he'll send me a postcard or two – maybe even bring me a present.

'What do you think?' asked Ken.

'It sounds wonderful,' I sighed, 'and I'm more than a little envious.' And I really was.

'I thought it might appeal to your sense of fun because I have a proposition for you ...'

It was a bolt from the blue – me to go too! For all of it! 'Yes yes yes! But what about work?'

'Ah yes, well, let me tell you the rest of my plans ...'

Imprisoned once more in my cold empty flat I poured myself another glass of wine and tried to think it all through logically.

I could go, I could be with Ken, and the idea of flying around the world with him, and in such style, had my blood racing. But that was just the start! After that the plan was to sail *Zany Lady* to different countries around the world. It was like a dream. But there was the crunch – it meant giving up my career at Horizon where I was doing so well. What if it didn't work out? Where would I be then?

Ken had assured me that financially he would see I was OK, so could I really say no and just continue at work? How would I feel knowing that every day I sat in the office I could be out exploring and enjoying what the world had to offer? It was a chance many would give their right arm for, an offer unlikely to come my way again – a once in a lifetime opportunity. I ought to be sensible and discuss it with my parents before making any decision. But I could see myself being happy with Ken, and in my mind I was already transformed from office worker to a thriving wayfarer of the world.

Dawning of Inspiration

Six months later in August 1986 I said goodbye to the stability of the previous few years. Leaving my position as Accounts Controller for one of the largest holiday companies in the country, I expectantly leapt from the heart of land-locked Birmingham into the more exciting pursuit of globetrotting.

Flying around the world for six weeks was wonderful and by the time I returned I was truly ensconced in my new luxurious life. Ken and I had got on really well and were closer than ever.

Ken wanted to spend the first year on his yacht visiting some friends in Spain. So the plan was to leave the UK the following March and sail straight to the Mediterranean. Ken resigned from Horizon in January '87 and a couple of months later we sailed off into the blue.

Ken felt it was a good idea to do some chartering whilst in the Med – not quite what I had envisaged, but still, it was only going to be for a year, wasn't it? I was beginning to wonder. Had I given up my career at such a crucial time under a misapprehension? Even though it was enjoyable it was bloody hard work and chartering in the Med was hardly a sensible reason for having given up my job.

I voiced my concerns to Ken, and said I felt I ought to return. I really liked him but I wasn't married to him, and whilst I might have taken the risk of losing my career against the experience of sailing to faraway places, I had to consider my financial stability for the future. I think it's acceptable for anyone to take one year off and treat it as a sabbatical – anything else is escapism and I felt irresponsible.

Ken assured me sailing the Med was just the start and that soon we would travel further afield. He obviously couldn't charter without help on board, and as to finances, there was nothing for me to worry about. If ever we parted he would see me OK so why not relax and enjoy it? I did.

I quickly slipped into my new way of life aboard *Zany Lady* and discovered I loved this more colourful and less structured approach to living. Over the next four summers we sailed many thousands of miles from one haven to another, dropping hook in small harbours and sequestered nooks in Spain, Sardinia, Corsica, Sicily, Malta, Greece, Turkey, Venice, southern Italy, Yugoslavia – so many beautiful places. I loved being a nomad (though I wasn't so keen on the hard work involved in chartering) but I still liked my home too. To retain some sort of balance we returned to the UK each winter to spend time with family and friends and also to do a little consultancy work.

Life certainly hadn't turned out how I expected. We were still in the Med and chartering seemed to have become the priority rather than exploring. Ken and I worked well together as crew but had grown apart. Perhaps it was because I had recognised that I was just drifting through life, or maybe my imagination was still working on sailing to more exotic destinations, but on a day that outwardly seemed like any other, a new me began to emerge.

It was another hot day. I was enjoying some personal space, relaxing on deck and basking in the sundrenched heat of the Mediterranean. The warm crystal-clear sea was gently lapping against *Zany Lady*'s hull, and I was indulging myself with a nicely chilled glass of white Rioja, whiling the afternoon away reading Naomi James's book, *At One with the Sea*.

At that stage I wasn't an avid reader of sailing books, but I picked this one up secondhand along with many others that made up our constantly changing and slightly battered ship's library. I have an awful habit of speed reading, which means it doesn't take any time at all to get through my latest selection, but this time I found myself turning from the last page back to the first. Hers was an amazing achievement. With hardly any sailing experience Naomi had set off in 1977 to sail single-handed and non-stop around the world. Trouble with her self-steering gear forced her to make two stops for essential repairs, but she didn't give in, and in 1978 she returned triumphant to Dartmouth, having completed this awesome circumnavigation. It was a truly wonderful and inspiring book. I found I kept wanting to read more. I just couldn't put it down. I'm not sure how many times I fingered those pages before I recognised the strange feeling of excitement bubbling inside me for what it was ... Had anybody done it without stopping? I desperately hoped not, I just knew it was for me. I could do it, I was sure I could. I had to do it.

The idea was crazy, far fetched even, but one day I found myself telling Ken. To my astonishment he wasn't surprised and said in a rather dry voice, 'I've watched you over the last few days and I knew this was coming.' Hardly encouraging, but I knew he was worried about how it would affect his plans, so I suppose that was to be expected. I think that almost to the day I set off he was convinced it would all fall by the wayside – still, he wasn't to be the only one!

A few weeks later in September 1990 we returned to the UK, and after a few months at home set off to Africa to spend six weeks in the desert with some friends who were part way through their trans-Africa expedition.

On our return I told Ken that I was opting out of sailing for the next season so that I could work on my project. He wasn't happy, but all his logical arguments fell on stony ground and I wasn't to be dissuaded, however crazy he thought it was.

So in April when Ken returned to his yacht in the Med, I remained behind at his house in Edgbaston. I didn't explain this unexpected change in my lifestyle to anyone. The truth was I actually wasn't brave enough (or crazy enough) to voice loudly my newfound ambition until I had spent a few months quietly doing the groundwork.

Firstly, had it been done? If not, what was it really like in the Southern Ocean? What sort of boat did I need? How much would it cost? Was it really possible to turn this daring adventure into reality or was it merely a pipe dream?

There were no records over here of anyone having achieved it, but some relatives of Ken's in Australia said that a woman called Kay Cottee had sailed around the world non-stop in 1988. I was devastated. They sent me her book as a consolation and I was glad they did. Yes, Kay Cottee had sailed around the world from Australia, but apart from popping over the Equator to round some rocks just a few miles north, her circumnavigation was entirely in the Southern Hemisphere.

I wanted to be the first woman to follow the recognised full antipodal circumnavigation as established by Chichester, but like Robin Knox John-ston I wanted to try and achieve it without going into harbour and without assistance.

The record available would be set under the rules as per the World Sailing Speed Record Council. They confirmed that no woman had attempted this particular record. This was great news. What Kay had done was fantastic, but I was glad she had still left something for me to achieve. I was elated and filled with renewed excitement.

However, the more books I read the more frightening it sounded. The Southern Ocean sounded like something from another world – stories of monstrous freak waves nicknamed 'greybeards' that travelled round and round the world increasing in height and strength up to a towering hundred feet, and appeared out of nowhere to swamp even the largest ocean-going vessels; the Cape of Storms off South Africa where, in bad conditions, the shallow Agulhas Bank with its fast-running current collides with the waves, making it difficult for any ship to survive; icebergs; the notorious Cape Horn, graveyard to many a sailor – the list of dangers seemed endless.

I could see it was going to be a real test of character to put it all together and then carry it through. I knew that one of the most critical points would be how would I cope with being on my own for so long? There would obviously be times when I would feel depressed. But how depressed would I get? Would I pull myself out of it or would I sink into a pathetic blob and be too apathetic to do necessary things on deck? The pressures on the mind are appalling and people have been known to crack up and jump off ship. But I wanted to do this. Surely that would make a difference. Wouldn't it? Well, there's no point running away from something before you've even tried and I felt driven from within. I realised I would never be satisfied with my life unless I tried. I just had to go for it.

I decided to chat it all through with an old friend of the family, Peter Gross. Peter wasn't a sailor but I knew he would give me an honest opinion. We'd always got on well together and I felt sure he would be straight with me and tell me what he thought. He was brilliant. Not only did he believe I would do it, he offered to use his marketing expertise to help me get a sponsorship folder together. He made it very clear that, with the economic climate not being so good, it wouldn't be easy to get a sponsor, especially for a high-risk project. But the idea was exciting and might catch somebody's imagination. So we put together a simple prospectus with the main points in mind. It had to be clear but exciting, informative but punchy, totally honest, and both Naomi James's and Kay Cottee's achievements would have to be clearly acknowledged.

Pretty soon I realised that the first step would have to be a trial run at single-handed sailing. The fact that I had already sailed well over 31,000 miles was a bonus, but there had always been at least one other person on board. It doesn't matter that sometimes they are asleep – in times of danger there is still comfort to be gained from another's presence. I knew that if I was to have any chance of succeeding I had to be completely sure in myself, sure that the loneliness aspect wouldn't negate my confidence and logical thinking in times of crisis. If I could prove myself in this I would be in a more creditable position to make my intentions public and start the hunt for a sponsor.

How was I going to find a boat to do it in? I couldn't afford to hire one and the problem of insuring against such a venture would be another headache. If I'd been in a yachting environment I might have been lucky enough to borrow one, but I wasn't, I was in Birmingham, and the only person who had a yacht and might possibly be persuaded was Ken.

Considering he felt I had let him down it was a little cheeky, but I sent a fax to him in Corfu. After all, I comforted myself, it was Ken who had introduced me to sailing, and even though his initial reaction to my future venture could hardly be described as encouraging I felt sure he would approve of the vigilance of a trial run (though I was equally sure he wouldn't be immediately enthusiastic!). Eventually he agreed, though rather reluctantly. I would fly to Corfu in October, we would both sail the boat to Spain and then I would sail her back to the UK. Great – only one problem to go. Peter had organised a press conference for my return, to announce my further venture. What was the best way to broach the subject with my parents?

Mum and Dad were already convinced that I was facing some mid-life crisis – why else would their thirty-two-year-old daughter be thinking of walking away from a life of luxury to an unknown future? So, understandably, I was keen to put the idea across in a positive way. But the more I thought about it, the more complicated it seemed to become. Eventually

I decided to try it out on Dad first. His reaction was one of stunned silence quickly followed by, 'I'm not sure it's a good idea to mention this to your mother just yet.' I knew what he meant, Mum is not the adventurous type. She has a mortal fear of heights and is frightened of the sea. However, time was running by and I was shortly leaving on my trial voyage, so I opted for taking them both out for a meal – convinced that the convivial atmosphere and a few glasses of wine would help. I chose one of their favourite restaurants and after two glasses of wine I was feeling almost courageous. I winked at my father.

Unfortunately this was spotted by my mother who promptly said, 'I suppose you are going to tell me that you are running off to get married.'

'Oh Mum, were it that simple. Actually . . .

I was amazed and relieved. Her simple 'Oh yes' made me feel as though I had made a mountain out of a molehill. Having considered that I'd sold her the idea I really enjoyed the rest of the evening. However, wishful thinking had blinded me to the truth. Just like I was hoping she understood my dreams, she was hoping I hadn't really voiced them. To her the idea was so outrageous she had blanked it out altogether!

In September 1991 I flew off to Corfu full of excitement about my forth-coming trial challenge. I received a very dubious welcome from my Corfiat friends, who having only really seen me in party mode were astounded that I should be considering sailing back to the UK on my own. My desire to achieve proved impossible to explain, so keeping 'mum' about my further plans, I tried to smile away their concerns and cryptic comments until eventually Ken and I set sail for Fuengirola in Spain.

Surprisingly it was an adventurous crossing. *Zany Lady* had been an expensive yacht but now really was in need of some serious work and by the time we arrived in Spain things weren't looking too hopeful – a situation not helped by our Spanish friends who tried to charm me into a change of heart.

Ken was understandably getting nervous. The rigging was a bit suspect, the oil sump on the engine had cracked, which could mean no power for the batteries, the weather was really bad and the forecast from the Met Office wasn't showing any improvement. News was coming in of terrible conditions in the Atlantic and many fishermen lost at sea. On top of all of this was the knowledge that it was impossible to get insurance for a passage across the Bay of Biscay at this time of year.

I was resolute. If I didn't do it now I would probably never get the chance. Ken's argument against me going was based more on the lack of a reliable engine as back-up rather than the conditions I would face. The weather and insurance I couldn't have argued about, but the engine – well, she was a sailing boat, wasn't she? So what if the engine didn't work? I wouldn't be able to use one if I went around the world, so it would be good for me to have to rely purely on my sailing skills.

As a last-ditch attempt to get the engine fixed we sailed to the better facilities at Gibraltar, but were given the same prognosis. Without taking the engine out altogether it was impossible to fix.

Eventually Ken capitulated and I ran around getting my last-minute provisions, and a hot-water bottle to replace the heating which, without an engine, I couldn't use.

I saw Ken off to the airport and then, full of exhilaration, set off myself. For some reason I wasn't at all nervous and I guess this was partly due to the sheltered weather in the Med and the fact that I knew *Zany Lady* so well. I'd also spent a whole week checking her over, identifying the potential problems and where possible setting up failsafes. I knew that I was mentally well placed to cope with whatever went wrong and this gave me a great feeling of confidence.

As I left Gibraltar it was glorious, but pretty soon I was out in the Atlantic and bashing into the steep seas caused by days of gales. I had a long and trouble-ridden trip as everything that I had thought might go wrong did. One of the stays sheared and the mast wasn't held securely but I held it in place with the spare halyards that weren't being used to hoist the sails. I tried to use the engine to power the batteries but even though I filled it up with oil before starting it, within minutes the oil had run out into the bilges. Then the water impellor, for the cooling system, seized and the engine overheated and was rendered useless. The rigid dinghy on the stern was moving about so I lashed it as best I could. *Zany Lady* had very shallow bilges and all the oil from the engine was running over the sole of the cabin. Every time I tried to pump it out it clogged up the bilge pumps, and I seemed to spend more time trying to repair the bilge pumps and cleaning the floor than sailing. The seas were so steep that poor old *Zany Lady* kept dropping off the waves and crashing into the hollow behind. Doors came flying off and equipment came shooting out of its casing.

The list of damage was horrendous, but in myself I felt good. Nothing had happened that I hadn't been able to cope with. I hadn't got frightened, I hadn't wished there was someone else on board. I was very happy sorting it all out myself. In fact I felt a renewed confidence in myself. For the first time in my life I had had to cope on my own, with nobody else to turn to, and I felt stronger for the experience.

After twelve days at sea I was on a real high as I sailed triumphantly into Dartmouth, and confidently announced to the waiting press and television my plans to sail around the world on a record-breaking voyage.

I was more sure than ever that I could do the 'big one'.

My euphoria quickly evaporated when I learnt that my Nana was extremely poorly. I rushed off with my parents to see her but I don't think she was aware I was there. It was the last time I saw her before she died a couple of days later. I'd loved her very much and we'd been great friends. I knew I was really going to miss her.

1992 and the Hunt for a Sponsor

Ken went off to a convention in Spain and I got down to the time-consuming task of compiling my 'hit list' of potential sponsors. There's no doubt that my idea was interesting enough to get to the right people. At first the sound of the post through the door had me running to pick it up, but as the weeks went by I found my confidence waning and some days I could not even bear to open it for fear I would see another nicely written 'sorry, but good luck' reply. All the stories seemed to be the same: if the budgets had not already been allocated for the foreseeable future, they had a policy not to sponsor individuals, or projects with a high risk factor. I fell into both of these categories and there was no way I could alter the project to overcome this.

I started to get selective and, by fingering each envelope, split the post into two piles – the hopeful and the definite refusals. I was sure I would be able to feel good news if it came. But eight months later I was not much further forward and things were starting to look bleak. It certainly wasn't for lack of trying – I had even gone to the extreme of hand delivering proposals to a few well-known anglophiles and been escorted off the grounds for my cheek. I didn't need friends to tell me the economic climate was not right, but I still couldn't give up. I had to do it somehow!

Then I got a phone call which brought my world crashing down. Sir

Peter Johnson from the World Sailing Speed Record Council told me that he had just been informed that a Japanese girl Kyoko Imakiire was nearing the end of a circumnavigation that would be considered antipodal.

I felt totally crushed. My dream had gone out of the window. What would I do now? I really believed that I was meant to do it. How could I be so ill fated?

For a while I went round in a dazed state. I couldn't imagine where I was going to go from here. I knew I couldn't return to chartering in the Med, and Ken and I had grown further apart. I mooned around for quite a few days and just couldn't get up any enthusiasm for anything. Then I got another phone call from Sir Peter. Kyoko Imakiire had had to receive helicopter assistance to get essential spares to her, and since outside help wasn't allowed she wouldn't be able to claim the record. I feel guilty now that I didn't have more sensitive feelings for how disappointed she must have been, but the honest truth is I didn't. I was so elated that the record was still there that I thought of nobody else but me. I simply added her achievement to my sponsorship folder and breathed a sigh of relief that my chance was still here. I was utterly selfish, and am now not a bit proud of it.

So I was back with my dream, although it was becoming obvious that nothing short of a miracle would see me presented with a boat, and I decided I might have more chance if I could raise my profile by doing a single-handed transatlantic crossing. I was in the middle of negotiating a boat for this purpose when things took a different turn altogether.

Finding the Boat

I had a phone call from Bill and Jean Melling, some very close friends up in Lancaster. They had been flicking through the *Exchange and Mart* and seen that an old steel hull was for sale in Cumbria. Although a little dubious, I decided to explore this further so gave the owners a ring. However, although I could just about cover the price, they had already sold it. As I put the phone down my heart sank – for the second time I felt my chances were just slipping away. The thought was unbearable and I knew I had to call them back just in case the sale fell through for any reason. So I picked up the phone again.

When I told them why I wanted the hull so badly it seemed my luck had taken a turn for the better. Paul Gillespie, the owner, had originally bought the hull because he too had had a dream to sail around the world. Unfortunately, a dream was all it stayed, which was why the hull had sat outside and been weathered into a rather rusty state. Because his dream hadn't materialised, he would love to see someone else's dream come true. He hadn't yet banked the cheque, would I like to go up and have a look? Would I!!!!!!

In a frenzy of excitement I threw some things in my little Fiat (I had recently taken a crash course in driving and passed my test after only three days) and raced up to Lancaster so that Bill and Jean could come and give me their opinion as well.

I was still wearing my silly grin when I arrived, and Bill offered to drive the rest of the way. I wasn't sure that arriving in a Bentley was going to project quite the right image to match the poverty I was pleading, but glancing down at my well-worn jeans and baggy jumper it was obviously not me who was well heeled, so I gratefully got in and we completed the journey in style.

Bill and Jean had built one boat before so had some idea what to look out for. She appeared magnificent to me on first sight but as we looked round reality started to clear my glazed vision and I found myself inspecting a rather ugly vessel that had been sitting outside for a few years and deteriorated into a rusting derelict shell. She had never seen the sea, let alone been afloat. Still, she was definitely strong, and at thirty-eight feet not too much smaller than I was used to (although admittedly smaller than I would have liked for this particular voyage). More importantly, she was all I could afford. Bill seemed quite positive so I took the plunge and bought her with practically every penny I had – a grand total of £7,500!

Feelings were running high as we left her behind and went back to Lancaster to celebrate with a few bottles of champagne. We spent a silly evening opening pages of the dictionary at random picking a name for her. Jean chose *Scintilla* but she wasn't to keep that name for long!

Early the next morning, still wrapped up in the euphoria of my recent positive mood, I jumped back into my car and raced down the M6. In my dreamy state I drove straight past Birmingham and found myself well on my way to London. It was late morning by the time I eventually got home and by then the excitement had somewhat dissipated and I was wondering what on earth I had let myself in for.

The Beginning of a Headache

Having got over my initial elation, I was now faced with the problem of what to do next. The hull was still in Cumbria waiting to be moved. I had no idea where I could put it, and to help matters my finances were down to the princely sum of just £200. I had been earning a little money from consultancy work but knew that I would now have to throw all my energies into turning this wreck into an ocean-going vessel.

By now Ken had returned from his sailing exploits, and when I told him the latest developments, his muttered 'Oh God' left me in little doubt that he thought I had finally gone too far. But in all fairness to him, he did sit down with me and help me to work out a new approach. I felt that we might be able to get lots of small companies to give materials and equipment even if they couldn't give cash, especially if we could get Birmingham City Council to back it. The project *Spirit of Birmingham* was conceived.

The first person to receive a hand-delivered copy of this new exciting venture was the Lord Mayor of Birmingham, Councillor Peter Barwell. He was very excited, and phoned me straight away to see how he could help. I told him I needed somewhere for the hull and within an hour he had found a space in secure surroundings, but outside.

However, with the onset of winter and the need for electricity and an on-site office, I decided that instead I had to find an empty building.

Finding somewhere in the centre of Birmingham was so complicated and drawn out that it is almost a story in itself. There was no shortage of buildings but none of them had access big enough to get *Spirit* in. Eventually, after a cocktail party with the Fifth Battalion of the Royal Regiment of Fusiliers, and also with the help of Peter Gross, the University of Birmingham came to the rescue. The Vice Chancellor, Sir Michael Thompson, was looking for innovative ways to encourage students to the university. Sir Michael was also an avid sailor so could thoroughly understand the magnitude of my plans and the beneficial effect if I pulled it off. I was given one of the laboratories in the School of Manufacturing and Mechanical Engineering.

My crazy project had found some credibility and stumbled forward another step. Everything had been worked out in detail: the route the hull could be brought in, taking into account low bridges, narrow roads, tight corners; the entrance to the university campus, and the most critical bit – into the laboratory itself. This was going to be very tight as the hull was only an inch or two smaller than the opening into the laboratory and it would have to go in at an angle because there was a low wall and a building right opposite.

Whilst this easy step was being worked on in Birmingham, unbeknown to me horrendous things were happening in Cumbria. I had received lots of irate messages from the contracted haulier, none of which I was too concerned about as I couldn't understand what the problem could be. Obviously I couldn't fix a date until the site here was secured. Eventually I called him back and suddenly it became painfully clear. The company grounds where the hull had been were now in the hands of the receiver and so my boat had been whisked away weeks ago and since then had been sitting on his lowloader – it was costing him a small fortune in lost revenue! The only reason he had been at all patient was the fact he felt attached to the rusty relic. He had been the original haulier to take it from where it was built (in Birmingham!!) up to Cumbria, and was enjoying the irony of bringing it back down again in a worse state than it had been in before.

It all took so long that Ken had once again gone off abroad, but eventually everything was planned and my hull would shortly be approaching Birmingham. My father was driving up to the services on the motorway to meet the lowloader with the hull and lead it along the agreed route to the university. Things like this normally run behind schedule, but not today! Security got a phone call from the driver to say he was already through Birmingham city centre and fast approaching the university. All my carefully laid plans were falling around my feet – he was approaching on the wrong road and would get stuck on the small hump-back bridge. The proud visions I had had of stirring headlines in the local papers were replaced by the horrors of more newsworthy stories as I envisaged the embarrassing scenario of not even being able to navigate the hull to where it was going to be worked on – let alone navigate it around the world!

I jumped into my car, and screeched across the campus just in time to see the lowloader approaching. Mindless of the danger I leapt out and flagged it down. My father arrived in hot pursuit. 'Oh,' said the driver, 'I saw this guy driving up the other side of the motorway flashing his lights and pipping his horn – didn't realise it was you.' Still, it was too late now. There was no way of turning the lorry round and a nice little traffic jam was piling up behind.

We rushed off in my car to remeasure the small bridge – it would be touch and go but now we had to risk it. Somehow we manoeuvred safely over that obstacle and having removed the barriers were now inside the campus. Phew! That was close.

Rounding the final bend by the laboratory we slowed to a standstill as everyone looked in disbelief at the next task. *Spirit* looked far too massive to be negotiated into its new home. Working it out with paper models I'd been sure it would just about go in, and the postgraduate students who were using it as a case study thought the same. But seeing it here in real life I could feel stirrings of uncertainty. Had we somehow miscalculated?

I put on a brave face and with a beaming smile said, 'It's amazing, isn't it? I mean, it doesn't look as though it could possibly go in, but I'm sure it will.' With relief I noticed a few wry smiles. What a great team – they had the right attitude. It was now a challenge, and if there was any way of getting it in, we would.

Narrowly missing the windows of the facing building, inch by inch, we gradually managed to tease it inside. She was home!

Dad lent me some money to pay the haulier and then we stood there looking up at her. She looked massive and one thing was for sure. Whatever work we did to her couldn't include making her any higher, longer or wider – or we'd never get her out again!

Planning Ahead

My project folder at least looked impressive – I had been successful in my career and knew that a good business plan was essential.

I designed the interior of the boat to suit the voyage. I knew I couldn't afford to be thrown around so reduced that risk by planning a partition down the centre of the boat. One side would be the 'snug' area, just big enough for two bunks, so that whichever way the boat was heeled I would be able to sleep comfortably, read and generally relax. The other side would be the workshop for making all the repairs. The navigation area would be sited near the cockpit, to one side of the companionway steps, and would be bigger than normal, as I knew I would be spending much of my time there. The galley (kitchen) could afford to be small with just enough room for me to stand in front of the gimballed cooker. It was important to leave enough room for it to swing freely, so that regardless of the heel of the boat, the saucepans would stay level and not fall off.

A lot of area would be needed for storage both forward and aft. The heads where I would wash and shower would run from one side of the boat to the other with the loo placed amidships, which would make it usable whatever the angle of the boat. There would be as many cupboards as possible and no space was to be wasted. The seventy-five-gallon water tank would be built to fit under the bunk nearest the centre of the boat and the fuel tank would be under the cabin floor. There would be a water chamber like a porch by the entry hatch so that I could shut off the inside of the boat from the outside elements before I opened the hatch to go on deck, which would greatly reduce the risk of being swamped by an errant wave. Throughout would be designed so that any water that got into the boat would quickly drain away to the bilges where it would automatically activate the bilge pump and get pumped into the sea.

She wasn't going to be pretty but she was going to be practical and very sturdily put together. I made an inventory of every bit of kit I required, including all the food, tools and spares that I would need to take, and everything was costed.

The timing of the project was related to weather en route and was therefore a key factor. If I missed the departure slot one year, which for me I worked out would be late August/early September, I would have to wait almost another twelve months before I could set off.

I worked out a critical path to follow in the hope this would keep me on target. The problem was going to be cash – if I had had the money there on hand it would have been realistic, but the whole project was to be dogged by a lack of funding.

I was also having some difficulty in adapting to life in the academic world of the university. I wasn't actually used to taking on postgraduate students, and had been accustomed to forging ahead with ideas and plans without having to follow lines of command. In a bid to get some good PR I invited the Lord Mayor to pop down to see the boat and have his photo taken for the local paper. I very soon found myself up before the Head of School. As I sat there in his office I felt myself bounding back in time to my schooldays and being chided by the headmistress. Didn't I realise that it was the privilege of the Vice Chancellor to invite people of such importance? VIPs were entitled to red carpet treatment and certainly not a faxed map with 'follow the arrows – I am here' scribbled on it. I was extremely hard put to keep my face straight, and couldn't resist a few witty retorts, but underneath were stirrings of misgivings.

I had already been asked to respect the fact that there were some offices at the farthest end of the lab so would I please not make a mess and be as quiet as possible. How on earth could I shot blast the rust off and work on a steel boat without contravening both of these requests? I could either do all the worst bits when nobody else was around or I could smile sweetly and carry on regardless. A combination of the two proved to be the most reasonable, if not the most satisfactory, solution.

Work progressed slowly – primarily because there is little you can do without any cash, but also because I was still only a team of one. However, my attempt at PR had proved fruitful. The front page of the *Birmingham Post* was taken up with a colour photo of the Lord Mayor and myself standing on the boat with glasses of champagne. My secret was well and truly out – now everyone knew what I was up to.

The reaction was mixed. Whilst many people were unsurprised to learn that I wanted to achieve something ambitious, many of them were also daunted by the enormity and loneliness factor of my plans – was it really possible for such a gregarious person to cope with being on her own for that length of time? Luckily, however, some very good friends were excited by my ambitious project and gave me a kick start by coming on board as my first sponsors. Gerald and Lynda Walsh own a top-drawer lingerie shop in Stratford-upon-Avon, a rather unexpected line of sponsorship but very welcome – it was cash not goods in kind they were offering! After that more local companies started to be helpful with building materials.

Ken was once again about to depart to the Mediterranean but before he went agreed to make loans to me of £10,000 – £1,000 for personal necessities and £9,000 to be used towards *Spirit* only if I believed it was turning into a viable proposition.

Life was hectic. My days alternated between writing off to potential sponsors, trying to secure the interest of an independent film company so that I could guarantee coverage to any sponsor, and sitting on *Spirit* poring over books on 'how to build your own boat'.

Trying to marry up the plans of the boat with the actual hull itself provided further problems. The only plans I had were for a slightly different design – a centre cockpit ketch – and I had an aft cockpit sloop. That wasn't really a problem as I was designing the interior myself, but why was the transom reversed, why had the bow been changed, shouldn't the skeg to hold the rudder be a little further back? I couldn't find any notes to back it up – would it affect her performance or seaworthiness?

I spent ages unsuccessfully trying to track down the designer (who was last heard of in South Africa) and then the Birmingham builders (who had since closed down). I was mentally accepting that some of the cash I was so carefully guarding would have to be spent on professional advice when I got another lucky break.

The local press had been contacted by someone claiming to be a round-the-world yachtsman. Apart from being a single-hander he also claimed to have been a skipper on the Whitbread Round the World Race. He was keen to help and amazingly he lived in Birmingham!

I have to say I was impressed. He was full of enthusiasm and obviously knew a lot about ocean sailing. What's more, he seemed to have all the contacts I needed. He'd also invited some nice guys who immediately offered to do some photos of me to help improve my chances of sponsorship – the next morning his friends took the photos and soon these were included in my sponsorship folder.

I suddenly felt much better about everything. Oh what fun it was going to be now there was an experienced team of two on the project! Now I could discuss all the structural details with a knowledgeable person as well as bounce other ideas around. He also had all the contacts within the marine industry which would make life much easier. I was really buoyed up by this new injection of confidence into the project. Combined with the postgraduate students who were using it as a case study for one day each week, surely things must start to come together more quickly.

I had also by this time met one of the senior technicians in an adjoining lab. Carl proved to be a gem, was very keen on the project and prepared to spend all his spare time helping me out. He also had good contacts within the university which proved to be very useful.

As the days and weeks passed, excitement was growing at the university – my advisor was great at promoting my project and everyone liked him. However, my spirits were being slowly eaten away by niggling doubts. At the very beginning, I was prepared to accept the overriding advice of my new and more experienced team-mate – after all, my reasoning was based more on logic and instinct, whereas he *knew*. But eventually I reached the stage when sleep was eluding me altogether. As I restlessly paced the house my mind was racing. How could I agree to structural changes and work on key areas of the boat when in my heart of hearts I still felt that it was me who was right?

As time went on I began to realise that this nice guy who was so willing to help me was guided more by wishful thinking than reality. Through him I'd heard of a professional designer/boatbuilder who was working on a new boat for the next Whitbread race, and I decided to put my mind at rest by seeking a third opinion. I rang him and pleaded with him. I knew he must be busy designing this Whitbread boat but I desperately needed to get his advice.

'No problem,' he replied. 'I'll be up tomorrow.'

The moment he turned up I was happy. He was fairly quiet and very pleasant. As he chatted through my concerns we seemed to be in accord on most things. He took a lot of measurements, the plans that I had, and came back with calculations on the key areas. This time it felt right. It was £200 well spent. I would have loved to keep him involved with the project but unfortunately I was too tight on cash. Still, the most important concerns were now sorted. The other professional advice I needed I would have to get from people supplying the equipment or from the resources within the university.

I felt guilty and sad having to say goodbye to someone who had tried to help me but I knew I had no choice. The boat couldn't be built on dreams and the project had to retain credibility, so I wished my advisor well in his own ventures and turned my thoughts back to my immediate problems. Not least of these was my own self-confidence – how could I have been so stupid? In the end I just had to accept the honest truth. My desire to have a team had blinded me. It had been a hard lesson to learn. Now I was back on my own.

1993 – a New Year and a Fresh Start

So far I wasn't very impressed with myself but there was no point in brooding on past mistakes. It hadn't been a totally wasted two months and I had to move on. In future I would put greater store in myself. I could understand that my venture might appeal to the emotions or imagination of others, but that didn't automatically mean that they would actually be of help.

Carl was a godsend during this time. With a heart of gold and a great sense of humour he helped me to laugh off my bad experience and slowly get back on course. Every lunchtime and often for a few hours in the evening he would come along to the lab to help. We put strengtheners into the keel which came up into the sole of the boat and up through the hull. This would take away any worry of the keel snapping off, as any stress would pull along the whole of the rounded hull instead of just on the weld. We reduced the stress on certain other areas and moved the rudder skeg back to improve steering performance.

The ballast proved to be one of the most complicated elements. Should we use lead ingots or ballbearings? Carl tried to convince the university to melt the lead for us but apparently this caused too many problems with the Health and Safety at Work Regulations. So I purchased four tons of lead ingots. When they arrived we were horrified. They looked as though they would fill half the boat. My brother Paul came to help Carl and me load them into the keel. It was a job and a half, lifting them up on to the deck, taking them below and carefully lowering them into the keel, and instead of the expected few hours it took days. We kept placing them in until the keel was full. It was no good. There was still a pile of ingots to go, and even worse it was supposed to be in the bottom third to get the right stability.

There was only one thing for it – we would have to creep in when no one else was about and melt it in. We thought we had packed the ingots in tightly but were amazed to see the lead almost disappearing as it started to melt. It was a beautiful and mesmerising sight as it dissolved into a shimmering molten waterfall and we were delighted with the result!

I kept in touch with the photographers who'd helped me and they came along to film critical parts, but all in all progress was horrendously slow. At this rate I would be drawing my pension before she was finished! I knew that in order to retain the credibility of the project, things would have to be seen to be progressing much more quickly. It was nearly three months since the hull had arrived and it didn't look too much different.

I needed to be able to brainstorm ideas and also to get help fitting *Spirit* out – it simply wasn't possible to achieve everything myself.

Dipping in and out of every different aspect wasn't making for efficiency in any area.

Some key business people, who like me were members of Priory tennis club, could see I needed help. They got together with John James, who was big in the city, and targeted likely people to sponsor me. Every few weeks we would hold a progress meeting, but the news was not good. Even after a great deal of effort and with all their contacts, nobody was found to back my rather ambitious project. I think my parents were quietly relieved.

In the meantime, despite being short of cash, I had decided to tender some of the fitting out to a local boatbuilder, in the hope that soon I would be able to afford to retain them permanently. John Pinder & Sons were based only a few miles away. Most of their work was with narrowboats for canals but a lot of the same skills were involved. John Pinder seemed a nice guy and confident they could do the job well. Without moving the boat to the coast there was no other option and I felt sure that with a combination of their knowledge, the different specialists within the university and the knowhow of the suppliers of various pieces of equipment, I could pool everything and come up with the right result.

Another area of concern was my ability to keep going. I was starting to feel very tired – the sort of weariness that only comes with constant battling against a situation that seems impossible. I was also getting very unfit, working crazy hours every day, and eating convenient junk food when time permitted. Gone was the healthy lifestyle of the past few years. I knew I would have to put my life back into some sort of order if I wanted to cope and win.

I needed to get fit, but once the day had started there just never seemed to be the opportunity to take time out. I approached my tennis club, the Priory, and they agreed to let me use the pool before the normal opening time of 7 a.m. This was great. My new regime started at 5 a.m., when I would jump out of bed and straight off to swim for an hour or so and sometimes even use the gym as well. Apart from starting to feel more energetic I found the swimming therapeutic, so that by the time I left I was more than ready to start the day. I was also in tune with what I was going to achieve.

Priory also let me include a flyer in their newsletter to members, and this produced some lucky results, not on the side I expected but from the media – the BBC. They were very interested and soon I found myself being interviewed by Richard Uridge for BBC Television. That went down so well a meeting was arranged to meet key people within the network to discuss a documentary and other possible coverage.

With February came the Boat, Caravan and Leisure Show at the National Exhibition Centre in Birmingham. I went along to try and get a bit more PR and found myself being introduced to someone connected with the PR for the show. He was extremely interested in my undertaking and offered to take over the huge problem of finding a sponsor so that I could concentrate my time on building the boat the way I wanted it.

Wonderful – or was it? My emotions were mixed. I was elated about the possibility of being relieved of this burden, but also nervous that I might be making a mistake. What if I ended up losing control again? I discussed it with Ken who was once again back from his travels. After all, he was an extremely good businessman and didn't want to see me get into a bigger mess than he already considered I was in, so he agreed to come with me as advisor at the arranged meeting. My fears appeared to be unfounded as it all went well. Mr X (as I'll call him) was a leading figure in PR and would work towards getting a sponsor on a success-only basis. That is, he would only take a fee if he secured all the sponsorship I needed. Ken was impressed.

This was also a relief to the businessmen from Priory who were glad that I now had the professional help I needed. Whilst Mr X was trying to attract a major sponsor I continued trying to get as much equipment sponsored as I could. Funnily enough some things were much easier than others. I had already been offered a full range of navigation equipment, when another company approached me and then thirdly the company I finally chose. I was impressed by the latter, which was VDO, not only because they were bringing out a new, very clear-to-read LOGIC range, but also because they were based in Birmingham.

I had also got a very good deal on the most endurable and reliable steering equipment on the market. This Whitlock rod steering would connect the wheel directly to the rudder and meant I would have no hassles with broken cables – a problem I could well do without.

The rigging was a critical area. The mast needed to be extremely strong, as did the stays that would hold it in place. I was keen to have a single-section extrusion mast and was surprised to find that not many companies could provide this. Also the chainplates and fittings connecting the stays to the boat would have to be exceptionally tough – we wanted the boat to be able to survive a 360° roll (though I hoped it wouldn't be tested), so made the chainplates well over scale, heavy and long, and we once again used the strength of the hull to take the stress. Apart from being strong the connectors also had to be easy to replace at sea.

I was really taken by Eurospars. They could supply what I wanted and were extremely helpful. Birmingham is hardly the ideal place to be building a boat but Eurospars didn't hesitate. With their help we decided that *Spirit* should have two roller furling forestays, one for the larger foresail and one for the inner staysail. This would split the sail area and make it easier to reduce quickly the amount of canvas as I would be able to roll it in rather like a roller blind on a window. We would also have an extra forestay so that I could fly an extra sail if I wished. This would also be used for the storm sail in very bad weather.

Because of the rigours of the trip there would be more stays than on a normal boat, including two twin backstays holding the mast to the stern of the boat, so that at least if one broke the other would hold it in place whilst I rigged up another one.

Nothing was too much trouble for Eurospars. They came up from Plymouth to give advice, and when I kept going back again and again about certain aspects they seemed pleased rather than hassled by my constant stream of questions. I knew that they thought my task was enormous and that I would be hard put to achieve it but even so they gave me all the help they could.

Now I was starting to enjoy myself more. I could really concentrate on the area I wanted to – ensuring the boat was built the way I wanted it and that no corners were cut. Mr X seemed to be doing well. I took him with me to the meeting at the BBC which went very well and things started to look very hopeful indeed – with their backing surely we could easily secure a major sponsor.

Mr X kept in regular contact and soon had three interested parties. At this stage Mr X decided to make a career move of his own. With my project and a few other important clients he felt it was the ideal opportunity to set up on his own. At first I was shaken and considered looking elsewhere but soon my confidence was restored when he announced that he had secured the interest of a main sponsor. Not only that, they were prepared to inject a great deal more money than I had asked for to ensure that everything would be done in a professional manner. Well, this was a change in events. From having to scrabble round for every penny I would soon be a viable commodity. I really started to perk up. This new deal would also take care of my personal finances which to date were looking pretty pathetic – yippee!

Mr X had shown me some of the papers relating to the deal, although nothing very specific. I was still suffering moments of anxiety but Mr X's excitement was infectious and Ken seemed relaxed about it all. The boat was coming on well. Most of the work now was on the inside. The steel work was basically finished, the fuel tanks were in, the water tank had been made, the polystyrene lining had gone in, the plumbing was finished, the woodwork was well under way – everything was starting to take shape. However, a sinking feeling of *déjà vu* wouldn't completely go away. Why hadn't the sponsors been to see the boat? Didn't they want to meet me? How could they possibly put so much money into a venture when they hadn't satisfied themselves about the person who was going to achieve it? Mr X poohpoohed my concerns and I tried to quell my disquiet.

As the date got closer for the signing I became paranoid. Why was the signing at my home? Wouldn't it be more normal to go to them? The day everything was to be completed I was up early and couldn't settle. The meeting was planned for two o'clock. By 2.15 the sponsor hadn't arrived and I was sure it was a no-goer. I hadn't been able to contact Mr X – where could he be? At about 3.15 the bell rang. Feeling sick with foreboding, I asked Ken if he would go to the door with me.

I knew instantly, the smile didn't fool me. I felt myself go cold and hard as my defences built up to take the now inevitable blow. Why do people always broach these times with the phrase, 'Well, there's good news and bad news'?

I realised that my long-term feelings of doubt were well founded and this fantastic sponsor was no more. Mr X's manner was nervous, the explanation was weak and the reasoning unconvincing. I could barely hold myself still whilst he went on to the so-called good news which sounded even more implausible. I was mortified and in no mood to listen any further.

I excused myself and quickly left the room. My first reaction was that this was a night for having too much to drink and trying to blot it out of my mind, but thinking ahead to the morning, when I would have to cope not only with the reality of this crushing blow but also the inevitable bilious aftermath of over-indulging, I realised I would have to pull myself together.

I decided to get the embarrassment out of the way and phoned the BBC to let them know. Richard Uridge was magic. Within ten minutes he had come round to cheer me up and talk it all through. It was such a relief to get it all off my chest. Richard seemed to be so understanding, so I opened up and told him all the previous hiccoughs as well. I was starting to feel quite depressed at my track record to date when I looked up to see a slight twinkle in his eye. Suddenly we were both laughing at my bad luck – or was it my naivety? This was the beginning of a great friendship.

My chat with Richard had helped me put everything into perspective and life didn't look so bleak any more. It was just another hurdle and I would have to find another way forward. Ken went back to his life aboard *Zany Lady* and I was left trying to pick up the pieces and start again.

It was now April and I had accepted in my own mind that departing this September was looking more and more unlikely. Actually I wasn't too disappointed about that as I'd never really expected to get it all together in only a few months, and I was quite relaxed about putting it off for twelve months until September '94.

Richard set up a meeting with Martin Holmes, who was a local specialist in sponsorship for motor racing and yachting. Martin and I were both strong characters and I was already a little sceptical about anyone who said they could get a sponsor, but Richard managed to smooth the way and Martin agreed to start work on finding the backing I needed. I was therefore surprised and quickly horrified to hear that there was a potential sponsor but that my departure date would have to be brought forward a few weeks to coincide with the launch of their new perfume.

Feelings of panic were running round in my head. Martin was right when he said that a large professional team with plenty of finance could finish the boat in no time, but would I be mentally prepared if everything was a last-minute rush? Once again I was experiencing qualms inside. I'm not sure whether I was glad or sorry that it all came to nothing, but one thing was for sure – I was heartily sick of the whole project.

What I needed was a break. I decided to get away from it all for the weekend so went up to visit my friends Bill and Jean in Lancaster. They were just about to go off for a few weeks on their yacht and were thinking of moving it from Mallorca. I suggested they make the hop to Corfu where I could put them in touch with my Corfiat friends – it's a lovely area to sail and it's also useful to know someone in case problems arise. So off they went and I returned to Birmingham.

Suddenly I was tired. I had been working crazy hours, my nerves had been to hell and back and now when the pressure was off I felt like collapsing. I met up with Helen, a friend of mine who had also had a hectic year, and over a few glasses of wine we started dreaming of all the things it would be nice to do. Wouldn't it be lovely to be in the sun, even better to be sailing. Lucky Bill and Jean, fancy being able to go off just like that. We treated ourselves to another bottle, and life was starting to look very amusing. Towards the end of the second bottle we were both giggling. Wouldn't it be fun to be there when they sailed into Corfu – imagine the surprise on their faces!

The next morning it still seemed a good idea. They'd have to enter Greece officially therefore they would have to go to Corfu Town. So why not? What was to stop us? Using my contacts within the travel industry I made a few phone calls and off we went.

I think my brain must have been on overload – how I could ever have thought that going to Corfu would be a rest when I knew so many people there is now beyond me. We did have a great time but returned absolutely shattered, having only slept for a few hours all week and over-indulged on the local wine.

Still, I soon redressed the lack of sailing by arranging to fly out to the Azores a few days later to meet Ken and the guys on *Zany Lady* and had an enjoyable sail with them back to the UK.

Fourth Time Lucky

By September I was back at the boat, with the same old problems: no sign of a major sponsor and very little cash to keep going. We had had to move the boat to another lab within the School of Electronics & Electrical Engineering. I'd had the hull for nearly eleven months now and there was still a long way to go. But Ken Stout, Head of the School of Manufacturing and Mechanical Engineering, gave me a great psychological boost when he started to show a lot of interest in the project. This was great, I could now be sure that I wouldn't lose the support of the university, which was proving to be an important endorsement of the project. He had also hinted that if I could prove the project was a viable investment then the university might be willing to inject some cash. I was filled with a renewed sense of well-being and confidence. I could do it and I would – somehow!

However, my feelings of confidence weren't reflected by Ken, who decided one day that if I was determined to carry on with this crazy project would I please move out and at least let him get on with his own life. He was right, we weren't going anywhere, but it was still a shock. Everything I had was invested in a pretty shaky project and now I had no security from my private life either. Moving out meant living somewhere else, more expenses but no income. Luckily I still had my old flat. After ten years together it was over. Contrary to popular belief there is no such thing as a common-law wife and I was not entitled to anything. All those years of working with Ken and sharing his lifestyle were suddenly behind me and now for the first time in my life I really was on the breadline.

It was a bitter pill to swallow. There was little I could do but shrug my shoulders. Although we'd become distant I'd enjoyed most of my time with him; now that was all over. I had to move on, build up a life for myself and find a way to finish the boat. I was determined not to let the project or my circumstances defeat me. It was a real case of sink or swim.

Sweeping up my pride off the floor I threw my clothes into bags, dumped them at the flat and threw my energies back where they were needed most – in the boat lab.

It must be a quirk of nature – or maybe it's my character, or perhaps more simply it is typical of people who are already busy nearly every minute of the day – but when your life seems full to overloading it's strange how one nearly always wants to fit something else in. I had been impressed by the amount of interest shown by local schools and had already shown many children around the boat, giving them little talks about the project and trying to answer their engaging questions. I was really touched by their curiosity to know everything about the boat and what I was going to do and suddenly it seemed an awful shame that this project couldn't be more wide reaching. Wouldn't it be great if my project could be followed by all the local schools?

I soon found myself sitting with Terry Martin, the headmaster of one of the local schools, and the External Funding and Promotions Manager for Birmingham City Council's Education Department, Peter Harding. We were discussing a cross-curriculum package for all the schools to follow for the next year. I knew I wouldn't really have enough time to be part of the team putting it together but was hoping to encourage some other people to take it on. Unfortunately this never quite came together, although it wasn't wasted time, in fact far from it: it was one of the luckiest moves I made and proved to be a turning point in the whole project.

Peter Harding was already extremely active in many areas and the reason he was so good at what he was doing was his vision and total commitment to any project he took on. Peter had seen something in me that inspired him. He says now that it wasn't just the burning passion in my voice but also the fact that I was clearly 'hands on' with the project: 'Although you were dressed beautifully, you had obviously got ready in a hurry and presumably on the boat – there were traces of paint in your hair, under your fingernails and on the heels of your smart boots.' Peter's a believer in 'first impressions' and on this one occasion I was later glad I had been forced into a hasty transformation from boatbuilder to businesswoman.

Peter came to see the boat, and as soon as he stepped on board seemed completely spellbound by the enormity of the task I had undertaken. He knew absolutely nothing about sailing so left without making any promises. But I could see he was captured by my dream.

Over the next few months Peter's involvement increased. Initially our meetings were infrequent as he tried to find someone to come on board as main sponsor. As time went by, though, Peter's involvement increased, until after normal office hours he would come along to the lab and be 'hands on' with the project.

Peter actually loved this side of it and many an evening was spent with Carl, Peter, myself and Jason, who was employed by his father's business John Pinder & Sons, working together. All dressed in overalls, and covered in paint or varnish, we looked a right motley crew. But we worked hard, had a lot of fun and gradually began to see rewards for our efforts. Inside, *Spirit* was starting to look great. The woodwork was finished and shining bright with varnish. All the navigation instruments were on and the galley was finished apart from linking up the taps on the sink. The cushions were being made for the snug and from a quick look round she appeared finished. She wasn't of course. The engine wasn't fitted and there were still a great many other things that needed to be done, but she was coming along well. For weeks on end the lab looked a tip as the rubbish and beer cans piled up. It was one of the most satisfactory and memorable periods and we all worked tremendously well together. It was a great feeling.

We were now frantically trying to get her presentable for the Boat Show in Birmingham. Obviously she wouldn't be completely ready inside but she still needed to look the part. Within a fortnight of the date we were due to show *Spirit* at the show, we were spraying the final coat of paint on to the hull. All the undercoating had been done over the last few days – working day and night to cater for the gaps between coats. She looked a little better and at last we had covered up the awful name of *Black Pig* that some anonymous witty person had daubed down one side of *Spirit*'s hull.

Sunday morning I was up early and bursting with excitement at seeing *Spirit* – overnight she had had her last coat of paint. For the first time she would have her top coat on. She would be glossy white instead of matt grey and I was hoping this would transform her from the ugly duckling into the beautiful swan.

As I stepped into the lab, my first reaction was that she hadn't been painted at all – was she white or was she still grey? I felt like weeping. This top coat had made no difference to her at all – in fact she looked worse, the gloss of the paint accentuating the unevenness of her lines rather than hiding them. Oh God, I couldn't bear the embarrassment of showing her off. Placed between two fibreglass boats who would be boasting their beautifully moulded lines, it would be more like showing her up.

Perhaps she looked worse because of the lighting in the lab. I kept moving around to eye her from different angles, then I inspected the deck. God, it was awful. Twice I walked out of the lab hoping that I had previously been too critical and that all of a sudden a fresh look would see her standing there proud and pretty. But nothing changed – she looked terrible.

I phoned Peter and asked him to come and have a look. He confirmed what my mind refused to accept – she looked a mess and would have to be repainted.

Just ten days to go – what a disaster! However, Monday brought me back to my senses and I was phoning Masons Paints asking them if they could sponsor with their paints. They were terrific and within a couple of hours they had promised me all the paint I needed, though if I really did need it there and then I would have to go and collect it. I left the rest of the team rubbing *Spirit* down with sandpaper and dashed up to Derby to pick up the new paint. By the time I returned she was ready to be repainted.

This paint suited her much better and she looked the business. At last we could move on. Peter called in a signwriter to paint the sponsors' logos on the hull and make spraydodgers and banners for the boat.

In the meantime Dad and my brother Paul, who had their own engineering company, had been custom-making some of the large pieces of deck fittings such as the pushpit and pulpit which would be sited at the bow and stern respectively to stop me falling off the deck, and granny bars and handrails to give me security whilst moving around on top.

There was so much still to do and time was being eaten up. It didn't matter what time I got up in the morning, there just never seemed to be enough hours in the day any more. Gone was the exercise regime of last year – with the pressure of imminent deadlines, every minute was sacred.

I was still hopeful that the university might put cash into the project and on the day of the meeting to finalise this, I was in my office making sure I had all my facts ready.

Carl came in to see me. 'God, you look shattered.'

I looked up in horror. 'I do?'

'Yeah, you look all done in.'

Well, it wasn't really surprising, but that certainly wasn't the image I wanted to put over trying to secure the investment of the university.

I decided to pop back to the flat to have a shower and freshen up. The flat is only a couple of miles from the university and I left it in plenty of time, and headed back. The next thing I knew I was being ricocheted across the road. I couldn't believe it. Apart from a couple of cars waiting opposite to cross over, the road had been clear. But here I was in a three-car smash! Luckily no one was hurt but all three cars were write-offs. The police kindly got me to the university in time for my meeting, but as soon as I sat down shock set in and I was in no state to convince anybody of anything. I sat in my office and the tears racked my body – how could it have happened?

I had been balancing a tightrope of tiredness, and now everything came tumbling down around me. I was sure I could arrange another meeting about the university investment but I couldn't manage without a car and I had no money to buy even the cheapest runaround. Without one I couldn't possibly pull this project together. Was this to be the final stumbling block?

Luckily Ken came to my aid. He would get me a car in return for the shares I still owned. I signed them over and was once again on the road, in a pretty little Metro Rio.

Sunday 6 February 1994 and just three days to go before she was moved to the NEC. I was totally wrapped up in making *Spirit* look presentable when Peter asked what I had in mind for the show.

The rather blank look he received told him everything. Apart from getting a free holiday to raffle off, I hadn't even thought about it. With the same dexterity that had produced the banners and signwriting for the boat, Peter worked out what we still needed to help promote the boat and got on to the Ed Doolan Radio Show . . . printers to produce leaflets, lottery tickets, more banners, help to man the boat at the show, and a crate of champagne!

I was cringing with embarrassment, sure that we wouldn't get a response, but within minutes the phone started to ring as amazingly local people rallied round to help. The only thing we didn't get was the champagne – I guess it was hardly an essential item! I was amazed by the terrific sense of camaraderie and this was my first real taste of how the people of Birmingham help each other out.

On the day we would transport *Spirit* to her first public appearance I woke up with an unusual sensation of calm. I sprang out of bed and looked out of the window. Under the clear blue sky, everywhere was pure and sparkling under a fresh blanket of snow. So quiet, no traffic was getting through – would we manage to transport *Spirit* to the NEC through this? But I wasn't worried. I love the snow – and if we couldn't get to the show nor could anyone else. I still had an underlying feeling that even though *Spirit* looked her best, she would be shown up once alongside the smart fibreglass boats.

By the time I was ready to leave a few cars were managing slowly to make their way through. Passing those that had been abandoned I reached the university. As long as one drove slowly it wasn't too bad – but would anyone else turn up? John Butlin Transport had offered to move the boat whenever I wanted but surely it was expecting a lot for them to turn up in this! I needn't have worried – they were brilliant.

I set out champagne and glasses and soon the rest of the team arrived. Slowly we hauled her out of the lab. What a wonderful sight – what a day for her 'coming out'! Following *Spirit* to the NEC I felt my first vestiges of pride – she was splendid and she was mine!

After she was craned in there was still a lot to do. Treadmaster arrived to lay down their non-slip deck, and the floor covering was put down on the inside. The pushpit, pulpit and other deck fittings had to be put up but by the time the show opened she looked magnificent.

With the help of my parents, Carl, my brother Paul and volunteers, both Peter and I agreed she was the star of the show. Paul Tilsley, the current Lord Mayor, came to visit us, and seeing his obvious enthusiasm for the project, rather cheekily I asked him if the Council would consider 'lending' us Peter for the duration of the show. His help and expertise would be invaluable in currying favour with potential sponsors.

It was a long, tiring eleven days for all of us but the effort was rewarded by seeing the public swarm to see our prize possession. It also brought other benefits. A very nice chap called Bill Jermey who had experience in victualling boats for long passages offered to help me with organising and obtaining all the food I would need for the voyage. The Vice Chancellor of the university, Sir Michael Thompson, and his lady wife came to see us and were impressed. This was the good news I needed. With Sir Michael's support we could probably secure the extra investment from the university.

Then it was back to the University of Birmingham to get her finished. To help ease the administrative side Peter managed to get a sponsored secretary from Pertemps and a photocopier from OCE. Then armed with my vast shopping list he began the difficult task of phoning round potential sponsors to support the project and provide everything I needed – from washing-up liquid to the engine. I passed him all my previous correspondence and soon he was back asking why I had such things as sails and an engine on my list when offers for these had already been made. They say beggars can't be choosers but in many cases I knew specifically what makes I wanted and didn't really want to accept anything less. Muttering something under his breath he told me to leave it with him and he'd see what he could do.

Peter was great to work with, always full of energy and brimming with ideas. We worked crazy hours but it was satisfying and often fun. Peter was now a major part of the project and became the project director.

Peter certainly has a novel approach to achieving his goals. One of the things I felt I needed was an engine. A pretty funny item to want when planning to sail around the world but the reasoning was sound. I would need to be able to provide power to keep the batteries charged, and whilst I was taking some things that would get power from natural sources like the sun, I also wanted a reliable back-up that would give the batteries a good boost now and then. So the choice was between an engine or a generator. I plumped for the engine in the end because it would give the facility to be able to manoeuvre the boat in and out of harbour during sea trials (and of course be useful after the voyage), but it would also be an emergency back-up. I wouldn't be able to use it on the actual attempt except out of gear, to power the batteries and run the watermaker, but if I got dismasted and needed to make my way closer to land or needed to go to the aid of anyone else I would have more control. I had already approached Volvo Penta and been offered a good price but I certainly hadn't been offered a free one. I wasn't hopeful that Peter would succeed – after all, having been approached once it was unlikely they would change their decision.

Peter had no hesitation. He made the link between the Volvo engine and the fact that John Butlin Transport used Volvo Trucks. Peter sold the idea to Volvo Trucks who put him in touch with Volvo Cars who then put him in touch with Chris Davis, the MD of Volvo Penta. Chris was keen on helping and asked how much we could afford. Bad question but good answer – nothing, we were still financially broke and this was only one of the expensive and essential items on the list. Fortunately Chris became convinced, the engine was ours and soon I was having a course on engineering. Chris's enthusiasm for the project was obvious and he became a great friend to both Peter and me.

But you can't get everything for nothing so it was with great relief that I welcomed the university, who had already given so much support, on board as a major cash sponsor. This was a great vote of confidence in me and the project which was nice as I was really feeling very much at home there.

Spirit went on show a few more times at various events around the city and became quite a celebrity. One memorable moment was when she was being displayed in Victoria Square in front of the Council House. A true Birmingham wit leant out of the bus and shouted, 'Yow waiting for a flud, mate?' She was raising considerable interest, and was in great demand, but we couldn't get wrapped up in everyone else's excitement, there was still too much to do. So we decided that the rest of the work could be just as easily finished closer to the sea, and away from Birmingham. We also felt it was important that the project should be seen to be nearing its objective. It was almost four years since I had first had the idea and I'd now had the boat for eighteen months.

I had never considered departing from anywhere but Dartmouth. However, now we were being asked to make the departure from the Southampton Boat Show. Understandably Peter was really buoyed up about the idea. It would raise the whole profile of what had to date been very much a local project and the departure itself should get excellent coverage. But I was unshakeable. I wanted to leave from the River Dart. I couldn't really explain why, except that I had always sailed from there, it felt right for me, and this seemed tremendously important.

After a quick visit to Dartmouth and Kingswear everything fell into place. Suddenly Peter seemed to understand my desire to leave from there. We had a successful meeting with Simon at Westaway Sails about making the sails and he agreed to try and get Haywards to provide the sail cloth. After discussions with the Royal Dart Yacht Club it was also agreed that I would base myself at their cottage which was very handily next to Dart-haven Marina where the boat would be. I was really happy about everything. Dartmouth is incredibly picturesque and from our base on the Kingswear side of the river we would get the best of both worlds.

As the days grew closer to my relocation I found myself sitting in my nice office on the university campus and realising how much I was going to miss it. But still there was the excitement of the next step to look forward to.

After twenty-four successful years in local government Peter had decided to set up his own company and this meant he would be able to spend more time on the project. How fortunate I was. He was working for the love of it (which was lucky since I couldn't afford to pay him!), because he believed in me, and was also keen to promote Birmingham.

My contentment was complete when my mother offered to come down to Dartmouth with me to help me out in any way she could. Knowing how much she didn't want me to go, I was very touched by this and found I was really looking forward to spending some time with her.

Journey to Dartmouth

My old four-foot-high stuffed dog Bernard was roped to the deck as we made our way down south. Mum and Dad were already down there in the cottage that was to be our home for the next few months.

We had a great deal of fun getting her down through the narrow winding and steep lanes that lead down into the valley. Plans had changed slightly so although we had arranged a police escort it didn't quite match where we wanted to go. Peter and I went off in my nice new sponsored Rover car and did a trial run. At every low-hanging branch or low-lying telephone line I would jump out, stand underneath and Peter would try and judge whether the boat would go under. We still weren't really sure but knew we had no option: this was the only way down and at least it was one way. If necessary we'd have to jump on the deck and lift the lines. It was a tricky ride down, but finally, strewn with broken branches, she proudly entered Darthaven Marina, Kingswear, Devon.

The weather was glorious and it felt rather like being on holiday. However, there wasn't time for that. The first evening we all sat down and had a serious chat. There could be no room for hangers on. We had to work hard during the day and enjoy the evenings when we could – anyone who came to stay would have to pull their weight. All eyes fell on Bernard – what use was a stuffed dog?

The next morning started a crazy tradition. Every day Bernard had to be seen to be doing something. Dressed in an apron and a huge pair of slippers he spent the first morning sweeping the courtyard, then togged up in his lifejacket spent a day practising in the dinghy. The next he started to deliver the post through the clubhouse door. When it was time to relax he was to be found lolling in the deckchair wearing dark shades and cradling a can of beer. Now, the Royal Dart Yacht Club is one of the oldest (if not *the* oldest) in the country, is very respected and steeped in tradition. They just weren't used to such crazy goings on. We could understand the slight difficulty in relating such a serious project with such abject tomfoolery but were amazed to see members walking right around Bernard as if he wasn't there! However, our sense of humour finally won through and we got to know what a great crowd they were. We formed some very close friendships down there.

For the first week or so everyone stayed down. Soon though normal life had to resume. Dad returned to help my brother Paul run their engineering firm in Birmingham, Carl had to return to the university and Peter decided it was easier for him to work from his office in Birmingham than from the cottage. So just Mum, Jason (who was our only employee) and I were left behind. Peter continued to work hard on the lists of things still needed and I seemed to spend more time on the phone than on the boat. Jason was working on *Spirit* all the time and Mum threw her efforts into wherever she could help most – either in the office we had set up at the Royal Yacht Club or on the boat.

At the weekends Peter, my father, and often Carl and Paul would come down to Kingswear. Nobody ever took a day off, there just wasn't time to enjoy the beautiful surroundings. Our energies were completely focused on the mammoth task in hand.

Eventually we reached a stage where *Spirit* could be put in the water and worked on there. This was an important milestone. Everyone seemed to be around that day – Peter was there, as were my father and my brother and his family. The BBC came down and watched as the mast was hoisted and she was rigged. It all seemed to be taking for ever and I could barely stand the suspense. This would be the first time she had ever been on the water. Was I just about to witness my recurring nightmares becoming a reality?

Then the big moment came as the crane slowly moved her towards the dock. Whilst she was still suspended way above the water I leapt on board with Peter and my parents. The champagne corks had already been popped, a little too prematurely to my mind, but I was in dire need of a drink to calm my somewhat tightly strung nerves. Down and down she went till we could feel her start to float.

When she finally settled on the water she looked great from the deck. Two swans paraded regally behind us as we were towed round to the pontoon where I immediately hopped off and stared at her in amazement. She hadn't sunk! *Spirit* was floating beautifully and she was well balanced. What a relief! She looked splendid and we all felt very proud of her. Now we could really enjoy ourselves!

Jason went below to check for leaks and to our horror found one. The champagne was immediately forgotten as we all frantically rushed below to find the offending problem. I tried to push to one side the vision of *Spirit* slowly sinking on her first day afloat. It turned out to be not much more than a pin hole in one of the welds but the water was coming in surprisingly fast. We hammered a nail into it to stem the flow and made arrangements for her to come back out the next day.

Once she was back in the water it was time to push on with the remaining work. Everyone else returned to Birmingham and so once again Mum, Jason and myself were alone.

Things continued well for a while and I took a day out to return to Birmingham to present the awards for prize-giving day at my old school, the Edgbaston Church of England School for Girls. It was lovely to see the young pupils, so innocent and enthusiastic about life. They'd also held a reading competition and presented me with a cheque for £1,000. I was absolutely amazed and delighted. They really made my day special and I felt refreshed from my problems by the time I left.

All too soon I was back in the fray and once more trying to cope with all the complications that seemed to go hand in hand with the project. I think in all fairness if there had been a team of guys working with Jason all might have been well. He'd been great in Birmingham but I think he felt quite lonely in Dartmouth – guys working together have a particular rapport that is just not the same when the only other person is female.

I was concerned by the slow progress and not feeling relaxed enough to mess around. The weekends were a little better because then the men came down, but during the week it was difficult. Mum and I did occasionally take Jason to play darts at the pub, although it wasn't really the answer. Jason had to pass the Royal Dart pub on his way to and from the boat and it was natural that he should pop in for a pint or two. As time went on he appeared to become less and less enamoured with the work.

After a few weeks Peter relocated to Dartmouth and set up in the sailing office at the RDYC. This was great as he was literally three steps away. I was worried that he was spending all his time helping me instead of setting up his new business, but he was adamant. There was so much we still needed. A means of communicating was one of the key areas. I was really in two minds about this. Yes of course I would need to take a long-range radio but did I want to take anything else? Wouldn't it be easier to adapt to my new life if I wasn't constantly in touch with home and being reminded of all that I was missing?

In the end it was the involvement of the media that was the deciding factor. Richard Uridge at the BBC had flown to America and arranged for us to take the large new Inmarsat system that would enable me to send back live television broadcasts via satellite. However, even though the university had designed how it could be carried, I felt it was too big to be standing above the deck. After speaking to Mike Golding, who had the previous year sailed around the world, we decided to go for the much smaller and better-tested Inmarsat C. Using a laptop computer I would be able to send and receive faxes via satellite, thus maintaining the surest link with the base camp that would be set up in Birmingham. Funnily enough we couldn't get such a good deal on this, and with just a few weeks to go I was once again in the red.

I started to look at what we could cut back, but Peter was determined. I must go with everything that would help. Forget about the money – it was a problem that could be sorted later. Well, if he was willing, I was!

Even after several discussions, the situation with Jason didn't really improve. He clearly wasn't happy and neither was I. It was a real shame. I didn't want to see him go but understood that, having been with us for so long and now spending so much time on his own, he was not getting the same level of enjoyment out of it. We had a long chat and agreed that he would be happier back home. There was no point carrying on, and then, with the inevitable pressures we were all under, falling out. He had been a valued part of the project.

47

Another of the ongoing problems was the electrical wiring and fitting of electronics. Charles had been really helpful whilst I was up in Birmingham but after the move to Dartmouth things became complicated. Quite understandably it was much more difficult for Charles to come down to Dartmouth to help us out, especially as he was doing it all free of charge. His wife Alison was getting close to having their first baby – an important time in anyone's life. We were getting desperate – time was running short. I didn't really want to bring in someone totally new as I know it is difficult to take up where someone has left off, so we pleaded with Charles to send someone down – even if it meant us paying.

Unfortunately Charles's replacement was not at ease with either himself or us – partly, I am sure, due to the fact that he was recently diagnosed as diabetic – but whatever the reason, the vibes were bad. He was staying with us at the cottage and things became uncomfortable.

My mother, who can normally cope with anyone, was getting to the end of her tether. Did he not have any faith in women? He certainly wouldn't heed anything I said and was scathing to the extreme. This was exceptionally frustrating as it was obvious that he was getting confused with everything, and I was having to pay him. I tried again and again to talk it all through but he didn't want to listen – he thought he knew everything and didn't want some female telling him what to do. The wiring was starting to look like spaghetti, but even worse I could see he didn't understand the importance of placing tuners near antennae. When I talked to him he got very muddled, mixing up in his mind all the different pieces of equipment, and finally blew his top. Enough was enough. However much it cost I wouldn't be happy until it had been redone. Well done, Lisa – another fine mess you'd got yourself into!

At this stage Peter was away for a couple of weeks. He'd booked a holiday with his family months before. He was worried about going but he'd had practically no personal time with them and it seemed unfair to cancel it. I insisted and reluctantly he went.

By now we had completed and sent off the Notice of Intention for the attempt to the WSSRC. They wrote back and said it was 'very exciting news', sending a shiver up my spine. Suddenly it all seemed real and I suffered a moment of panic as I realised there was under four weeks to go and I had rather a wreck of a boat on my hands. It wasn't the only wreck – I was beginning to feel much the same. The constant worry and stress of trying to pull it all together without the money to do so properly was really showing.

Mum phoned my Uncle Dick in Thurleston and he got hold of a specialist in marine power. If I could get the boat to Plymouth by the next day he would see what he could do, but timewise it was all a bit tight. Confidence in the project was definitely shaky. I decided that to retain any credibility I would tell everyone I was going off on trials.

At 4 o'clock the next morning Mum awoke to find me sitting on the end of her bed. She said that for the first time I looked defeated and she didn't think I was going to make it. The trouble was a mild case of panic. I had woken during the night sure that the revised fuel filler position hadn't been fitted and I couldn't manoeuvre in harbour without the engine! But of course as daylight approached common sense prevailed and with Dad's help we fitted the fuel system and were ready to go.

We had a cracking sail down to Plymouth and Nick Nutt came to look at the electrics. My fears were confirmed. Nick said it was horrendous, and it couldn't be put right quickly – in fact to try and identify what had already been done was going to take as long as it would have taken them to do the whole job. Whilst they tried to sort out that ghastly mess I was desperately trying to fit all the other pieces of equipment still in storage. God, I couldn't possibly do everything myself and be ready on time.

Every day Peter phoned from Spain but it didn't really help either of us. Peter was unable to relax at all and the last thing I wanted to talk about at the end of the day was an update on the current situation. It was a frustrating time for both of us.

I telephoned my father's cousin David up in Yorkshire. He was tremendous and was soon down in Plymouth. Apart from being practical he was also great moral support and I really enjoyed him being around. With David's help things started to go well and we fitted the self-steering gear. Like most sailors I had always relied on an electronic autopilot or a real live helmsman. However, it would be impossible to have enough power to run an autopilot and I couldn't be steering every hour of the day for nine months. So I needed this wonderful piece of kit that was powered by natural sources – the wind and the sea. Trying to see how it worked we realised we had yet another major problem – there was too much friction for the system to work. The rudder must be too tight. Oh no! Was someone trying to tell me something? Was I not meant to get off? Well, I wouldn't give up now – not now that I had come so far. I'd put nearly four years of my life into this. We'd have to take her out of the water and try and make the rudder swing more freely.

David was super – in no time at all he'd fixed the rudder and we were back in the water finishing off the electrics. However, it had all taken much longer than we thought and there would be no time now for trials – I'd have to learn as I went!

Back in Dartmouth everyone was with me. Peter had come straight from the airport, my father was down there full time and my sister had flown over from America. I was so surprised to see Sara. It was wonderful that she had come over to help, and quite out of character for her to leave Anthony and the three children to fend for themselves. I evaded all questions about the sea trials – how could I possibly admit publicly that I hadn't had time?

The last two weeks were hectic as we did everything from loading *Spirit* to last-minute shopping. *Spirit* was sinking lower and lower into the water with the huge amount of stores. It seemed impossible that anything else could fit in, but it just kept coming. Over half a ton of food, miles and miles of spare ropes, clothes, sleeping bags, pillows, books, normal-size buckets for general cleaning, huge plastic containers for washing clothes in, right down to every single screw, washer, fuse and every tool that might conceivably be needed to replace or repair everything over the next nine months. As each item went on board it was ticked off the list and its location noted. Every cupboard had been labelled and everything was catalogued. With such a vast inventory it was essential that I could go straight to what I wanted and not be hunting around ransacking every cupboard. It was an awesome task.

A final check through the list of things now stowed on board *Spirit* confirmed that everything was on. Was there anything I needed or wanted that wasn't on the list? 'Pickled onions,' I said, 'olives, shampoo – I don't have any shampoo.' Peter said it might be a good idea to walk round a supermarket and mentally tick off what I had and see if there was anything else I had forgotten. He phoned the Plymco supermarket and they agreed to sponsor whatever I needed. So off we went.

When we arrived I was welcomed with a bouquet of flowers, coffee and cakes. They had invited a reporter to come along from the local paper to follow me round. They would cover anything up to £700-worth of goods. I couldn't help but laugh. 'I'll never spend anywhere near that!' I was wrong. When I started looking round there were lots of things I wanted, from CDs to socks, mustards to some fresh foods. As one trolley was filled up so another one appeared. I spent an astonishing £1,000! It was tremendous fun and I just prayed that I would be able to find enough space to stow it.

I managed to fit in one day at Torbay Hospital learning everything I might need to know if I was ill or badly hurt on the voyage. South Birmingham Health Authority had provided me with an extremely comprehensive medical kit which would be mostly useless unless I knew how to use it. I can't stand the sight of needles or indeed blood but I knew I couldn't afford to be squeamish so listened and watched intently as they taught me the procedures I hoped I'd never need, from splinting broken bones to stemming blood loss after the loss of a limb. The staff there were great but I think they all decided I was barmy.

Peter Kemp, a friend from Birmingham, came down to help and we spent an hour running through the computer program so that I would be able to communicate via the satellite fax system.

The BBC film crew had been down for a few days filming the last-minute preparations. We managed to fit in a quick run out to sea to get some more filming and then spent an hour going through how to use the cameras for the TV documentary.

Richard Uridge had remained a good friend and gave me a going-away present of twelve half bottles of champagne, three bottles of home-made wine, some poetry books, and about thirty envelopes with silly messages in to be opened at various points on the trip. Looking through the envelopes some were obvious – 'to be opened on your birthday' – others daft, like 'to be opened when you realise you have forgotten something' or 'if you're feeling down'. It was lighter moments like these that kept me sane in the final run up to the big day.

As the departure grew closer Dad was beginning to accept that I might really be going. This combined with the long journey to and from Birmingham he had been making each weekend started to prove a bit of a trial. Not that he ever said anything. He was as lovely and hard working as ever but he looked totally worn out. Mum and I had become really good friends and whilst there was an underlying worry about the enormity of my challenge she managed to hide her concerns and get on with the job in hand. All in all, though stressful, it really pulled the family together and we were closer than we had ever been.

The penultimate night before I was due to leave we had a big party at the Royal Dart Yacht Club. I was presented with a beautiful Omega watch – safe up to 120 metres under water(!) – which was a joint gift from Omega and Roundy, a friend of mine who is a jeweller. The Royal Dart Yacht Club presented me with a red ensign and burgee defaced with the crown and arrow in gold – the signature of the club, and a great honour. To thank them for all their support I gave them a signed limited edition print of a painting done by my Uncle Dick showing *Spirit* leaving the River Dart. It was an evening I knew I would relive many times over the coming months.

The next day was horrendous as we frantically finished packing all the stores. I kept racking my brains. Had I forgotten anything? Had I really got everything I'd need for the whole voyage? I knew I couldn't afford to forget anything – the rules forbid taking anything on board after departure. Considering I normally find it difficult to pack to go on holiday, it was a mind-blowing exercise. Ken turned up on *Zany Lady* and helped us during the last day. It was late in the evening by the time I was happy that everything was on board and stowed away.

I didn't feel at all nervous. It all seemed to be happening, but it didn't feel that it was happening to me. I calmly went off to bed. It never even occurred to me that I wouldn't be sleeping there the next night, I just didn't give the next day a thought. I slept like a log.

Part two

False Start!

The morning was hectic and before I really had time to take in what was about to happen I found myself being escorted down through the crowds to *Spirit*. There was a buzz of excitement in the air, but inside I didn't really feel anything. After the emotional goodbyes to my parents and close family I stepped off dry land. I realised with a sinking heart that I was shaking. Something inside me was starting to understand, but my brain was shielding it from me.

Surrounded by a flotilla of boats and wellwishers, I was towed off the pontoon. The sails went up and with just a light breeze I had a slow and tricky start goosewinging downwind to the harbour entrance and the official starting line. This is the most tricky point of sail; with the wind from behind and one sail out either side, it requires having to swap them over frequently to retain control. It was the sort of challenge I didn't need in front of so many onlookers, and with so many boats around. I neared the castle guarding the entrance to Dartmouth, and tried to quell my nervousness as I smiled at the TV cameras and floating crowds. I felt rather like an actor on a stage, and tried to play my part as was expected of me.

As I slowly got further away from the protection of the land the wind started to pick up. Feeling the gradual but steady increase in our speed through the water I knew I would soon be on my own. Taking a deep breath I turned towards HMS *Exploit*, the naval training boat, and putting on a brave face gaily waved a final farewell to my parents.

Sunday 4 September 1994

Now *Spirit* and I are alone. The wind intensifies and I anticipate the feeling of exhilaration that comes with the sensation of speed. But instead I feel my first pangs of disquiet. My mind, still a little numb from trying to restrain my emotions, is finding it difficult to understand why we are moving so slowly.

Normally with this strength of wind I would be considering reducing the amount of sail I had up. But here we are, with full sail flying and struggling to make decent progress. Good heavens, surely she wasn't going to be this slow? I'd made my calculations on timing for this 30,000-mile voyage by presuming that we would average between 4.5 and 6 knots even taking into account periods of complete calm. And yet here we are with 20 knots of wind and not even making 5 knots. The world would take for ever at this pace.

I feel strangely alienated – not just because I am suddenly alone and setting off into the unknown, but more because I feel a total lack of togetherness with *Spirit*. Of course I know how she was put together and where nearly everything is, but I don't have the feel of her. Instead of feeling at one with her she feels as hostile as she had been the day she went in the water. Not knowing her or yet understanding her, I feel she rides under me like some cumbersome weight. She is still inauspicious. I know this won't change until the initial awkwardness has been overcome and we can get on to a more intimate footing. However, I am already concerned that she might be too slow to sail well enough to please me.

There is no use worrying pointlessly – what can I do about it? If she is slow, at least she is strong and well equipped. And so what if she isn't the fastest, sleekest boat around? She is mine and she is my only chance, and instead of whingeing I should be feeling jolly lucky! I can't help wishing that we had been able to become friends before we set off. Yet here we are – total strangers setting off on a long, lonely and hazardous journey.

As the adrenalin rush dissipates, most of my nervousness goes with it and I start to appreciate the day. Gosh, it is lovely to be back at sea again. And I've made it, I've really made it. After all those years of struggling against the odds, my dream has come true. I am here at sea and setting out on a once in a lifetime adventure.

The stress slips away, and I feel in its wake a galloping rush of weariness. So so tired. I can't be tired yet – not until I am out of the Channel and well clear of the shipping lanes, some of the busiest in the world. Just another two or three days then it will be safer to luxuriate in some desperately needed sleep. Maybe even an hour or two at a time. For now I need hot food and coffee to sustain me and give me the energy to sail *Spirit* and survive these first few hazardous days and nights at sea. It only takes twenty minutes for a ship to approach from the horizon, so I will have to be almost constantly on watch. I won't be able to manage without sleep altogether though, so I have decided to set my three alarm clocks to go off within minutes of each other so that should the first one fail to wake me the second or third will.

The first day has been unkind. The north-westerly wind went westerly, and I have been forced to head for the French coast.

Just my luck, if it stays like this it won't be easy to get out of the Channel. The wind's really picked up. Would have liked better conditions for my first day especially as I am trying out this newfangled self-steering gear. I don't feel happy with it yet but I've got to keep at it. Still, if I get into a mess I guess I can always resort to the electronic autopilot for a while though I don't really want to start using battery power just yet – unless I have too!!!

By nightfall I was having to cope with the busy shipping routes and sailing closehauled was experiencing fairly rough seas. To produce some power I have thrown the towgen off the stern. This turbine attached by a long rope will spin in the water and produces power for the batteries.

I don't seem to be able to sail as close to the wind as I have on previous boats, so I've decided to try her on the other tack. When the wind is coming from the direction you want to head, you can't sail directly into it. To get power into the sail and propel the boat through the water you have to get as close as you can, which probably means being 40° or 45° away from your intended path. The distance you have to travel to reach a certain point can be tripled as you zigzag (or tack) along to make progress. It's the slowest and most frustrating point of sail, and is called beating. Each time you change tack you have to swap the sails over to the other side. I've tacked before by myself many times but not on this boat and not with self-steering gear. The result was enough to make me groan.

As I turned the boat through the wind, the towgen spinning out behind got caught around the self-steering pendulum under the water. Pitch black, with the waves smashing against the stern, I couldn't see enough from the deck. Biting my lip, I held on with my feet and leant right over the stern of the yacht. Water splashing in my face, the salt stinging my eyes, I was near to tears with frustration and tiredness. It was no use, I couldn't clear it. I knew I couldn't afford to lose the towgen so early on, so the easy option of cutting it loose was out of the question. Great! My first night at sea and already I was doing something I had hoped I would never have to do. Carefully I climbed off the deck and lowered myself down the steering frame.

Scared but determined I wedged myself in the frame and gripped tight with my legs. The blackness of the night meant I could see very little so I pushed my arms down the rope until I felt where it was caught. The sea breaking against my face and the bouncing of the stern made everything so much more difficult. My muscles were rigid as I relentlessly tried to hold myself safely in position. Then after what seemed an eternity I realised it was finally free.

Feeling slightly shaky and a little weak I slowly hauled myself back on to the heaving deck. Shivering with exhaustion I put the boat back on course and went below to change into dry clothes and get something hot to eat.

Analysing where I had gone wrong with my tack and wondering if tacking with the towgen streaming out behind will be a constant problem, an even more daunting realisation hit me – I hadn't been wearing my safety harness. Lisa, I reprimanded myself, Lisa, oh Lisa, what a complete idiot – you might be tired but you are going to have to pull yourself together if you are hoping to get even halfway round the world! At this rate you'll be lucky to survive the night!

Thursday 8 September 1994

Well, I might not have had time for a trial sail before departure but we've certainly got a feel for it over the last few days. Increasingly strong headwinds have meant very little progress and bad seas. It really is fool-hardy trying to beat into it, but frustration has been building up inside me and desperate to be getting somewhere I bash on fruitlessly.

After four days I should have been miles away but with the wind as it has been I could have turned round and been back in a day. The wind has shifted a little and I have started to make better progress down past Ushant on the north-west tip of France.

However, I am concerned that we are already battle scarred. Amongst other things the rope, called the sheet, which controls the foresail has frayed right through, and the sprayhood in the cockpit which gives me some protection against the wind and sea has partially collapsed under the weight of the seas. But more worrying than any of these are the problems that are rearing their ugly heads below.

I have considered my position. I am still close to the UK, close enough to return and sort all the problems out. This will give me a better chance for the rest of the trip and I won't have these problems hanging over my head. And what have I got to lose, apart from a few days? Negative publicity – that's what – but why worry about that and ruin my chances later? It is time to discuss it with Peter.

For the first time I really appreciate the satellite fax system. Instead of trying verbally to explain my problem I can just type it on to the laptop computer and 'send' it to a local satellite which will redirect to the office in Birmingham and be with Peter within minutes. At present though there is a slight problem, and I am sending via Peter Kemp who has been a great help in setting up the computer programming as we wanted it.

....

08 SEP   FROM: BT INMARSAT-C FAX   TO: PETER KEMP

....

Peter, will you please pass this to Peter!

Peter, thanks for your note. Yes, ironically the wind direction and seas have improved but I am seriously considering whether or not I would be better to come back, get things sorted, and leave again next Tuesday or Wednesday, more confident that things may hold out.

Problems:
- Leak forward hatch.
- Big leak around the base of the mast.
- Leak in navigation area possibly from the genoa track lifting.

(The latter two are the main concern – if I can't stop them leaking then sooner or later I will lose all the electrics. I am already having some problems with the navigation equipment which I believe is linked with this. Also, if the genoa track is the problem might it rip out of the deck under strain?)
- Water gushes through the air vents.
- I would be happier with more patches on the sails.
- Need some sort of protectors over shrouds otherwise will have continual problem of fraying sheets.
- I cannot use express and transmit on the computer.
- The packing system for files will not link in with the BT system and is therefore useless unless a new version can be transmitted to me – wish we'd had time to test and learn to use this before I set off!

Anyway, think on it – speak to you tomorrow re a final decision.

Ciao for now!
Lisa.

....

Thursday 15 September 1994

After conferring with Peter, I turned round and headed for home. With the wind in my favour I made rapid progress back to Queen Anne's Battery Marina at Plymouth, where eager friends were waiting and the press were flocking round. Some might have seen this as a negative move but Peter handled the media well.

In retrospect I now believe it is the single most important decision I ever made. It has been a week well spent. Whilst Andy and a few others helped strengthen and repair some of the weak points I tried to reduce the weight of stores on board. Obviously spares and tools have to stay but I took off most of the food, decided what I needed and restowed. Some books and boxes of wine have been damaged and these came off as well. I am left with just two boxes of wine from the ten that John and Amanda Wilmott so kindly gave me. I decided that I can manage without replacing them if it will help my speed. Repairs have been done, many things were improved, and everything has been looked over. Peter Kemp came down with a revised computer program. Everything that can be done, has been. Everyone here is terrific. We have worked extremely hard and everything seems to have a positive feel about it.

Now I am once again ready to return for the restart at Dartmouth.

The Real Thing!

This morning's departure saw a much quieter gathering. Apart from a few people from the media there were only the officiators and a few friends from the RDYC. We hadn't invited anyone else but unexpectedly my parents turned up. It was a lovely surprise although I couldn't help noticing how pale and drawn they looked. I would love to have been able to laugh and joke and quell their nervousness but was too preoccupied trying to sort out the latest problem.

We'd topped up the diesel tank but now the filler cap wouldn't screw back in. Dad rushed off to try and get a new one but couldn't find the right size. It obviously needed to be watertight otherwise the diesel would get contaminated with seawater and be useless. But the option of delaying my departure for a few hours whilst we tried to locate a replacement was more than any of us could stomach, so we pushed it back in and smothered it with sealant. It will just have to do for now. I'll keep a careful eye on it and if necessary think of a better repair later. After the problems I have already faced in such a short time at sea it was hardly confidence-inspiring and each of us fell silent with inner disquiet.

I gave Mum and Dad a big hug and stepped back on deck. As the final warp released *Spirit* from the pontoon the towboat pulled us clear. No shouting and cheering this time. Each of us pale and pensive with apprehension, the mood was sombre and the smiles strained at the significance of this second send-off. It was with a sigh of relief that we were off and away.

Blanking out thoughts of how those left behind must be feeling, I busied myself with *Spirit*. In no time at all my feelings of weariness and wretchedness were dispelled as I settled back into life on board.

This time I feel more at home and quietly confident. Pleased that I was big enough to go back whilst I still had the chance, I am filled with an inner glow and feel secure in the belief that I now have the best chance for success – if I am meant to make it I will.

My route around the world will be out of the Channel into the Atlantic, then south over the Equator to the Cape of Good Hope. Then across the Southern Ocean south of Australia and New Zealand to Cape Horn where I head back up to the UK. Navigationally it's simple. Just keep turning left until I'm back at the Channel! I've decided to follow the old sailing routes which will keep me well clear of hazards such as the north-west tip of France and the Bay of Biscay. Not necessarily the most direct but should average the best winds, and avoid much of the current shipping.

My first day at sea again has been good with 25 knot north-westerly winds giving me a beam reach on my course to the south-west.

18 September (Day 2)

During the night the wind backed around to the south-west, the very direction I wanted to go. How frustrating. I had no choice but to start drifting north-west and hope that a favourable wind shift would soon see me back on course. I'm only 100 miles into a 30,000-mile journey and already going backwards!

By dawn the south-westerlys had strengthened and with the rise of the waves came an unfamiliar and most unwelcome noise. What on earth could it be? It seemed to be coming from behind the cushions in the snug area and sounded like a loud sharp banging on the hull. Perhaps something was hanging over the side? I checked but there was nothing there. Perhaps someone had left a tool down there from the repairs in Plymouth. But it was a strange sound, almost as though the steel plates were being pulled and then popping as the tension eased. The only way to get to it would be to dismantle totally the snug area of the cabin – a ghastly thought. The sea was already quite lumpy and unless I really had no choice I didn't want to be surrounded by ripped-off sheets of plywood, and to be quite frank I didn't have the energy. I faxed Peter and asked him to check with Andy who had done the work at Plymouth. Peter's fax assured me that everything was rock solid, but nobody could figure out what it might be.

I've decided to keep an extra-vigilant eye on the deck – any sign of stress and I will start to strip the inside, otherwise I'll wait and see if it wears off. One thing is for sure – whatever the problem is I'll have to fix it at sea. There definitely isn't time to turn back again unless I'm prepared to forgo this year's slot, and I can't face the thought of that!

Throughout the day my temperature has been rising and now as darkness falls and I'm writing my log I don't really feel at my best.

19 September (Day 3)

This morning I feel better. My temperature is more normal, despite my being up every half hour checking the course and keeping a look-out for shipping.

The winds veered to the north-west which has also perked me up as it means I can now start sailing in the direction I want to!

With the change of course the knocking's disappeared but confused seas mean progress is a little disappointing – I'm beginning to wish that *Spirit* was a much longer and sleeker boat. However the increase in wind is raising my spirits – I'm enjoying myself!

....

20 SEP   FROM: BT INMARSAT-C FAX   TO: PETER HARDING

....

Mucho vente! A gale – nobody mentioned this ... *tant pis – c'est la vie, n'est ce pas!*

Some really big seas now. Yawing a bit. Still taking it easy whilst I get the feel of how she will handle – well, at least I'll get to know her quickly in this!

I have done hardly any downwind sailing – quite scary really. But it's certainly exhilarating. Going to have to get used to putting the spinnaker pole in to make a good course straight downwind, but not yet feeling brave enough. It could be disastrous to try it out for the first time in bad weather. I think I shall save the experience for lighter and more settled weather!

Anyway, I am fine. Hope you are settling back into a more normal lifestyle now. You've been great – thanks!

Speak soon,
Lisa.

....

21 September (Day 5)

Well, *Spirit* certainly isn't fast but I'm starting to feel very much at home with her. I feel safe and believe that as long as I look after her she'll look after me.

I don't have any particular routine except that every day I carry out a thorough inspection of everything on deck. Every single shackle pin, rope, screw, all are checked – I know preventative maintenance is the real key. Things will undoubtedly go wrong at some stage anyway and most likely in bad weather but at least I'm minimising the risks by taking action ahead of time.

With these daily tasks out of the way it's time to sit down and write Lisa's Log for the Midlands newspaper, the *Evening Mail*. Six days a week for the duration of the voyage – will there be enough to write about? But once I got started I was pleased to discover I quite enjoyed writing it.

22 September (Day 6)

Five and a half days into the voyage and I have really started to settle into life on board – that's not to say that it's all relaxed and lovely, because it isn't, and I'm missing some things too; but in general I'm now feeling more at home in this yacht that is rolling its way through the Bay of Biscay. For the last three days I've had favourable winds, though fairly strong – much of the time gale force – with quite a few squalls and dramatic skies. I've actually spent most of my time in the cabin, as with some of the seas breaking over her it gets jolly wet on deck, which isn't much fun when you can't get dry again. I even battened the hatches yesterday after one wave came pouring in. But today the sun is shining, the winds have dropped to force 6 and it's quite glorious. I'm also now well clear of the main shipping lanes which means I don't have to be so vigilant about my watchkeeping. Apart from nipping on deck every now and then I do as I like. For the first time in many years I now find myself with time to let my mind drift.

Here I am just 230 miles west of Cabo Finisterre on the north-west tip of Spain. How I enjoyed my previous trips along the quiet northern coast. It's southern Spain I really love, not the well-traipsed haunts of the tourists, but the real Spain that only the locals can reveal. Andalucia with its feisty gypsy guitarists, and the flamboyant flamenco. The ferrias and horse fairs, the three-day pilgrimage on horseback to the mystic town of Rocio. How lucky I have been to enjoy all that. Wouldn't it be lovely to be there now ...

....

22 SEP   **FROM: BT INMARSAT-C FAX**   **TO: PETER HARDING**

....

Dear Peter,

Have you ever seen the real Spain? I'm sure you would love it. Are you busy tonight? Perhaps you could fly over and meet me for dinner.

We'll go to a back street trattoria for a glass or two of ice-cold Jerez and some *entremeses* – freshly sliced *jamon serrano*, wild goat's cheese, large green and black olives stuffed with anchovies and herbs. Then we'll stroll around the town until we hear the chatter and laughter of the local Galicians. We can go and join them for a steaming bowl of *caldereta asturiana* (fish and seafood stewed in sherry and peppers) washed down with some fine Rioja wine – Marques de Caceres. The gypsy guitarist is sure to be there, and who knows, maybe we'll be lucky and Señora Maria Jose will grace us with some fine old traditional flamenco – you can hear her shoes stamping and her castanets clapping as the tempo gets faster and faster, and the whole *casseta* gets quieter and quieter – apart from the beating of the drum and the rhythmic clapping of the old Spanish *hombres* with their impassioned cries of ... *Olé!*

Actually you have probably missed the flight and it's the wrong part of Spain for flamenco!!!!

Oh well, dream on, Lisa ...

P.S: Don't worry, I'm feeling quite sane really!

....

23 September (Day 7)

The wind's back to force 8–9 but the motion is quite comfortable and *Spirit*'s riding it well. There weren't too many problems on board so I curled up in my bunk and started reading Robin Knox Johnston's account of his voyage around the world. Heavens, was he unlucky or what. Fascinating though it is, it's enough to put anyone off. So I put it down, switched on the CD player and sang along to Dr Hook whilst pottering round in the galley concocting something for my evening meal. It often used to make me laugh that in bad weather most people went green at the thought of eating, let alone cooking. But I'm lucky. I don't suffer from seasickness and really enjoy producing something tasty to eat.

Tonight I opted for frying onions and then adding peas, tuna fish, potatoes and mixing it all into parsley sauce. I don't know how sailors used to manage to cook before the gimballed cooker was invented. It's such a brilliant idea. Whatever the heel of the boat the cooker swings to compensate and stays horizontal so the food stays on top. There is a down side of course to eating on a wildly rolling boat, and that is you have to eat out of a dish angled just right so that gravity can't have its way and throw it into your lap. All in all this normally simple act of eating can be extremely frustrating and messy, and if it gets on to the floor it's downright dangerous. So mealtimes in bad weather are never really relaxed. You have a choice of either getting it down as quickly as possible in stilted gulps, or like tonight, find a comfortable niche where you can wedge yourself in and leave both hands free to dance the bowl in accompaniment to the rhythm of the boat.

There isn't much that is easy on a boat in bad weather but whilst I'm coping as best I can with life on board, Peter's trying to cope with life back in Birmingham.

I think we both believed that once I had left, Peter's part would be mostly over and he would be free to get on with making a success of his own new business. But with the amount of interest being generated amongst the people of Birmingham and the need for us to cover costs this has actually become a fulltime job.

Peter's first requirement has been to learn how to type. Now that he has set up his own business he's having to do everything himself. There's no money for a secretary so Peter is doing everything from making coffee, answering the phone and trying to generate income for the project. We discuss everything between us, passing faxes back and forth trying to decide the best way forward.

The one thing I hadn't anticipated was Peter's conscience now that he's helped me so much. Trying to explain that I would have gone anyway and that all he did was to make it better for me hasn't dispelled his feelings of responsibility. He's tired and under pressure but wants to feel in complete control and is finding it difficult to do what he needs to do most – delegate some of the workload. My parents have offered to help as have a few others but Peter feels that things will be clearer and simpler if everything's channelled through him, and the logic of this is easy to understand. But it means a great deal of unexpected work for Peter and, as the complexities and problems of the voyage unfurl, I can't help feeling he will dig his hole deeper and deeper.

A further complication is that Peter isn't a sailor. So far this hasn't proved to be a problem, indeed it has meant our skills complemented each other – I the sailor, Peter the seller. But now as things start to go wrong it isn't so easy. We'd recognised this would be something of a predicament so set up a system whereby we both have copies of the same manuals. But this really didn't solve our dilemma. I can read the manuals but not always find a solution. So I literally have to paint a picture of the problem so that even without seeing it Peter can understand enough to be able to discuss it with specialists. It might not sound too complicated but imagine sitting in your lounge with a TV that has gone wrong and then trying to fix it via the telephone and through a third person who isn't an expert. Still, it just goes to show that with practice anything is possible, as so far we are managing it.

24 September (Day 8)

Got up at 0800 hours this morning having been up four times during the night to alter sail or course to suit the changing direction and strength of the wind. It's lovely this morning, but the winds are rather light and the leftover swell of the sea means the boat is rolling about a bit. Managed to find two slices of bread that were not too mouldy – I might make some later on.

I wish the wind would pick up a bit. I had hoped to be passing Madeira within three days, but at this reduced speed it's more likely to be four or five, and if it dies altogether ... it could take for ever.

Oh well, I'm bound to have quite a few days like this. I really could do with a day without this swell though – there are quite a few things that need seeing to but it isn't easy with the boat rolling wildly from one side to another. I wish it was one thing or the other, wind or no wind, but up and down like this means the swell never abates. It really would be nice to have a shower too, but the motion needs to be more constant for that. Not that I haven't been washing, mind you, but it isn't quite the same just splashing yourself with water out of the sink and there is a growing pile of laundry to wash when I get a nice quiet sunny day.

It looks as though it's going to cloud over shortly so I think I'll go on deck and make the most of it. I might even treat myself to a beer – only the second since I set sail a week ago!

2200 hours: Money's still a critical worry. I've swanned off into the blue with quite a large overdraft at the bank. NatWest has so far been terrific. I've signed my flat as guarantee to the debt, but will they hold off till I get back and have time to repay it? God, I hope so. Suddenly it seems very important to have something to go back to. I've read about families who get wrapped up in the romance of sailing off around the world and sell up everything lock stock and barrel to do so, only to find it is not all it is cracked up to be. The transition back is never so easy – particularly with no home to go to.

I don't want suddenly to find myself homeless and can't help worrying about the potential mess I've made for myself. Money still owed to date is one thing, but what about the cost of communicating from sea for eight months? This will surely double my debts.

We've obviously tried to find ways to cut down on costs wherever we can and have had some help to set up a system so that any text I write can be reduced into computer language and thus be up to fifty per cent cheaper to send. However, at present there appears to be a problem with retrieving it. This means I'm having to send in normal text, which is an expensive exercise.

In a bid to keep these costs as low as possible I've suggested to Peter that perhaps we should just communicate once a week, but apart from the fact that this would cause problems with Lisa's Log for the papers it would also put extra pressure on both myself and the people at home.

....

24 SEP
FAX TO LISA – NORTH ATLANTIC   FROM: PETER HARDING
....

Dear Lisa,
Damn the expense at this stage. If necessary I will pay for it – just make sure my name is still on the side of the boat! Take great care. Will fax later,

Peter.
....

25 September (Day 9)

The sky was clear last night for the first time. What a truly wonderful sight – I'd forgotten how brilliantly the stars shine at sea.

26 September (Day 10)

Another day without much wind, but the sea's slightly flatter so I decided to have a look at the spinnaker pole and see if I could discover what was wrong with the cup that holds it on to the mast.

Well, I couldn't. Everything looked as it should, and the pole's clipped firmly into place – I can't understand why it's fallen out so many times. Anyway, having got the pole down I decided I might as well make use of the little wind there was and poled out the foresail. Then to boost my morale I used the opportunity of fairly flat seas to have a shower – what a delight! It really was a gloriously sunny day and I went up on deck to dry my hair. Then it was time to tackle the laundry. The worst thing about the sea air is that it permeates the material and it never feels perfectly dry again – retains a sort of tacky feel. Ugh, horrid. I also can't understand why I always end up with an odd sock. I've got a drawer full at home waiting to find a mate!

Did some useful maintenance on the self-steering gear this afternoon so I am pleased that that is off my mind. It's started to rain now – but maybe it will bring the wind as well.

27 September (Day 11)

During the night everything started to go wrong and I felt a little depressed. Nothing seemed to be working properly and the wind was unstable. One minute it was quiet, the next it was gusting and seemingly coming from all over the place. Suddenly I realised we were not on course so I carefully gybed the boat to get the wind on the other side, let the mainsail out and put her on course again. Having made sure she was fairly settled I moved down the deck to change over the preventer which would stop the boom of the mainsail swinging violently back should the wind shift again later. It was stupid and careless. I was undoing the original preventer line when I realised something was not right. For a second I froze, then as the boom came crashing back I threw myself down on to the deck.

I looked down into the dark confused mass of the ocean, my mouth was dry and I felt shaken as I realised the close escape I had had.

My mistake was to have felt quite safe and relaxed – I thought the boat was under control – how could I so easily forget one of the first rules of the sea? Never take anything for granted and never underestimate the fickle nature of the wind and the sea. Still, as it happens no harm was done except to give me a bit of a shaking up and a pretty good reminder to take more care in future. There are enough times when you have to pitch yourself into dangerous situations without creating them. I've decided to look at the whole system and see if I can set up something that will enable me to control it from the cockpit.

I was feeling more positive later on and decided to treat myself by making some bread. It's really so easy I don't know why I don't make it at home. I guess it's a bit of laziness really when it's so easy to buy, but the difference – the gorgeous aroma as it's baking and the lovely texture when it's done. Such a shame I don't have any fresh salad stuffs to go with it – the thought of crisp lettuce, greenhouse tomatoes and fresh fruit is enough to make my mouth water.

I am just about to pass Madeira and in my mind I can scent the heady fragrance of the wild orchids, feel the shimmering heat reflecting off the cobbled square and I'm enjoying a nice ice-drenched glass of dry white wine before indulging in a light lunch of fresh fish blackened over the charcoal fire, served with a simple olive oil and fresh lemon dressing.

Oh well, guess I had better bring myself back to reality and go and choose a tin for lunch!

I'm now aiming for the Arquipélago de Cabo Verde, a group of islands about 300–350 miles west of the border dividing Mauritania and Senegal.

28 September (Day 12)

Last night was terrible. The wind was up to its tricks again, shifting, dying then gusting – it was impossible to have the right amount of canvas up or to have the *Spirit* stay in one direction. I eventually gave up at about 0530 and went to bed frustrated and exhausted with my efforts. I awoke this morning to find *Spirit* was sailing well and then within an hour the wind had died and I was once again left drifting round in circles waiting for something to happen. I could see dark clouds all around me and four different places where it was raining but I was sitting in the middle of a hole. I know that Tropical Storm Ernesto is affecting the area south of the Canaries (where I had hoped to be tomorrow), so why am I sitting here in the middle of nothing?

Still, there's nothing I can do but get on with some bits and pieces until it starts to blow. Because of the lack of good sailing I haven't been able to generate power for the batteries from the propulsion of the boat through the water. If it doesn't pick up soon I will have to top the batteries up with the engine alternator.

29 September (Day 13)

The sun returned this morning and I unashamedly spent a few hours on deck. I made some bread and let it rise with the heat of the sun. It was a beautiful day with the sun shining, the wind to keep me cool and the sea a dazzling greeny blue.

Although it was a nice day I still followed my daily routine of checking all the kit and doing any necessary preventative maintenance. I started on deck, by checking all the ropes and sheets for signs of fraying, then the shackles to make sure they were still secure (in fact I have wired most of these up so they shouldn't come undone, but I check them anyway). I check for any loose fitments or signs of stress on the rigging and other pieces of deck equipment, inspect the sails for sign of wear or tear and generally give the boat the once over. Down below I check for loose wiring, or plumbing, and then do the housekeeping. It's essential that everything is in its right place or locked away, so that nothing is flying about and I can lay my hands on anything immediately. But even with all this, by the evening things were going haywire.

Instruments that had been OK earlier suddenly started to give out strange readings and I just couldn't see why. I am having quite a few problems with some of the electronic equipment, which means that from down below I can't tell what direction we are going in or indeed know where we are. I guess I'll have to replace the fluxgate compass which will at least give me a sense of direction but I can't figure out what is wrong with the GPS, the Global Position System. This should pick up an average of three fixes every few seconds, from different satellites, to pinpoint where I am. But I seem to be in some sort of black hole as this isn't happening.

Then the spinnaker pole fell out of its retainer and I had to battle to get it back in. It seems to be one thing after another. This combined with my slow progress is really getting me down.

---

29 SEP   FAX TO BERNARD   FROM: PETER HARDING

CONFIDENTIAL
Hi Bernard
Look, I'm writing to you because the skipper doesn't seem very communicative today. Tell me, is she OK? or do you think she is fed up?

Don't let her see you writing to me but please reply ASAP.

Hope you, Edward and TK are enjoying yourselves.

Love from
Your friend
Peter.

---

29 SEP   FROM: BT INMARSAT-C FAX   TO: PETER HARDING

Hi Peter
Yes well we know what you mean. She was great this morning but now she's not very good company. We've decided to play dead for a few hours in the hope that she won't think to take it out on us!!

If I were you I'd give it another hour or so – she's bound to be feeling better by then.

We're OK most of the time but it's not exactly a holiday!!!!

Lots of love
Bernard, Edward and TK.

---

29 SEP   FAX TO LISA   FROM: PETER HARDING

Look Lisa, you are very much like me. We have both taken on a new challenge and some days are more difficult than others. I feel like that, up and then down. We are both used to being in control and keeping our inner thoughts to ourselves. I think it would be helpful if you discussed your inner thoughts with me. I have with you, and you have given me the confidence to move forward. I know you are frustrated with your slow progress but you are doing just fine. And what can you do about it anyway? Pour out your frustrations to me if you like but please don't let it get you down.

....

....

29 SEP   **FROM: BT INMARSAT-C FAX**   **TO: PETER HARDING**
....

Hi Peter,
God, I feel so fed up today. I really thought I would be enjoying this much more than I am. I was fine this morning but now I feel lousy. It's pathetic I know but I can't seem to help it. I hate going so slow – it's driving me nutty! I hope I don't have too much of this type of weather as I really can't bear it.

Lisa.

....

30 September (Day 14)

Light winds today so decided to fly the spinnaker. This voluminous light-weight coloured sail balloons out in front of the boat, and is a truly wonderful sight. But its beauty has a price – it needs constant care. It is a very fickle sail and if not set exactly right collapses and can quickly wrap itself around the forestay. It's almost impossible to believe that something so big can get into such a tangled mess but I've been caught out before on a fully crewed boat and had to repair to harbour to get it all sorted out – not a problem I need now! The other hazard occurs if it picks up a gust of wind, as the size and shape of the sail can mean it has tremendous sideways force and may heel the boat right over. This can be disastrous.

I had an added hazard I realised. I have been carrying a spare forestay only some seven inches in front of the main forestay and if it got wrapped up between the two it would be impossible to unravel. So I took the precaution of using a spare halyard to net between the two and hopefully prevent the spinnaker from getting between them.

I took my time, checking that all the sheets and guys were led properly and then hoisted the spinnaker up and she started to balloon. I nipped back to the cockpit to set her properly and soon she was flying. How lovely it looked and what a wonderful feeling it was as we started to glide across the sun-dappled water.

At about 1800 hours I decided I had to take it down. I'd been at the helm for hours now tweaking and adjusting to keep it full and I didn't dare risk trying to fly it at night when I wouldn't be able to see it clearly.

I ran through the process in my mind over and over again until I was sure I had it all in the right order. I was really quite nervous in case I got it wrong. It's so important to release the wind and get it down quickly. But I did it without a hitch – *yes yes yes*! I feel really pleased with myself and now I can't wait for the opportunity to do it again.

1 October (Day 15)

I'm so frustrated. No wind, or not enough to sail, and I'm just rolling about in a slight swell. The sails are slapping and banging and creating the most horrendous din. Even when there is some wind it's swinging all around the compass and every time I try to sail it defeats me. The steering can't cope with so little wind, the instruments are going haywire and I'm totally fed up. I need to run the engine now as the batteries are getting low, but having checked the fuel filter I saw it was three quarters full of water again. How can there be so much water? Where can it be coming from? Is the fuel contaminated or is it seawater getting in, maybe through the filler cap? Still, whatever the cause, writing about it won't cure it – I need to get down to it and drain it off.

1800 hours: God, why is everything so difficult on a boat? I know they say you have to be a left-handed dwarf to do any repairs or maintenance on a boat but this was really pushing it. I thought I must be turning the bleedscrew on the filter the wrong way, but having checked it found I had got it right and eventually with the aid of a marlin spike managed to unscrew it. I happily drained all the water off, went to tighten it up and it fell off in my hand. The diesel was happily pouring out of the bottom, into the engine room, and try as I might I couldn't get a grip on the thread. I started to feel a mild sensation of panic – this was not a good day. My face was burning and I had a terrible headache – probably a touch too much sun and frustration with the day. I kept telling myself to keep calm, it must go back in. If only I could see what I was doing – but there was no chance of that. It took another twenty minutes of futile turning before the obvious struck me – I was turning it the wrong way. It easily went back then. What a complete imbecile. The whole day has been one that I would be better off forgetting.

Don't think I will tempt fate by trying to run the engine tonight. I'll wait till tomorrow and hopefully make some water, using the desalinator, as well.

2 October (Day 16)

I've been at sea now for sixteen days and apart from the sea and the sky the only things I have seen were tankers in the shipping lanes in the Channel, one container ship making its way towards the Gibraltar Strait and a fishing boat off Madeira.

However, I have had a visitor for a couple of days, who turned up really needing a bed for the night – in fact he stayed two. He looked tired and had obviously travelled a very long way. He didn't speak the same language as me and I have to admit at first I was a little nervous. He came on board and without a by your leave went below to inspect the quarters. Having obviously satisfied himself that it would do – no other option seemingly available – he proceeded to make himself at home. I was a little nonplussed at first, having my home invaded like that, but decided, since I didn't appear to have much option, to offer him some food. He obviously didn't have the same taste in cuisine as I did and turned his head. I tried him with a few varieties of things but he really wasn't interested. He didn't want any water, and he even refused the wine. Well, there was nothing left to offer so I just let him get on with it – I didn't expect him to stay long.

Yesterday, his behaviour seemed a bit erratic but I honestly didn't know what to do about it. In hindsight maybe I should have tried something, as unfortunately his capricious nature proved to be his downfall ... Flitting from one place to another he divebombed the spinnaker which was bundled up in the sail locker, was momentarily stunned, got up, moved about and then wobbled over to the shower tray where he lay down for the last time.

My poor sweet little birdie had died. I felt mortified. He was such a tiny little thing, and even now I can't get rid of the feeling of foreboding – it's amazing how superstitious one gets at sea. I hope it's not a portent of things to come ...

3 October (Day 17)

I feel a bit peeved today. After such a short time the papers are already wanting more exciting reports of my trip. I thought the idea was that I would write my diary to give a feel for life on board. I have taken some trouble to do this and write it in a format that is not too technical that I thought would appeal to people in general. I have been more than honest about what has happened, and having reread the pieces en masse I think they read anything other than 'what a lovely time I am having – aren't I the lucky one.'

03 OCT   FROM: BT INMARSAT-C FAX   TO: PETER HARDING

Hi Peter,
Look, re the copy for the papers. I am sure they would like me to fall overboard nearly every day, but I *won't* be doing this – sure, it's a dangerous trip and as it progresses it will get more hairy and life threatening, but it's unrealistic to think that every day is going to be a totally black day. I am not a lunatic who's gone off on a suicide mission.

The bottom line is I have been doing the best I can and if that is not what people want then I'd rather not bother.

Lisa.

03 OCT   FAX TO LISA   FROM: PETER HARDING

Lisa,
Listen, don't worry. The paper have said everything is great and to carry on. You're doing just fine!

We had a frost here this morning. Winter really seems to have set in – lucky you being in the sun!

Speak later.
Best wishes,
love, Peter.

I accept what Peter says but I don't feel in the mood today – I still feel a little negative about it all. I've spent my life trying to hide my feelings and pretend everything is OK when it really feels anything but. Now that I am being more open it isn't enough. I am not finding this easy at all, I'd like to retreat back inside myself and not feel so exposed.

4 October (Day 18)

I am now halfway between the Canary Islands and the Arquipélago de Cabo Verde, which is about 300 miles west of Dakhia in Mauritania. I know that many people at home have huge maps on the wall to follow my progress, so every few days I give them my position to plot. It seems to me that sometimes their crosses must be almost on top of each other – I've hardly moved anywhere for ages.

I never imagined I was going to have such light and fickle winds for such extended periods of time.

5 October (Day 19)

Well, since I've felt so utterly depressed about my progress I decided to have a look back and see exactly how lousy it was. Had I cut the course finer and crossed through the Bay of Biscay then my distance to Cabo Verde would have been 2,340 nautical miles. However, because of the winds I gave the Bay of Biscay a very wide berth and I have already done 2,244 nautical miles with another 368 to reach Cabo Verde. I must admit that I can understand why racing yachts have autopilots instead of self-steering – they keep a much more accurate course, whereas the self-steering gear doesn't seem to hold course quite so close to the wind. Also any slight shift in the wind means that you can be off course without realising it. What this boils down to is I have managed to average 4.5 knots towards my destination (even withstanding those days I didn't really get anywhere) but in reality have been averaging nearly 5 knots over the course I have travelled – so I am now not so downhearted as I was. But it sure doesn't feel like good progress!

05 OCT   **FAX TO LISA**   **FROM: DAN AND GWEN CLAYTON**

Hello again,

It's nice to hear from you and know that you're generally OK. It's inevitable that some days are better than others – all you can do is be positive about each one, and make the most of it, whatever form that takes.

You asked how we were settling in after Dartmouth, and the answer basically is that life is not quite the same without you. You are very much in our minds all the time. We are not worrying about you as we both know you have the good sense not to let day-to-day problems overwhelm the knowledge that you are making good progress, and that every day that passes by is one day nearer to your aim.

We look forward to your next fax.

All our love,
Mum and Dad, Paul, Theresa, Daniel, and Hannah.

Well, I guess I should be lucky that Peter and my parents are not pushing me to make better progress. I hear what they say and I know it makes sense, but being safe seems a lousy option at the moment when all I want is speed!

Thank goodness I have this wonderful facility to send and receive faxes. What a difference it makes to be able to communicate whenever I want to. It's great getting encouraging faxes from Mum and Dad. Peter is a constant source of moral support. It's funny but I've already got to know him much better through this impersonal route. He also seems to be doing wonders with raising support and many people and friends are helping where they can. He has also mentioned a possibility of coming out to Cape Town with the BBC so that I can drop off film and get a bit of a boost to my morale before I enter the Southern Ocean, but I am not sure I am too keen on the idea. I am scared that if I see human faces halfway through I'll be tempted not to go on. Oh well, I've plenty of time to think about Cape Town. It's still 5,500 miles away.

All the same, it does also make me realise I have missed everyone, and I'm feeling a bit homesick right now. I think I had better pacify myself and make something nice to eat. I'd quite like to escape into another book but I'm going through them at such a pace I won't have anything left to read. I could be good and do some filming for the BBC documentary but I don't think I'm in the mood – I hardly ever am, come to that. I'm not sure I like these feelings of responsibility.

When I first thought of this voyage I wanted to go off quietly without anyone knowing and enjoy the sense of freedom. Time to discover myself and what I am capable of. Yet it doesn't seem like that at all. I still feel bound by convention and expectations.

I wanted to use this voyage to understand more about myself, but instead of having the solitude I expected nothing has really changed. The only difference is I am here and not there. I am still thinking as I would if I were with people. Pathetic stupid things like wondering what I'm missing at home. I know it would be unfair of me to not keep in contact because then everyone at home would be worrying whether I was all right. But I'm torn. I like being in touch and yet it's taking away a large part of what I was hoping to experience. It's just not possible to explore your inner self when outside influences are present. I guess I am not thinking clearly because I'm not actually feeling a hundred per cent at the moment – a sick sort of head, a bit weak, so I guess I shall retire early tonight. At least I'm still sailing with a nice steady motion, so that's pleasing me. Haven't really seen any sign of shipping so hope I'll get some decent sleep – weather permitting.

6 October (Day 20)

Not feeling so good today. I didn't think you could pick germs up at sea but I'm definitely not on top form, feeling quite weak, and my headache is worse. I've got a difficult decision to make. I know some screws have fallen out of the mast, I've managed to screw three back in that I can reach from deck, but there's another one that must have fallen off something else way up the mast – I can't see from down here what it can be, but you can be sure it's there for a reason.

The trouble is, without knowing what it is, and how serious it might be, it's difficult to balance the risk of my climbing the mast when I am not feeling strong enough to do so, against leaving the problem until I feel capable of getting up there, by which time it might have created a more complicated and dangerous problem.

I keep going on deck, to see if anything looks amiss, and I can't see anything obvious, even through the binoculars. In fact I'm finding it difficult enough to balance on deck and when I look up the fifty feet to the top of the mast, and see it swinging wildly from side to side, I'm tempted to risk leaving it till I feel more capable.

I think I'll go and get an hour or so of sleep in the hope that I'll then feel slightly better – I know I shan't stop worrying about it till I've been up there and checked everything.

I am now 380 miles west of the islands in the south of the Banc d'Arguin so parallel to the border between Morocco and Mauritania.

7 October (Day 21)

Still feeling a bit apathetic today. It's such an effort to do anything. Gybing the main and transferring the pole over to let the foresail out on the other side seemed to take ages, and it took me three attempts to get all the lines led right. I should be flying the spinnaker really but I don't feel up to it. I'm just completely devoid of energy, and my mind feels all woolly. I haven't been up the mast again, as there's simply no point whilst I'm not thinking clearly. The weather isn't helping either – it's very over-cast, lots of thunderclouds around, and the air is very heavy, oppressive really.

I should be feeling wonderful – I will be passing the Cabo Verde islands tomorrow, but I can't say I'm feeling much of anything right now. Still, no doubt tomorrow I will be feeling better and will get childishly excited about seeing land!

Nothing of much interest has happened over the last couple of days except that I found two flying fish on the deck. There were scales every-where, presumably from their first nightmarish landing on the deck and their futile attempts to get back overboard, poor things – what a way to go. I really can't bear the thought of eating them. Anyway, I'm not sure that you can.

8 October (Day 22)

At first light I could see the lie of land on the horizon. But it wasn't clear which were the islands and which was low-lying cloud. As I got closer, the cloud lifted and I could make out the different islands.

I am at present wending my way past the island of San Antonio (at least I think that's the translation). We cut close to the headland and at one point we were just a mile off, but our course takes us past it, so now it is a few miles away. I haven't seen anything apart from rock but it's really wonderful to see any form of land again after miles and miles of ocean. I desperately wanted to stop for an hour or so, go and buy a few local provisions, and just see people, hear them laughing and chatting, but in reality the only sign of life I have seen is a masted boat on the horizon. I think I'll have to come back one day and share the experience with someone.

Apart from seeing a hazy outline of Madeira, this is the first land I have seen since leaving England. It's my first real milestone – 2,500 nautical miles off the journey. I've actually sailed 2,840 but not always in the direction I wanted to go!

I'm amazed that I haven't seen a single dolphin yet. I've seen hundreds of flying fish and I heard and saw the outline of a whale. I was becalmed about midnight, and putting the floodlights on the deck I went up to put the genoa pole back on the mast. Kneeling down at the bow I heard this peculiar noise. A slow but constant *fffrugh!* (well, that's the only way I can think of to describe it). I leant right over, and saw a large black shape moving through the water. I've no doubt it was a whale, and I was both excited and slightly nervous. I wanted to see him but I was anxious that he might come and investigate further – one flip of his playful tail could be disastrous. Anyway, I stayed quietly on deck for some time but he didn't reappear. I'm not sure whether I was glad or sorry.

9 October (Day 23)

Gosh, I do wish I felt better. Certainly Nurofen, Dioralyte, dark glasses and keeping out of the sun are helping a little, but my head feels tender in patches and I've got that sick sort of feeling that comes with a migraine. I guess I must be dehydrated as my skin is also dry and hot and that might explain these blisters in my mouth.

I could kick myself really. It's always really riled me in the past when people have been careless enough to get sunstroke and yet I have been sitting out in this strong sun without a hat! Well, although it is late in the day I am trying to make amends by making one. Goodness knows what it will turn out like. I have cut up one of the cardboard drums holding the spare ropes and with an old T-shirt should be able to make something – and what does it really matter how I look!

10 October (Day 24)

I really am feeling like my old self, thank goodness – what a relief. Today sees me slightly frustrated because of the lack of wind but I have made use of it. I have taken the furling genoa down and checked all the fitments at the top – all OK – and retired the bowlines as they were chafing. I tightened the block shackle for the downhaul (can't find the seizing wire anywhere), checked everything else on deck – all OK. Have made two more trips up the mast (how I hate climbing up those thirty-one steps that take me fifty-five feet to the top) and everything seems to be OK, with the exception that even with a very careful inspection I still cannot find where those screws have come from – there are just no screws missing anywhere, which is crazy!

But all that suddenly went from my mind when I saw smoke billowing out of the boat. I shinnied down the mast like greased lightning, raced across the deck, down below and switched off the engine which was generating power for the batteries. I could hardly see anything through the thick acrid smoke, so picked up the nearest fire extinguisher ready to douse any flames. Carefully I opened the door to the engine room but apart from a lot of smoke I couldn't see brightness from any flames. Gradually the smoke started to clear and I came out into the galley to get some air. But it wasn't much better out there and I was just looking at the awful mess, the blackened cooker, blackened kettle – a blackened kettle without a handle! Oh crikey, it hadn't been the engine at all! I must have put the kettle on to make a coffee and well and truly burnt it dry. I'm not sure whether it'll be any use now but I'll clean it up later and, if it's worth it, try and make a new handle. What a twit!

Anyway, I've left it for now. I've faxed Peter and done my copy for the *Evening Mail*, and made some bread.

I went for a quick swim. I dived off the boat and swam off about forty feet to get a fresh view of *Spirit* (but I suddenly remembered Robin Knox Johnston's story of the shark so I was fairly quickly out again). Barmy, I suppose. There wasn't any wind and it was unlikely to suddenly blow out of nowhere, but the sails were up. Still, I am a good swimmer and it was lovely and although I would have felt happier with someone else around, I shall no doubt do it again.

I did a bit more towards completing my sunhat but sewing really isn't my forte. I had home-made bread for lunch with cheese and pickled onions and a glass of water!! I've tightened up the fanbelt on the engine (I knew that crow bar would be useful for something – I used it to jack up the alternator!). Then I greased the self-steering locking pin and a few other bits and pieces, filled the lighter, sent faxes to my mum and dad, then ran the engine to make loads of water and top up the batteries. I have also spent an hour reading through the literature on the self steering to see if I can improve it – only trouble is I'm going to have to read it a lot more than once before I know the answer!!!! I've also restowed the tapes and glue locker, and restored the manuals, etc. On top of that I have spring-cleaned the boat and done some filming – not much, but at least it's a start.

1800 hours. I now have a little wind so have poled out the genoa and am moving gradually along. I've also made a very effective repair to the kettle – it now has a carved wooden handle instead!

11 October (Day 25)

I've also lost sight of the islands now. My next sight of land will be the Cape of Good Hope some 5,000 miles away, and my course to get there is not direct. I have so far followed the passage recommendations as given by the Hydrographic Department of the Navy. This route should in theory give me the best constant winds, the least likelihood of being in an area notorious for exceptionally bad weather, and help me to avoid being stuck too long in the doldrums. It's a longer route and not the natural one you would imagine if you were to look at a map or chart – the distance from the Cabo Verde islands to Cape Town is 3,940 nautical miles. To sail it I will have to go with the winds which will first take me away from Africa before I will get the right winds to take me towards it, and so I will travel at least 5,200 nautical miles.

I really do seem to have been exceptionally unlucky so far in that even having followed the recommendations I have already spent more time sitting around in areas of high pressure with no wind than I would have expected to spend caught in the doldrums – and I've still got those to come! At the moment, I'm feeling more than a little frustrated – I have just spent three solid hours baking in the heat of the sun, tweaking the fractious spinnaker, and my effort has rewarded me after all that time with a pitiful five miles! It hardly seems worth the effort.

It's such a beautiful day, azure sky, ultramarine sea – perfect holiday weather, and I never thought I'd get sick of that – but I'm not on holiday. I've got a long way to go and every day wasted like this means another day extra on the journey.

Oh, what the heck. I'll give it till lunchtime then take the sails down for an hour and go for a swim!

I've got a funny feeling that all is not right at home. Strange really but I feel I must contact Peter and make sure all is well. I'm still feeling concerned about the financial state of affairs back home and can't help wondering if it would help if I sold the flat and cleared it all. Whilst I can see that if I am successful then it might solve both of our problems, there is the 'if' to consider, by which time Peter and I will have spent more money on communications. Oh God, what a mess.

1900 hours: I was right sensing something was not right with Peter. He is feeling really pressured and down at the moment. I said I would give him a call through Portishead Radio but although they have been great and have suggested lots of different frequencies, we still keep losing each other. I've given it up as hopeless for now so have faxed Peter and let him know. But I feel I have let him down a bit by not getting through.

12 October (Day 26)

This morning brought a nice surprise – a little bit of wind – *yippee*! So I can now really start sailing, though it's weird to be sailing away from my destination until I pick up some favourable winds way down in the Southern Hemisphere in about five weeks' time. It's going to be rather difficult to gauge my progress.

I was so excited about the wind this morning, tweaking the sails, feeling the breeze on my face, enjoying the sight of *Spirit* cutting her way through the water. Now I've started to sail I could put the towgen spinning out behind the boat to produce some power for the batteries. I was being so careful (or thought I was), but all of a sudden something slipped out of my wet hands, and I watched in disgust as my half-inch spanner (one of my most useful tools) hit the water and quickly started to sink. I'd been dreading this happening. Still, there's no point crying over spilt milk, and after a few choice words I carried on with that I was doing.

Not that I deserved it after losing my spanner, but I decided to treat myself and call home. I was quite disconcerted to hear my own voice was a bit croaky but since I don't spend much time talking to myself (not yet anyway) I suppose it isn't really that surprising. I think I shall have to consider singing every day to keep it in practice!

I've received a nice fax from my parents today as well as some from wellwishers in Birmingham. Mum and Dad say everything is 'fine' although I am not at all sure they would ever let me know otherwise. But I think I'd know inside, and I just sense that they are OK. I feel good today.

13 October (Day 27)

I'm absolutely drenched. I've just hit a thundersquall – the sky is pitch black, the raindrops are huge and heavy and vainly attempting to flatten the surface of the sea. Visibility has almost disappeared and *Spirit* is swanning through it all famously. My average speed during these 40-knot-plus squalls is around 7 knots, which is brilliant. I just wish it would stay that way. But they never last for long and then I am left once again trying to cope with just the odd variable light breeze. Consequently I cannot fill the sails long enough to move more than a few yards before once again I am left going round in circles with the sails slapping and banging. Then all I can do is sit on deck hoping the wind will eventually arrive. I've gone hardly anywhere this week and it's driving me mad.

It is very difficult to get the balance of the sails right when there are such violent and sudden changes in the conditions. I can see from the weather information that my route is littered with thundersqualls all the way down to the intertropical convergence zone. I think I might be crazy enough to take my shampoo on deck and wash my hair during the next squall!

14 October (Day 28)

I'm definitely someone who works better under pressure. The more there is to do, the more productive I am. When it's like this, going nowhere, with so much time and only a few things to do, I seem to achieve almost nothing and find myself either putting off jobs because I can do them later, or even forgetting things that I had intended to do when I was stuck in a calm.

Over the last few days I've noticed my concentration to be way under par. My mind seems to wander from one thing to the next. This morning I started to type a fax to reply to my sister Sara in America, which prompted me to first finish writing up my log. That must have sparked off another train of thought, for the next thing I knew I was taking apart the self steering where it attaches to the main steering system and trying to solve that problem. Being in the sun made me hot so I made a drink, which started me thinking about lunch so I started to make some bread. Pouring the water into the flour I suddenly started to wonder if it was a good day to do some laundry. As I hung the clothes on the guard rails to dry I remembered that I hadn't quite finished making my sunhat and started on that. It was only when I saw the orange light on the satellite transceiver and realised there was some mail waiting for me that I remembered I still hadn't finished my log!

I've been at sea for almost one month and it all seems a bit unreal. In many ways it doesn't seem long but in others I feel as though I have been away for ever.

I've still got problems with the programming on the computer, it's sending up all sorts of messages. Still, it's an amazing bit of kit and this is hardly the ideal environment.

I really can't understand why Peter can't access the reports from the GPS. I know that my computer is sending them so they are on his system somewhere. It seems ridiculous to be transmitting automated position reports three times a week if they are inaccessible.

....

14 OCT   **FAX TO LISA**   **FROM: PETER HARDING**

....

Lisa,
Please give me your position and tell me what the hell all this is about distress messages!

    Peter.

....

14 OCT   FROM: BT INMARSAT-C FAX   TO: PETER HARDING

Dear Peter,

I am at 9.43°N and 24.22°W, 650 miles west of Conakry, just before the border between Guinea and Sierra Leone. Pretty pathetic progress.

Re your concern about these distress messages, there is nothing to worry about – this is typical of life at sea. I am in no danger but just so you understand I will give you more details. When an SOS message goes out it activates coastguard, shipping, etc. via radio telephone and fax, etc. It sets off an automatic audible alarm on the Inmarsat which doesn't stop until you have read the alert. Basically the first one was about two to three weeks ago. A forty-foot aluminium boat gone missing between the Azores and Spain. Left the Azores ages ago – never seen since. The next was reported last week or the week before, I can't remember offhand. About the same size, left the Gibraltar Strait heading for France – never seen again. The third was last week, just a distress call to say that there was a yacht at sea with no one on it. Then at the weekend or early this week there was a man-overboard distress sent at 2300 hours. But as it was still in existence eighteen hours later it would appear he wasn't found. The other was just a ship that sank – all crew saved but the life rafts were drifting around and were a hazard to shipping. I just rather fancied spotting one and having a look at it.

Anyway, don't start getting any silly thoughts into your head – this is always the case at sea. I remember last year in the Azores being amazed to see that there was a list of nine boats that had left the Azores or were making for them over the last three months and had never been seen again. It's a bit like driving a car – you don't always make your destination!

The positive thing to remember is that nowadays if some ship or other does get into trouble there is a fantastic network set up for rescue co-ordination, not like years gone by when no one would even be aware that someone might be in trouble.

On a slightly lighter note I hope to God that if something unlucky happens to me you'll organise a memorable party overflowing with champagne. No crying for me, please. I'd like you all to think, Bloody hell, she just had to do it, didn't she, couldn't be contented with a normal life – she had to go out there and go for it. For I'd certainly rather die at trying than not try at all, and it will be no one's responsibility but my own!!!!!

Be in touch tomorrow. Hope all is OK with you.

Bye for now,
Lisa.

....

15 October (Day 29)

I'm in fine fettle although had an awful night, possibly because I enjoyed a glass of wine too many and also because it is so damned muggy. I did contemplate sleeping in the cockpit but decided against it and consequently spent all night tossing and turning. I'm sailing quite well and thankfully able to make some power as I can now put the towgen out and the prop gen on. I've been running the engine an awful lot because the solar panels don't really do much and the batteries were run right down.

There's a diddy little butterfly keeps flitting around the boat, which is incredible when you consider I am more than 600 miles from land.

There's a great deal of lightning around today so I think I will keep communications to a minimum – with nothing else around to attract it I'm like a sitting duck.

16 October (Day 30)

I'm feeling a bit down again today and it's all related to lack of progress. They say the doldrums often bring on deep feelings of depression – but I'm not feeling that bad! I'm going to try and get the barometer working today. It's not been set properly since I left and yet I need it as a warning sign for approaching bad weather.

I've been part way up the mast a few times again trying to solve the problem with the fluxgate compass. I've taken it off altogether now so that I can try and work on it below. It's not easy coping with such fiddly nuts and bolts when hanging on a halyard.

17 October (Day 31)

I'm heartily sick with the wind. I can't believe I'm having such bad luck. It's really getting to me now – I've made so little progress. I find myself hypnotically drawn to the wind indicator instrument and spend hours watching the needle go round in circles, all the time willing it to stay in one position so that I can start sailing.

It's really quite pathetic – even if I get a glimmer of wind from one of the passing black clouds I'm out there trying to make a few yards' progress. For the last few days there has been a constant formation of thunderclouds, but even these only have momentary gusts.

I always thought that I would get frustrated in the doldrums – it's a well-known fact that it drives people to distraction (or worse!) – but today I feel really down for the first time. I can't be bothered to do anything, I feel totally apathetic. Just recognising this has worried me, it's been creeping on for some time now and knowing that I am normally so cheerful and positive about things seems to make it so much worse. I seem to just sit there staring and staring, looking for something that isn't there and unable to break myself out of it. I'm reacting as badly as I feared I might and I don't know what to do about it.

Even with all these clouds it's been unbearably muggy. My only activity is opening the hatches to try and improve the oppressive atmosphere, then quickly running round shutting them again to keep out the frequent bouts of rain.

I know everybody tells me that I'm not in a race and I'm doing fine, but I keep wondering if it's a lack of judgement – maybe if I was fifty miles further west or fifty miles further east I would have the wind I sought. Then again, maybe not. I keep trying to cheer myself up by comparing my timings with Robin Knox Johnston and Naomi James but even though I am doing better than them it doesn't seem to help.

18 October (Day 32)

The sails were slapping and banging and driving me demented so I decided to go on deck to see if I should take them down and give up any chance of any wind. The sky was dramatic – all around me were different formations of clouds, some towering miles into the sky, some as black as hell, and you could see the rain thundering right down to the sea. There was even a complete rainbow. However, where I was, nothing, just an overcast miserable-looking sky and the swell that foretold of wind around somewhere. I walked on to the deck and my attention was drawn to the sea, it was a mass of tiny bubbles. The ennui of the doldrums forgotten, I felt quite excited – what had caused them? Had I missed a passing ship? Was it some sort of sealife? I'd remembered reading of cases similar to this before and was sure that Naomi James mentioned in her book how mystified she'd been upon coming across the same sort of thing.

I went below and hunted out her book. It didn't take me long to find, yes, there it was: 'Two things have puzzled me this morning. The first was a series of long lines of foam on the water as if a ship had recently passed, but that is unlikely . . .'

How I wished I'd more books with me on the mysteries and wonders of the oceans. I delved into every likely book I could find – the *Mariner's Handbook* and *Ocean Passages of the World* – but nothing really seemed to give a satisfactory explanation. Eventually I had to admit defeat. Well, if nothing else it had been a welcome diversion from the frustrations of this part of the trip.

However, I couldn't help thinking about it again later this evening and wondering if, like me, Naomi had also found an empty bottle of washing-up liquid in the sink!

19 October (Day 33)

I've just come down off deck after yet another monstrous downpour. I've actually been reduced to wearing a waterproof jacket because it is so horrid (not just wet but cold). This is the eighth time so far today – I thought it was supposed to be warm down here. I'm still only getting wind in the squalls. How much longer will this go on?

I wish I could pick up a weather forecast but I don't seem to be picking up anything at the moment.

During the calms I have been working on various things. I have two huge gas cylinders that look like missiles, one each side of the boat. I've been using the number one tank since I left England, and to trim the boat I have switched over to the number two tank to start taking some weight off the other side. On crawling round the back of the engine room, I noticed that some water has got in near the transom – not much. I've been trying to trace where it's coming from, as if I don't stop it soon it will start to corrode the electrics, in particular the tuner for my ship's radio – I don't want to be without that. One of the possible places is the air vents which, although they are designed to keep the water out, aren't perfect. If they are letting in water now, it will be a real problem in the Southern Ocean. The difficulty really was how to seal them off. I knew there must be something somewhere, and then I found it – the plastic lids from the Marvel containers. With only the slightest modification, these now clamp on but can also be removed if I wish to get ventilation into the engine room – brilliant.

On checking the running rigging, I found that the halyard which hauls up the mainsail was quite badly chafed where it goes into the mast, so I've cut off the damaged piece and reattached it. It wouldn't have lasted much longer, and if it had chafed right through, the mainsail would have come tumbling down, and I would have had to climb to the top of the mast again to sort it out. The mast is fifty-five feet above the deck, and it's bad enough when the boat is flat. When the sea is rough – well, you can imagine.

The only other area of concern is the batteries. Not making any way through the water, I can't use my prop shaft generator or my towgen. And because I've not now had any sun for days the solar panels haven't been of any use. This has meant me having to run the engine for long periods to top up the batteries – I can't afford the diesel to keep doing this. I must admit I have often thought it a shame that I am not allowed to use the engine to propel the boat. But it's against the rules, and anyway it wouldn't take me far. It would also leave me short on battery power so it's a pretty daft train of thought really. I just want to move!

If I get a break in the rain I think I'll go just a short way up the mast and try and fit the new compass.

20 October (Day 34)

I can't believe this weather. I can't remember when I last saw the sun – it's been days. The sky is constantly black, and the rain is incredible. Even more surprisingly, the rain is cold. I seem to be constantly trying to dry myself off from the latest soaking, and gone are the days of a cool drink of water. Now it's hot chocolate to warm me up – this is the last thing I expected in the doldrums.

Still, I am trying to make the best use of the calm. I am avidly reading of other people's experiences of storm conditions and how they did or didn't cope with them – frightening! I've decided that now is an ideal time to check that I am as prepared as I can be for any potential disaster.

Looking around the boat I am surprised to see a number of things that could fall up, i.e. if the boat turns upside down not everything would stay in its place so one of my priorities is to make sure that apart from not being able to move sideways, everything is lashed down.

I don't expect to have to abandon ship but even so I must be prepared. The life raft is permanently strapped on deck, and with a quick flick of the emergency release I can throw it over the side. But what I think I will put together is an extra panic bag. Although the life raft is equipped for survival offshore there are always other things that are useful, things to keep my mind occupied, such as crosswords, pen and paper for writing, a spare watch, a small chart of the world, my emergency GPS navigator, handheld compass (not that I'll be able to choose where I drift but it's nice to know where you are), chocolate, water, brandy, a few tins, dried fruit, biscuits, fishing line, extra First Aid, suncream, and extra distress flares.

I shall also write up an emergency procedure, so that if there is an emergency I'm not trying to decide what to pick up first, the first line of this will read, 'Do you really need to abandon ship?' In a state of panic it's amazing how many people jump off a larger vessel in distress into a small piece of unstable rubber just because of the psychological security of the words 'life raft', when it's obviously safer to stay on anything larger that's even remotely floating, however badly damaged she is. I think I'll try and bear in mind that if *Spirit* isn't so low in the water that I haven't got to step up to get in the life raft, I probably don't need to get off!

21 October (Day 35)

The wind has been playing silly billies all morning. I've got so hot constantly trying to get her to sail on course, tacking back and forth, I can't seem to cool down. I would love to go for a swim but I am at last sailing! YIPPEE! So I think I'll go and have a cool shower. Of course I'm not exactly sailing the course I want to but beggars can't be choosers. At least I am moving. I'm heading west-south-west at the moment towards Guyana, South America, but I am making some progress towards the Equator as well and it looks as though I should have better winds further west. I've got the Equatorial counter current against me which is a bit of a nuisance.

Oh well, never mind, despite everything I feel good today.

I thought it was Wednesday today but it's Friday. I guess that is because every day seems the same. Over the last two weeks I've made abysmal progress. Still, if luck is now on my side (I'm tempting fate here) I should be able to cross the Equator and match Naomi's time and beat Robin Knox Johnston's by five days. They both made slow progress all the way: Naomi took 272 days and Robin 313. I hope it doesn't take me that long!

22 October (Day 36)

0620 hours. Woke at 0500 hours this morning knowing something wasn't right. I could hear the wind howling but didn't feel as though we were making way. I was feeling a bit groggy but crawled out of bed and put the floodlights on the deck. To my horror I saw the large foresail was in the water and half buried under the boat. I thought the shackle holding it up must have come undone but my first priority was to drag it back on board. Tussling with the unyielding canvas against the buffeting of the wind and the crashing of the seas over the foredeck, I managed to haul it aboard bit by bit. Lashing it to the guard rail I gradually secured it back on deck. It was then I noticed that it wasn't the shackle that had come undone, but in fact the halyard which had been chafed right through. I opened the forehatch and using my feet managed to jostle it down into the sail locker.

I put out a smaller sail and got moving again – I can't afford to waste any opportunities for progress. I'll have to wait until daylight though before I can go up the mast and see if any of the halyard is still there. But I think that is rather wishful thinking – it's more than likely slipped down the inside which is a nuisance.

What I can't understand though is why it has chafed through. OK, it was too much sail for the amount of wind, but even so I can't believe it wore through in such a short time. I don't ever remember this sort of problem on the 35,000 miles I sailed on *Zany Lady*, and we never looked after things like I do now. I also need to upgrade the windvane on the steering gear to cope with the stronger winds, but think I shall leave that till daylight as well.

2355 hours. Typical, as soon as it got light the wind started to become erratic – I'm being driven to distraction. Every time I set the sails the wind either shifts or changes in strength. The rain is torrential and over the last thirteen hours the wind has veered from south through west to north then east and now it's backing around the compass again. It's midnight now and I am wet, weary and exhausted. I've just opened a tin of curry which I couldn't be bothered to heat so have just poured it into a bowl. Looks as though I shall be sleeping at the chart table tonight all rigged out in my wet-weather gear and boots, ready to go on deck at a moment's notice. I couldn't bear to find I was travelling in the wrong direction.

23 October (Day 37)

It's glorious today. At times like this you realise that there isn't anywhere you would rather be or anything else you would prefer to be doing. I feel in my element. The sun is out most of the time, and the waves are sparkling and magnificent in their brilliance. The wind is more constant now and warm to my skin. *Spirit* looks absolutely fabulous as she cuts her way through the water. I'm so proud of her and can't help thinking how lucky I am to be out here doing what I am. I shall remember this as one of the sweetest days of my life.

24 October (Day 38)

Had a message on my computer from Portishead to say there was a call booked for me, and for ages I have been trying to get through. It's funny how important it seems to make that link. I can't think I would have felt I needed to respond quickly at home, but out here it takes on so much more significance. I feel that if I don't get in touch immediately then someone might be worrying unnecessarily. Although for all I know it could be someone I don't particularly want to speak to. Anybody can put a call in to me. At home I had the luxury of being ex-directory so only friends and family would call. I think I will fax Portishead Radio and ask them to let me know exactly who it is, then I will be able to gauge the urgency and feel-good factor of bothering to spend any more time trying to get in touch. It's not like picking up a phone and dialling a number, it always seems to take ages to get through. It's a lot of effort and selfishly I want to know if it is worth it before I have another attempt.

I'm also a bit cross that I have wasted battery power. I wanted to capture my conversation on film so lit up the cabin with the special paglight, and had that and the camera draining power from the batteries – all for nothing. What a stupid waste.

I've topped it all by flooding out the galley. I switched the water pump on and had a shower in the heads but when I came out I saw that the taps were on in the galley as well. This is one of the problems of having both a hand pump system and an electric pump. Having obviously turned on the galley taps and found the pump was off I used the hand pump but forgot to close the taps. Still, all I've done is waste some water and it's pushed me to wash the floor, so it's not all bad.

Anyway nothing could spoil my day today – not even the fact that the wind is forcing me more westerly than I would have liked. For some inexplicable reason I feel great!

25 October (Day 39)

YIPPEE! TODAY I SHALL CROSS THE EQUATOR!

I was up at 0430 hours and making fresh bread for breakfast. I'm going to spoil myself today. Recklessly decided to give myself a face pack – something I never had the time or patience for at home. I wasn't quite sure what to make it with but lack of anything else saw me cracking an egg and splitting the white from the yolk.

Stage one was a failure. Having plastered my face with the egg white, it started to harden and pull my skin really tight. Out of curiosity I couldn't help peeking in the mirror. One look was too much – the laughter bubbled up inside me and the next minute it cracked into hundreds of pieces and was ruined. So on to the next stage. Mixing the yolk with some honey I applied it to my skin (which remarkably did feel better even after those few moments). Yes, this was much better, but I don't think the warm weather was helpful, as it soon started to feel horribly sticky and I had to wash it off.

I shall wash my hair later and give myself a manicure, then sit down to a feast of salmon pasta and champagne.

Then I can enjoy my congratulatory faxes – I've already had two and hope to receive some more by the end of the day. I know I've got at least one present to open but if I can actually fight my way through to it I'm also going to delve into the enormous sack of presents – surely they can't all be for Christmas and my birthday!

By the end of today I shall have logged over 4,200 miles, and it feels good.

1500 hours: Well, I'm not there yet, still have twenty-seven miles to go. I've been through the Santa Claus sack and found loads of good luck cards and presents, including a lovely photo album that Mum and Dad put together of my last few days on land, and I can't stop looking through it.

I've decided to save the rest for Christmas, even if a few of them are meant for now, as I really don't know where I am going to put everything. The snug is festooned with cards and streamers and there is wrapping paper everywhere – it looks gloriously shambolic!

I am dead on schedule to cross the Equator at 2030 hours and the champagne is cooling in a bucket of seawater.

....

25 OCT   FROM: BT INMARSAT-C FAX   TO: PETER HARDING

....

PETER,
I AM ONE MILE NORTH OF THE EQUATOR ... SO OPEN YOUR CHAM-PAGNE. CHEERS!!!!!!

   LOVE,
   LISA.

....

....

25 OCT 22:28 FROM: BT INMARSAT-C FAX   TO: PETER HARDING

....

DEAR PETER,
I AM CROSSING THE EQUATOR NOW! ... YES YES YES!
   HERE'S TO YOU – THANKS FOR ALL YOUR SUPPORT. YOU'RE ONE VERY VERY SPECIAL PERSON. PLEASE SEND MY LOVE TO MY PARENTS.
   LET'S DRINK TO SUCCESS AND HAPPINESS ... CHEERS!

   HIC HIC HIC!
   LISA.

....

25 OCT   **FAX TO LISA**   **FROM: PETER HARDING**

Lisa,

Well done – brilliant! I've got my champagne here and I'm toasting you and your success. I've spoken to your parents who send their love and will be sending a message tomorrow. Fantastic – keep it up, you are doing *great*!

Love,
Peter.

I can't believe it – I've actually crossed it. I'm now in the Southern Hemisphere. It feels absolutely superb – oh, what a moment.

Well, whatever happens now at least I shan't feel I've let people down if I don't make it. When I think of some of the snide comments made before I left I am just glad that I can rightfully now ignore them. I just hope that when I get back I can say a big enough thankyou to all those who have helped, especially Peter.

26 October (Day 40)

The satellites must have been red hot with Peter and me communicating so much last night – there seemed to be so many different ways to express how marvellous it felt to cross the Equator at last.

I still can't stop looking through Mum and Dad's photo album, which with all the lovely messages inside the cards made me feel quite emotional. Not surprisingly today seems a bit of an anti-climax. This combined with the effect of very little sleep due to unsettled weather, and the surprisingly heady effects of the half bottle of champagne, has meant that all day I have been feeling a little out of sorts. My day has just disappeared in a haze of fantasy as I imagined spending hours with the people closest to me and the enviable freedom of being able to jump in my car and go off wherever I liked.

27 October (Day 41)

Had a busy night. Almost no wind one minute then a gale for an hour or so, dropping right down again. Each time I got snug on the bunk I had to get up again. This went on most of the night so today am not feeling too full of life. Guess I'll try and snatch some sleep today if possible.

28 October (Day 42)

Today, although after another night without much sleep, I am once again settled into my existence and thinking about my next milestone – Cape Town – now some 4,500 miles away. It's very difficult at this stage to say when I am going to arrive, basically because I am initially heading for South America to pick up the winds. Peter, not being a sailor, keeps asking me for an ETA. I suppose it depends how accurate he wants me to be. I can probably estimate within one week – approx. five and a half to six and a half weeks, but if my past progress is anything to go by I'll be way out! I will have a much better idea when I am actually heading for it.

Can't decide what the weather is going to do. It's not very settled but I shall try and go up the mast to sort those problems out. Then I might take the cabin apart to find the banging which from time to time reoccurs, although I must admit since it means dismantling most of the joinery I am rather loath to start such a complicated task. I don't have a jigsaw to cut a panel out easily and don't want to start it and then leave it in a state where I have to look at a mess. Oh well, one thing at a time. First up the mast to try and sort out the problems with all these chafing halyards.

31 October (Day 45)

The last three days have been a nightmare. I am going absolutely demented here as Peter has been sending me fax after fax asking me to confirm I am all right. I've sent him numerous to say 'Yes yes yes, I am fine', but he obviously isn't picking them up. My computer is confirming they have been received so they must be sitting in his mailbox somewhere. I cannot understand why this has suddenly developed a hiccough and ridiculously keep replying even though he isn't retrieving them.

I've tried to contact him via the SSB radio but Portishead tell me that I am breaking up too badly – hopefully, though, they will at least tell him I have been trying.

I know it's selfish but I do wish I could somehow let him know to stop trying. He's presumably worried which is why his faxes are conveying such a sense of frustration. He's probably going out of his mind, writing so many times and getting no response, but it's driving me crazy! I've got to the stage where I want to switch the bloody thing off.

1 November (Day 46)

To retain my sanity I decided to make sure that I had a nice day today. I have promised myself not even to look at the computer until later on as there is no point getting all het up about the fact that I can't communicate with Peter. So I have enjoyed a beer in the sun, given myself a manicure and been reading on deck. I am still sailing but the wind is very light.

It's strange but I dream a lot on the boat. I've hardly ever had a dream in my life, well certainly not that I remember, but just lately I have been dreaming every night. I don't dream about the boat, I dream about life in general. But last night it was mice – tiny clingy blood-sucking mice that were everywhere, all over the room (wherever I was), all over my body – they had started out as cats. I felt so bloody awful this morning I haven't felt good all day. I hate this sort of thing – it makes your head ache, you feel tired and can't understand what makes you dream such crazy things.

Am I going crazy? Yes, but I've always had a head start on that and believe it to be quite an essential requirement in order to have depth of character and an understanding of the world at large. Maybe it's because I have so much time that my mind can wander around itself picking up bits and pieces and chucking them all together to make a nonsense. I often imagine I am somewhere else, somewhere that I know, with people I know but who aren't associated with that place and we're having seemingly intelligent conversations about totally nonsensical things. At least I hope it is just that my mind is exploring, but I'm now not at all sure.

Hunting for a new book today I realised what a strange collection I had picked up. I had been offered a selection of books from The Works bookshop and found one on the meaning of dreams. I couldn't resist pulling it out and reading about mine. God, I wished I hadn't. Every one of them tells of having a close shave with death or being shipwrecked.

I've put it away for now and have decided to read a children's book on fairy tales instead! But I'm feeling a bit disturbed by what I've learned. For some reason I can't dismiss it as easily as I would like and I have to admit these don't seem like normal dreams.

2 November (Day 47)

I am currently still heading west of south towards Ilha da Trinidade, just 600 miles east of Vitória on the Brazilian coast. Hopefully some time within the next 400 miles I will start to pick up more favourable winds that will enable me to start heading at last for Cape Town. I've been amazed at how erratic the winds are down here – from all the information I have they should be pretty constant, but they have been far from that. I'm keeping my fingers crossed that I don't get too stuck around the Tropic of Capricorn where the winds are definitely not expected to be reliable.

I desperately want to make progress towards Cape Town, and yet at the same time I know that every mile I travel takes me closer to the Roaring Forties and the unfriendly Southern Ocean – a prospect which fills me with a mixture of exhilaration and apprehension.

The plan is to rendezvous off Cape Town to drop some film off to another boat. It will of course be lovely to see people, even if it is from a distance, but to be honest it's somewhere out of preference that I would steer clear of. Everybody thinks of Cape Horn as the worst place to be, but one of the world's most dangerous stretches of water is off the Cape of Good Hope. It's known as the Cape of Storms and a gale or storm off here opposing the fast-moving Agulhas current causes unbelievably high, steep seas and freak waves. Boats that have survived hurricanes have met their fate on this shallow bank. Chay Blyth had a frightful time here on his first attempt to sail alone around the world. He was knocked flat (i.e. the mast hit the water) eleven times whilst trying to cross the Agulhas Bank, and had no alternative but to give up – it must have been a terrific disappointment. I can only pray that fate is kind when I reach this notorious black spot.

3 November (Day 48)

It's taken me four trips up the mast eventually to feed a mouse down inside so that I can rethread the halyard. It was more complicated than normal because the spare forestay blocks the opening to the mast. Finding something that was small enough to push through yet heavy enough to ensure that it fell straight down the inside of the mast wasn't easy. Anyway, having gone up so many times I thought I might as well go up once more to see if I could get some spectacular footage for the BBC documentary.

It wasn't easy trying to hold on and film the deck at the same time. It's amazing how much more it sways around up there. Consequently I don't think my filming will be steady enough to be of much use but it was worth experimenting, even though I do have some rather nasty bruises on my arms from gripping so tight! I guess this is one occasion I should have bothered to use a safety harness but I find it just makes climbing the mast so much more complicated. Having to clip and unclip at every step seems to present more hazards than just climbing up freestyle.

4 November (Day 49)

I don't know what brought it about but I suddenly feel more content and able to accept my progress to date, and I've resolved not to spend useless time and nervous energy worrying about what to me seems slow progress. How arrogant I must be to think I should be ahead of Naomi's time when she was in a much larger boat than mine, which was obviously going to give her much better speed. Having set out purely with the desire to 'have a go', somewhere along the line I have turned it from a personal challenge into a race in which I am determined to improve or better not only the achievement, but the time as well.

Considering I would, if necessary, have set off in a bath tub with any old sheet as a sail, to be disappointed with what I do have seems to be churlish and ungracious in the extreme. *Spirit* is proving to be a wonderful boat, and if she is not light it is because she is constructed of steel – which I wanted. She is equipped with all manner of luxuries which are undoubtedly helping to make it a pleasant experience – but which I could if necessary have done without.

How extraordinary that I should be so conflicting in my emotions. One minute cursing her lack of ability to sail fast in light winds, whilst the next minute indulging myself by celebrating with some of the very things that contribute to this fact – good food, champagne at the Equator, and a bag full of congratulatory presents.

Still, I now feel purged – yes, it's a wonderful feeling to put things in perspective.

I wonder how long it will last . . .

5 November (Day 50)

....

5 NOV   FROM: BT INMARSAT-C FAX   TO: PETER HARDING

....

Hi Peter,

It's Bonfire Night tonight. What are you going to be doing? I wonder what my parents are doing? It's times like these that I find most difficult. The thought of everyone at home getting together round a roaring bonfire with fireworks and glasses of hot mulled wine is enough to make me wish I were there instead. Goodness knows how I will cope with Christmas!

Yes I know it's silly but that's just how I feel!

Anyway hope you have a good time – you lucky thing,

Lisa.

....

To keep things in perspective I have written a bit of verse today to try and remind myself of what I have so far achieved and why it is that I am out here.

It's pretty obvious I shall never be a poet though.

> 'Twas on a baking summer's day
> As I lay dreaming on my boat
> That inspiration struck me
> My future was afloat
>
> The spark ignited deep within
> Was only just the start
> Of many years of hardship
> As I tried to please my heart

What madness filled my days
And what sadness filled my soul
This was no easy task
To achieve this farfetched goal

My mind was bent on something
That my friends could not behold
But my vision was so clear
That no way would I be told

I wished to sail around the world
Non-stop and all alone
And to this end I gave my life
And all that was my own

It's impossible to understand
How much effort was required
To make the smallest headway
Towards the chance that I desired

But when you set yourself a goal
It's yours and yours alone
And only you can make it work
To make your life your own

So I struggled on against all odds
And began to see the day
When finally my assiduous work
Would see me on my way

And having worked so very hard
Support eventually came
I'll never forget the help I got
To help me achieve my aim

Now here I am and all at sea
And starting on my quest
I do not know how well I'll do
I can only give it my best

But if I fully succeed or not
Is really inconsequential
For I'll always know within my heart
That I tried to my full potential

And the thing that keeps me going
And why my enthusiasm refuses to pall
Is the belief that it's better to try to achieve
Than be afraid to try at all

6 November (Day 51)

Gosh, these halyards really are chafing through quickly. I've got to try and find out what it is. How on earth am I going to cope in the Southern Ocean? I can't possibly keep popping up the mast. I shall be risking my life every time.

Today I have been hit by a serious bout of depression that I can't seem to shake off. I'm tearful most of the time, and think it is the lack of progress that is getting me down. I hate it when it is like this – I'm not getting far and I'm moving in the wrong direction, which is like an omen that things are not going to go right. I haven't had any strong wind for so long that I'm almost getting scared of seeing a gale, let alone what I've got to face in the Southern Ocean. I'm worrying I'm letting everybody down, and also scared that I am not going to make it. With no control over the conditions here it's made me feel very vulnerable. I'm screaming inside and can't seem to get a grip on myself. I've never felt so out of control with myself before and it scares me.

God, this is so unlike me. What's happened to the positive Lisa? I guess it must be the lack of progress and total helplessness to be able to do anything about it. I'm hating it!

I'm feeling incredibly weak too. I keep falling asleep in the cockpit and banging my head, but that is probably a mixture of apathy and lack of food. I just don't seem to have an appetite at the moment.

7 November (Day 52)

The Ilha da Trinidade has been in sight since dawn which puts me about 770 nautical miles east-north-east of Rio de Janeiro. I really had hoped not to have come this far west but I've had no choice. I've been exceptionally unlucky with the wind direction which has meant that I have not met the more easterly winds which would have enabled me to travel towards Cape Town. Ironically, I am now much nearer to Cape Horn than to the Cape of Good Hope and more than once it has entered my mind to have a go at sailing round the other way.

I'm now moving into the latitudes around the Tropic of Capricorn where I must expect to have more fickle winds. However, every mile south at least takes me nearer where eventually I will pick up the prevailing westerlies, and of course, the distance west to east gets shorter the further south I go – so it's not all bad.

The night sailing at the moment is quite something. The stars are magnificent and seem to cover the sky completely. Also the sea is alive with huge fish and jellyfish. As darkness falls and *Spirit* sails gently through the water the complete blackness of the ocean is shattered by the startling brilliance of the phosphorescence. It's almost mesmerising – such a beautiful sight.

I've sent the paper a log of my day today:

0430 hours   Up to keep a sharp look out for Ilha da Trinidade 700 miles west of the Brazilian coast.

0440 hours   No sign of any navigation light, it's still pitch black outside. I need a strong cup of coffee. Position 20.06°S 29.37°W – should be able to sight the island at dawn at any rate. Poor progress again through the night. Only thirty-two miles covered in last nine hours and still travelling west of south which is disappointing.

0500 hours   Nothing in sight on radar.

0700 hours   Dawn just about to break but so much cloud around difficult to make out which is land and which is not. It's still a lovely morning – going to be hot later.

0800 hours   Spent the last hour on deck helming and singing along to *Phantom of the Opera*. Island in sight since dawn – looks very inhospitable from here. Fax to Peter.

0900 hours   Difficult to keep *Spirit* on course with such light and fickle winds – driving me crazy.

1030 hours   Quite a few birds about – not seagulls as I recognise. Don't fancy a swim, too many jellyfish. Daily deck and rigging check complete – no new problems visible.

1200 hours	Made some more bread again and left it to rise in the heat of the sun. Ilha da Trinidade looks like a half-submerged rhinoceros. Can't see any signs of habitation – maybe there's some the other side.
1330 hours	Just enjoyed lunch and a lager on deck. I wished I hadn't only brought eighteen cans with me – what was I thinking of?
1600 hours	What little wind there is is all over the place, *Spirit* has spent the day going round in circles. How I wish I was allowed to use the engine to gybe her back on course – it's testing my patience.
1700 hours	Changed the ship's compass to the Southern Hemisphere one.
1900 hours	Trying to change fluxgate sensor up mast but think I'll wait till she is on a more steady course.
2000 hours	Leaving Ilha da Trinidade behind at last. Position 21.05°S 29.32°W. Time for a glass of wine, something to eat and send fax via satellite to Peter. Too much sun I think today – given me a headache.

8 November (Day 53)

Another beautiful day, very sunny and just a breath of wind. *Spirit* is moving along at barely 2 knots.

I think one of the jobs I have got to do today is go through my sack of potatoes. I noticed a certain odour coming from them yesterday which presumably means that some if not most have decomposed and I might as well save any that I can. Fortunately the onions and also the eggs seem to be faring better, which is lucky as they are the only other source of fresh food I have apart from the bread I make.

The batteries are also getting low. Because I am not sailing at any decent speed, I cannot generate power from my two main sources. The solar panels provide a little, but not enough, and I have already used more diesel than I wanted to so early on in the trip. I do hope I get some good sailing winds soon.

9 November (Day 54)

It's another sunny day and with just a gentle breeze *Spirit* is gliding across the sun-sparkled sea. It's the sort of day that would entice anyone to take up sailing. The sea is almost flat, and the shushing sounds as *Spirit* paves the way ahead is tranquillising. When I can put to one side the pressing time factor, I know there is nowhere I would rather be than here.

The sea has a certain magical quality that is enigmatic. It never looks the same, and yet it does. Every day is the same yet different. It reminds me very much of the desert. There's just something about the endless miles and miles of isolation that draws you to its soul. I can't imagine ever being bored out here, life takes on a different meaning. There are days like today that are nearly perfect in their serenity, other days where the conditions are just as nice but I am frustrated through my lack of progress, and others where I would be happier sharing the experience. There are moments of fear, and the knowledge that soon I will be facing the daunting prospect of the Southern Ocean. The fear will be tempered with feelings of exhilaration and relief that I am making good progress. I know that at times I'm going to wonder what on earth I am trying to do out here all alone, and wish with all my heart I had stayed at home.

However, I wouldn't change it for the world. I feel at one out here, all my emotions are heightened, some good and some bad, but it's all real. There's nothing to hide behind – I am me, there's no point pretending to be anything else. There's something good about having to accept yourself as you really are.

10 November (Day 55)

Have been sailing well since yesterday lunchtime and have covered 126 miles in the last twenty-three hours, *and* in the direction I want to go. I am headed to cross the parallel of 30°S at 23°W, and from there shall aim to cross the Meridian of Greenwich at 35–37°S and head towards Cape Town from the south-west. Because of the spherical shape of the earth, the further south I go, the less distance there is between west to east, so even though this may seem a longer route than heading directly for Cape Town now, it is in fact a few miles shorter – and every mile counts! It's so nice to have *Spirit* sailing well again and to cross some miles off.

I do wish I had managed to get all those problems sorted up the mast, but I haven't yet so I guess I'll have to go up again. It's amazing how much more you roll when you are another fifty feet up, and whilst it's an amazing sight to see *Spirit* from way up there, it doesn't really compensate for my fear of heights! Going up the mast again is not a prospect I relish and it requires a determined effort to get myself together and start the formidable climb up. There are a couple of places, for example where the radome (for the radar) is, that are extremely complicated to get past, and whilst I don't enjoy any of it I really do hate those two hurdles. It's also acutely difficult to hold on and manage to accomplish intricate work when you are being swung from side to side. Every time I get back down, I'm covered in bruises and quite shaky from the sheer mental and physical exertion of keeping hold – it's definitely one of the worst complications of being on my own. How much easier if there were other crew on board and I could be hauled up in a bosun's chair – or even better, let someone else go up!

11 November (Day 56)

I was rudely awoken in the night with the knowledge that something wasn't right. I had been heavily asleep and by the time my brain was in gear, everything seemed to be OK. I was just dropping off to sleep again when I heard what had obviously alerted me before. A high-pitched screaming sound. It only took me a couple of moments to realise the gas alarm was going off.

It's such a terrible noise, and it's funny how noises like that really set your nerves on edge and make the situation seem more panicky. Unfortunately, for safety reasons, it is wired up so that I cannot shut it off.

I went into the engine room, armed with my gas detector set – a bottle of slightly watered-down squeezy with a brush on the top – and set to work. I've only got two huge cylindrical gas tanks, one each side of the boat leading to a vapour tank and pressure system before being fed to the cooker. I pasted everything but could find no sign of bubbles growing. I tried again and again, but found nothing.

I knew the alarm was sensitive, so started to look for other causes. A few rotten potatoes were giving off quite an odour so I guessed that must be it and removed them all to sort through again later. Sure enough it stopped.

However, this morning it's started again. I've once again retested all the connections and admittedly can't smell anything but if gas is escaping and sinking into the bilges I'll never get it out and next time I go to switch something on or light the cooker – well, we all know what that can cause.

At least I've found a way to stop the nerve-racking alarm whilst I am trying to sort it out – I've plugged it with Blu-tak!

12 November (Day 57)

I've got my fingers and toes crossed that I keep the wind through the horse latitudes. According to one theory they get their name from the early ships carrying horses to the New World, which were often becalmed in these areas and had to jettison the horses when they died of thirst and starvation. I wonder if this is how seahorses came about (ha ha!). Joking apart though, it would be nice to think that those poor creatures went on to become seahorses and live happy ever after in the water.

Got a busy day today. The self-steering gear needs to be looked at. The control wheel which attaches to the main steering wheel is partly broken away, and since last night it has been almost impossible to disconnect it. I obviously can't afford to put myself in a situation in which I can't control the steering – it could cause havoc – so I'll have to see if I can find a way to fix it.

13 November (Day 58)

I really could have kicked myself this morning. I started off in such a good frame of mind, and with my list of jobs set to work.

One of these was to repair or replace the topping lift. This is a halyard that goes from the bottom of the mast, right up the inside to the masthead, then down to hold up the end of the boom. Now, it's quite usual to keep moving ropes along to reduce the risk of them being constantly rubbed and chafing through, but just like the other side of the mast this was being worn down really quickly. If it went I would again be left with the problem of going up the mast to try and drop one down the inside again. So carefully attaching a thin line on a reel to the deck end I slowly pulled it through to the end of the boom. Unfortunately the small line spun off the end of the reel up the mast and the whole lot came tumbling down till it was trailing in our wake. Thus my attempt at preventative main-tenance has landed me with the very problem I was trying to avoid! Once

109

I'd calmed down I made another couple of trips up the mast and managed to replace it.

Since then I have been doing all manner of jobs. I have made a retainer for the wine box – definitely top priority! I have secured down the television and cut out some more indents into the foam to secure better all the camera equipment. I have also made a mug holder to prevent it sliding around and put in a couple more restraining bars in the cupboards to stop things falling out when I open the door.

I've done some filming for the documentary and now I think I will sit down and treat myself to a meal and listen to some music.

14 November (Day 59)

Not a good night last night. After my meal I went on deck for a while. It was a beautiful starlit night, although there was a dark cloud on the horizon. As usual I had watched the sunset to try and gauge the weather, but it's always a bit hit and miss. It had been a coppery sort of colour so I knew that meant wind – well, that was OK as I already had some. I glanced at the moon a couple of times and once when a cloud passed beneath it I could see a halo, another sign of impending wind, but the barometer seemed steady so I decided to get a couple of hours' sleep.

At 0200 hours I was awoken by the sounds of the wind in the rigging and knew that the force of the wind had increased significantly and with too much canvas up we were slewing up into wind. I really wished then I had taken down the lightwind genoa beforehand, but it definitely had to come down now. Not far off the sky looked very stormy and I obviously didn't have much time. It's a huge sail and very difficult to pull down with all the wind in it so I turned the boat downwind to try and back it (so that it would fall on to the deck).

I had about half of it down when a shift in the wind wrenched it from my grip. All my effort had been channelled into pulling it towards me and as it tore away my hand ricocheted back into my face, right into my eye. The pain was amazing, and for probably twenty or thirty seconds I couldn't see anything. At that moment something whipped me in the face, just below the same eye. I took a few seconds to compose myself before I eventually managed to alter course and once again try and bring it down. Then it was time to change the windvane, which involves leaning right out over the water, not easy with only one eye. Something hit my foot and went in the sea, and I still don't know what it was.

The wind increased to a force 9, and I went below to try and cool my eye. Within an hour the wind had shifted direction again and dropped to 5 knots, which wasn't enough to sail, and *Spirit* kept drifting off course. The radar was still picking up squalls a few miles off and at 0445 hours I was still unsure what the wind was going to do. By this time I was very tired and cold and decided that the only sensible course of action was to leave her to it and go to bed.

I've woken up this morning to good winds and a swollen eye with a weal underneath – very pretty! Shame I didn't bring that stuffed parrot – I could have done a silly sketch for the camera.

15 November (Day 60)

As at 1100 hours I had covered 6,224 nautical miles since I left. I am still suffering light winds and calms but Cape Town is only 2,000 miles away and the winds should get stronger very soon. I didn't believe it was possible to experience so little wind. Today I have gone absolutely nowhere. There is only 2–3 knots of wind – you can't even feel it. It was actually quite chilly this morning but now it's baking hot. At least I don't have to bother about what to wear on days like this and am enjoying a couple of hours' leisure time on deck. Fresh bread with cheese and pickled onions for lunch with a lager. Will probably pop up the mast later – as you do.

16 November (Day 61)

Been up since 0530 hours to take the furling sails down and check for chafing on the halyards. I'm relieved to see that they are not showing any signs, which is great because they are the only two that seem to be OK.

It has brought to light another problem, though. The staysail wouldn't come down very far, and I originally thought it might be connected with another problem I had up the mast, but in fact established it was the furling gear itself. I was quite relieved at first because it also identified where the screw had come from that I found on the deck some time ago.

However, after two hours I have to admit defeat. There are two screws holding the upper part of the furling gear. The one is partially unthreaded and preventing me from bringing the furling gear down, and the one underneath is the missing one. I've managed partially to screw the one back in, but not all the way and it is still blocking the track for the upper drum. I couldn't get the missing screw in at all – it must be misaligned slightly. I seem to have two options. One is to leave it as it is, and the other is to remove the resisting screw – I think the latter could cause even greater problems. So unless I come up with another solution I will just have to accept the fact that I'll never be able to get it down and will have to do any further checking and maintenance up the mast, which could be tricky.

I'm just about to go up to try once again to solve another problem that has so far defeated me. I have been up the mast now loads of times, and six of those to try and solve this outstanding problem of trying to drop a new halyard down the inside of the mast where the access hole is too small to take anything heavy enough even to pull the leading mouseline down. Still, today I am determined to solve it once and for all.

17 November (Day 62)

I eventually solved that halyard problem yesterday which was a great relief.

After a day with little or no wind, dark stormclouds, a purple sunset and halo around the moon were enough to warn me that the night would not be at all settled. Torrential rain came with each squall, and the wind direction kept shifting, but after three hours I was back with just a light wind again. I've hardly moved at all over the last few days.

In between squalls I've spent my time splicing and whipping ropes. It seems to be a constant task on this boat, so is a little frustrating, and made even more so by the fact that I could just as easily do them under way. When will I get some decent wind?

18 November (Day 63)

Today was a blistering hot day and I spent a few hours on deck just watching the sea. I had a funny feeling that I was going to see a ship or something and found myself constantly scanning the horizon and sea expectantly. In fact I did see lots of things in the water – ropes, a buoy, bits of boat that had either fallen off or were the remains of some unfortunate happening at sea and which must have drifted up with the current from the shipping lane not far south. But this afternoon I saw an almighty splash towards the horizon.

I was on my feet in seconds and straining to see more. I was so excited, I dashed below and quickly returned with binoculars and camera, found myself a precarious but excellent viewing point balancing on one of the winches on the mast, and eagerly searched for clues. Then I saw a smaller splash followed by what looked like a puff of smoke – whales! This particular one was at least two or three miles off, so he must have been vast, thrashing his fluke in the water. Then I noticed another just half a mile off. I was desperate for him to come closer, but he didn't. He just slowly lazed around in the water, blowing. It was the one furthest away that I was more fascinated by – he was obviously the lively one. When I saw him leap out of the water, 'Wow' slipped from my lips. I was absolutely stunned. I'd no idea whales could do that, but there is no doubt that that is what they were. Although it was impossible to judge their size exactly, they were magnificently enormous.

In retrospect it's probably quite a good thing they ignored me, as many boats have been severely damaged or sunk by whales. One playful flick of that huge powerful fluke would have been horrendous – a big price to pay for satisfied curiosity.

19 November (Day 64)

Lazed on deck all day!

20 November (Day 65)

Wind at last! From about 0300 hours I have been sailing well and am averaging just under 7 knots. It feels absolutely wonderful, and just to make life perfect the sun is now shining and the wind getting even stronger.

I didn't go to bed till about 0730 as I was enjoying helming too much. It was a wondrous night: full moon, almost clear sky, and the sea alive with luminescence. As the sun rose in the east the moon was simultaneously setting in the west. There can't be many places on earth where you can experience such a balanced and breathtaking sight.

After so little sleep I am a little tired but I'm feeling too exhilarated to care.

21 November (Day 66)

Had my best sail so far yesterday – it was magnificent. We were sailing along (or should I say surfing along) at between 8 and 10 knots. Because we were going downwind and it was fairly gusty we were yawing from side to side quite a bit, and *Spirit* was fairly waltzing down the waves. Whenever she went over 9 knots you could feel the boat judder, and at 10 knots it was amazing. Only once did we register over 10.5. I can understand how racing-car drivers get a kick – that sudden surge of power and speed is thrilling.

Unfortunately it only lasted about thirty hours and since then I have entered into a zone that is known to have light and infrequent winds.

Whilst the sun, when it is out, is still warm, the winds are much colder, and everything is starting to get just a little damp. Gone are the days of oppressive heat and wondering how to keep cool – now it's woolly socks and hot drinks. But it's lovely weather, in a way almost nicer. The dawn now has a fresh feel about it as though it really is the start of a new day, and I seem to have much more energy and not be so prone to those attacks of lethargy (or was it laziness?) that seemed to be a constant companion.

22 November (Day 67)

It was another night of disturbed sleep with the wind going up and down and requiring constant sail setting. So this morning I was not up until 0830 and feeling a little groggy. Thinking perhaps a cup of coffee might do the trick I sluggishly made my way to the galley to boil some water. I heard a noise on deck and thought . . . mmm, sounds like a whale. I must have been feeling really dopey because it didn't really register. Anyway, having by now noticed I needed to put more sail up, I put a hold on the coffee and ambled on deck.

I had just let out the rest of the furling yankee and was noting a ship heading towards me, when I heard it again. I casually glanced round. No more than fifteen feet away was a huge whale. Suddenly every nerve in my body was jingling. After a few stunned seconds I thought camera! I

Call of the Sea

Our home in Barnt Green

Sara (3), Lisa (5) and Paul (7)

(**above**) Safely back from my final single-handed sail on *Zany Lady*

(**below**) Force 10 on *Zany Lady* (*Peter Kemp*)

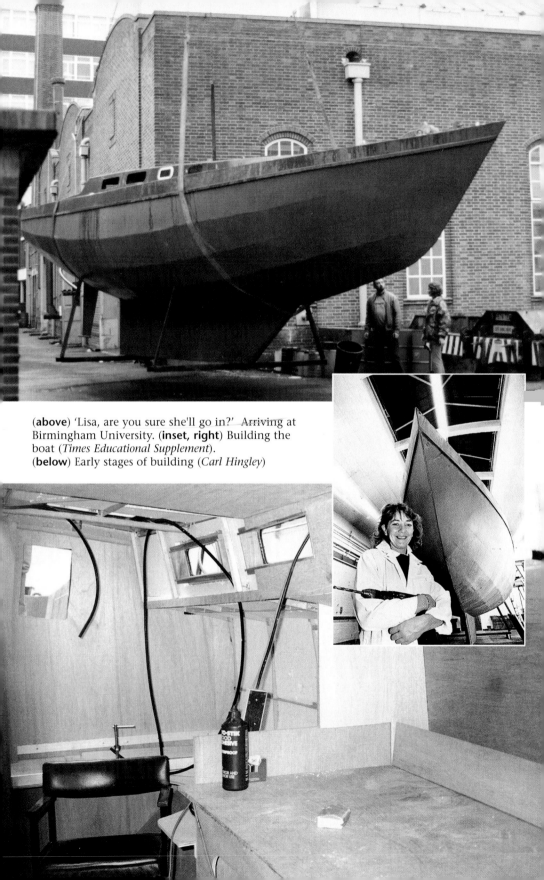

(**above**) 'Lisa, are you sure she'll go in?' Arriving at Birmingham University. (**inset, right**) Building the boat (*Times Educational Supplement*).
(**below**) Early stages of building (*Carl Hingley*)

(**above**) 'Gosh, she's heavy!' Pulling her out to go on show for the first time

(**inset, right**) Very Reverend Peter Berry, Provost of Birmingham blesses *Spirit* before departure

(**below**) All aboard! *Spirit* about to be lowered into water for the first time

(**above**) Provisions (*Carl Hingley*)

(**below**) Working on the Volvo Penta engine (*Mike Peters*)

(**left**) My home and work stations for the voyage (*Carl Hingley*)

(**below**) 'We've been on watch for hours. I thought she was doing this single handed.' Bernard, Edward and TK (*Howard Nelson*)

(**above**) High Seas (*BBC Television*)

(**below**) Fixing the furling gear

(**above**) Watching the sea. Glorious light   (**below**) Rough seas

dashed below, put in a new battery pack and rushed back on deck. I hadn't dared waste time putting the outdoor camera together and into its case, so was using the in-house one instead and praying the rain would hold off. My hands were shaking so much I could hardly get it in position; the extension arms kept flopping all over the place but eventually it was there.

He rose to the surface and blew through his hole – it was enormous – then he sank down again. All I could see then was his large shape under the water and was horrified to see it coming right alongside. He was still submerged, longer than the boat and only about four feet off, when I saw that we were going to collide. I ran to the wheel and released the self steering. My heart was in my mouth, my legs felt weak and shaky and I was suddenly praying that we would miss each other – I didn't think he was going to take kindly to being knocked, however unintentional it was. I didn't dare turn too quickly but gently eased the bow away. I was now aware that I was also on a collision course with the oncoming ship. Then the whale gave another blow and that was the last I saw of him. I steered to clear the path of the ship which passed about a quarter of a mile off.

I've checked my filming, and not surprisingly, trying to steer the boat and avoid the ship and a whale all at the same time resulted in pretty poor footage, but he's there in my mind to stay.

23 November (Day 68)

Been in one of those funny moods today – nothing has really happened, it's pretty gloomy outside, but I've been full of energy and feeling extremely mischievous – and I can't seem to get rid of it.

I've been on the deck and done the hoky-koky, gone part the way up the mast and yelled, 'Cape Town, here I come,' and spent the rest of the day sending ridiculous and nonsensical faxes to the office. I bet Peter is going demented!

I think it's because so much happened yesterday: first the whales, then two ships, and on the second one they waved to me – I was thrilled. I guess the fact that I am now less than 1,000 miles from Cape Town when I really will see people is also bringing home to me how much I do need that. I've been on my own for ten weeks and am getting excited and impatient at the prospect of actually talking to people face to face – well, it's far more likely to be shouting at each other from one boat to another, but I really can't wait.

Spirit is sailing beautifully without any help from me. I've done some work, already prepared the evening meal and am now positively bursting to do something outrageous.

There must be something I can try and channel this energy into, but I'm not in the mood to do anything serious, in fact I'm finding it extremely difficult to concentrate on this, so think I'll go on deck and talk to the seagulls.

25 November (Day 70)

Woke up this morning to the sun again and a fair wind to take me to Cape Town – lovely, I thought to myself, enjoying my morning coffee on deck.

I decided to do my deck and rigging check and suddenly all was not so jim dandy.

I had already recognised a problem with the staysail furling foil a couple of weeks ago and spent many hours trying to put it right but to no avail. However, today I saw the problem has become seriously exaggerated.

Whereas before it was only a problem because I couldn't bring the sail down for maintenance, now the foil which is in sections has parted halfway up the stay between the third and fourth sections and is swaying freely from side to side, which presumably means those screws have gone over the side as well. I was already one screw short further up; now I must be quite a few and I can't find the spares. I have literally hundreds of screws on board but haven't yet located these ones.

Even to start to look at the problem I need to bring the sail down – which means once again trying to solve the original problem. The trouble is I have no doubt whatsoever that if I loosen the one screw left holding the upper section I will lose it over the side, and then I'll have two loose sections. It's simply not possible to retain any balance leaning out at such a precarious angle from the mast and the only other way is to grip my legs around the foil itself – which I can't do with the sail there. Even if I manage this I have the problem of securing it all without the necessary matching screws. I have found some that have the same thread but are much too long. I suppose I might have to cut those down to see if they will do anything. But it's all rather frustrating, as they must be somewhere.

Well, I can't leave it – that is for sure. I'll have to try and do something however long it takes and regardless of how much of a botch it is.

I think I had better have a hearty meal and a bit of thinking time before I start.

26 November (Day 71)

I wasted two hours this morning trying to cut a dozen or so screws down to the right length. And all because I was too lazy to be bothered to root out the vice and set it up. In the end I realised I was being foolish and stopped for a break. Next time I don't feel in the mood to do a job properly I hope I remember not to bother.

However, the good news is that after my break I felt more logical and practical. It only took me ten minutes to get the vice out and set up, and within half an hour I had half a dozen screws sawn and filed. I've removed one of the lower screws on the furling gear to make sure they all thread and they do! Brilliant! I really had given up yesterday before I'd even tried. Pathetic. God, I hate myself when I'm like that.

27 November (Day 72)

When I woke up this morning I suddenly had an inspiration about where those blasted spare screws were. Oh well.

I can't help but feel hacked off about the lack of wind but I am starting to appreciate the warmth. At the back of my mind is the knowledge that these days are now short lived. Every day I am getting closer to the Southern Ocean, and whilst in a way I am keen to make progress, I am also now making the most of these easy days and bright sunshine. It's already getting much cooler, especially at night, and once I am a bit further south I do not expect to enjoy any days like this. I have already got my gear ready for colder and rougher climes – thermal socks, warm jumpers, heavy-weather sailing gear and my four-season sleeping bag – and I'm trying to attune my mind to the fact that for most of the next few months I shall be constantly damp. Ugh!

28 November (Day 73)

How infuriating! So close to Cape Town yet so far away from getting there.

I needed a course almost due east from here but with the wind coming from just south of that and the strong northerly current running up the west coast of South Africa I am being pushed way too far north. I could continue on this tack and get closer but at some stage I would have to turn to fight against both wind and current. And if the wind died I would just rapidly drift north, further and further away, a prospect that fills me with dread. So I'm having to sail on the other tack and go south in the hope that I can pick up the more westerly winds to take me more easterly where I can use the south-east wind and currents to take me to where I want to go. In the meantime I'm having to bite on the bullet and head away from where I want to go.

I feel devastated. Peter and the guys from the BBC have already been there days and are just sitting around waiting for me. How unlucky can one be? I've followed the recommended route but still have everything against me.

29 November (Day 74)

This all suddenly seems so ridiculous. I am now heading down to the very winds that will take me straight past the Cape of Good Hope and into the Southern Ocean and I'm beginning to wonder if I shouldn't just stay down here and get on with the journey. I know that in many ways I should go to Cape Town. I have the films that the BBC have so patiently been waiting for and I will be in a much better position to enter the Southern Ocean if I can do some pretty complicated repairs beforehand. Also I am looking forward to seeing Peter and human faces again. Actually to talk to people face to face would be wonderful, and yet, because I am already a little homesick and scared of entering this formidable ocean, I am worried that I might be tempted to do the safe thing and not continue my journey.

Against all of this is the urge just to carry on and not waste time by going north. I'm already manic about my slow progress and this deviation off route will cost me at least a week.

I'm desperately weighing up the odds. What if I spend all this time going all that way up to Cape Town and then conditions mean that I can't anchor off anywhere and get any repairs done? How will I feel then, knowing I have wasted a week of my time just to throw off some film to the BBC, shout 'Hi' to Peter and immediately turn round and head back down again?

30 November (Day 75)

At last! YES YES YES, I'm headed back towards Cape Town. After all my deliberations yesterday I have decided to give it a go. I really would love to see people, and whilst it will cost me a lot of time, if I *can* find a slightly sheltered bay to drop the hook then I will be a little more confident for the next difficult leg. I'm getting excited now.

Part of my decision lies in remembering how pleased I was that I had done those repairs in Plymouth when I had the chance. Much as I hate to lose a week or so I know I won't get the opportunity to do complicated repairs en route once I am past the Cape.

I have let Peter know at the Holiday Inn in Cape Town and he is positive I am doing the right thing too, so Cape Town here I come! How I wish I had a decent chart. The one I have is so small scale that I cannot fathom out exactly where Cape Town is. It's going to be a little like trying to find my way round London with only an atlas to guide me! Still, I have given them a suggested lat./long. position for us to meet up and then they can guide me from there.

1 December (Day 76)

Tomorrow I should be there and I just can't wait. They were all thinking of coming out from Cape Town today in a fast boat to say hello and do some filming but I really feel that forty miles is too far so we will meet up tomorrow. The forecast is good with 20 knot winds, and I should now have a good run in. At last things are going in my favour.

The only thing that has upset me a bit is a fax from Ken saying that I shouldn't stop and should just carry on in case any questions arise later. This is the sort of negative vibe I don't need. Does he think I'm stupid or what? It has been checked out with both the Royal Dart Yacht Club and the World Sailing Speed Record Council. As long as I don't go into harbour, have any help, use my engine to manoeuvre or take anything on board it will all be OK. Anyway, the Royal Cape Yacht Club have agreed to keep a watch and to ensure that the rules are adhered to. Actually I'm not really sure if it is that that has annoyed me or the fact that he says I've done the easy bit and the difficult bit is still to come. He's right, of course, but it's not what I really wanted to hear. I'd rather he had just said 'well done' for what I have achieved, rather then belittling it by making it seem that I haven't yet done anything special.

I've spent some time today packing together things that I want to get rid of as the boat seems to be a bit cluttered. I've also decided to chuck off my book on the meaning of dreams as I don't think it is doing me any good to be able to analyse dreams which foretell narrow escapes from death or worse. I've written quite a few letters to people at home so that Peter can take them back to the UK for me. Oh how I wish I was allowed to take things on board. I would love some wine, fresh food and more books to read, but the rules stipulate that absolutely nothing or no one can come on board from the moment I left the UK to when I get back.

2 December (Day 77)

Would you believe it? Despite the forecast the wind had all but died this morning, and I was left rolling about in a fairly large swell.

Because I now won't be near the coast until the late afternoon Peter said the BBC want me to hang around till tomorrow so that they can film me sailing in. What a bloody cheek. I was livid. I have come all this way and now they want me to hang around. Well, I've left them in little doubt as to how I feel and said a very definite no. Hell, I was cross – they must think it is like parking a car or something. What they don't realise is that to hang around like that would mean that I could not just go to bed and wait for tomorrow, I would be up all night making sure that I didn't get pushed too far north or have a collision with any ships. Bloody non-sailors!

During the afternoon the wind started to back round to the south; it was still a light breeze but was now coming from behind the beam. My annoyance of the morning forgotten, I realised it was a wonderful opportunity to fly the spinnaker – what great footage that would make.

Spinnaker-flying *Spirit* and I made a great entrance to the supposed meeting point. But where were they? Sure that they would arrive soon, I ignored the occasional gust in the wind and kept going. Surely after all this palaver they weren't going to leave me hanging around? But in my bid to arrive in style I kept the spinnaker up too long. I nipped down below to make radio contact once more and when I came up knew I could wait no longer to take the spinnaker down. Much as I wanted them to film me with it up I definitely didn't want to get in a mess with it, especially with the wind now gusting more frequently.

Just as I was letting it down the wind gusted and the next thing we were on our side in the water. God, what a mess. In trying to take the force out of the sail I let the sheet go and suddenly it was flying from the top of the mast. Everything was going crazy, the ropes were whipping backwards and forwards. By the time I had eventually managed to dunk the sail into the water I was exhausted and cross. The mess everywhere was awful. I prayed that they wouldn't turn up within the next hour whilst I tried to put everything a bit more shipshape. The drag of the sail through the water meant we were going nowhere and slowly I managed to haul it in without trapping it under the keel.

I was glad I had not put my ensign up as the post was now nothing more than a splinter. Just as I had finished tidying up they came into sight, just a few miles out of Cape Town!

At the first sign of the sleek yacht coming towards me I could hardly believe it was really them.

I was really nervous about coming in to anchor without being able to use the engine. I'd got an anchor but I hadn't bothered to take any chain as I really didn't expect to be using it. This was fairly simply solved by tying lots of my spare halyards together. It should be fairly easy to throw it over the side, but what if I made a mess of trying to handle the boat and the anchor and got into trouble? Oh God, please let me do it OK on my own.

All my fears were unfounded when I realised that it was a huge area I was going to be anchoring in, and using ship-to-ship radio they soon had me safely anchored. The yacht was from the Royal Cape Yacht Club and they were there to give me advice about where was the best place to drop the hook and also to ensure that I did everything myself and didn't contravene the rules of my attempt.

A tripper boat, the *Spirit of Victoria*, came out to welcome me to Cape Town and asked if it was OK to do a turn around us with every new boat full of tourists. No, I didn't mind. I couldn't see enough of people – even if I didn't know any of them!

Once I was safe everyone cracked open the champagne, and I opened one of my special half bottles. Peter had bought me some flowers and they let him out in a dinghy on a long line, and then per their instructions I threw him a line from my boat (he wasn't allowed to throw a line to me!)

so that he could come near enough to show me and the BBC could take some pictures.

It's funny how difficult it is to talk at these times. We discussed how *Spirit* seemed to look in good condition, and how healthy I looked, but basically we talked about a lot of nothing. I suppose that was because it had all been said by fax before, but it was great to see Peter and join in with their laughing and joking.

All too soon the excitement was over and they all went back to Cape Town to go out for a meal and celebrate my arrival. As I watched them go my heart sank. Sitting here now, I can imagine the sort of evening they are going to enjoy together and it is all too much. The thought of getting something to eat out of a tin and sitting all alone with no one to talk to is unbearable. I'm feeling numb and let down. I don't know what I had expected to feel – some sense of achievement, anything – but instead I feel nothing, just a sort of deadness inside. So I've got myself a drink and crawled into my sleeping bag with just my large stuffed dog Bernard for company. Well, if nothing else, with the wind direction as it is we're fairly sheltered so I needn't worry about the anchor being jumped out of the seabed, and I'm dreadfully tired and worn out so I think I'll take the opportunity to get some uninterrupted sleep.

3 December (Day 78)

I woke up refreshed after my night's sleep and keen to have a look at the messy problem of the furling gear. I knew that I had to dismantle it to fix it but was worried that if I dismantled it (or worse, only half dismantled it!) then I might not be able to either fix it or re-erect it.

I could either leave it as it was, which would mean that I would never be able to bring it down to do repairs and at some stage it would be rendered useless. *Or* I could have a go. The riggers had sent a fax with advice, but all of this was finished off with the comment that they had never fixed anything like this at sea and anyway not with only one pair of hands.

I got myself a hearty breakfast of tinned sausages in beans, two eggs and loads of coffee and by the end was feeling confident that it must be possible.

It was extremely difficult to see how the drum, etc. was held together at the base of the furling gear and I was dearly wishing now that I had watched them fit it in the first place. However, after a couple of false starts I started to make some progress. One thing I hadn't expected was that I would have to actually cut through the forestay itself, but there was no option.

Of all the parts I had for the rigging this was the one size for which I didn't have all the spares, so I would have to re-use everything I took off. Having cut the stay, I carefully started to let down the foil sections. As each one came down I disconnected it from the next foil, drilling out those screws that were stuck until all the foils were carefully laid on deck.

Peter had come out in a dinghy to egg me on and I needed it. I just couldn't clear the connector that I needed to use again to hold the forestay into the bottle screw. I was tired and felt totally beaten. If I couldn't free this one tiny little piece I might as well throw everything else over the side as it would be useless.

Peter kept shouting to have just one more go. I felt pathetic. I had already spent the last hour and a half trying to do it. Why would one more try make any difference? But I returned down below, once again put it in the vice, carefully placed the punch dead centre and with all my pent-up frustrations gave it an almighty whack with the hammer. I looked in amazement – yes, it had moved. Now that I had managed to shift it a bit the rest was easy and ten minutes later I was on deck dancing around holding it high in the air and shouting with joy.

I stopped when I heard Peter shouting and realised he was right. To drop it now in the heat of the moment would be foolhardy in the extreme, so I calmed myself down and considered what to do next. I decided to leave the rest of it for a new day, and instead got down to fixing the self-steering gear.

I seemed to be causing a great deal of interest and was included in the itinerary of the tripper boats which kept circling and shouting across questions and encouraging remarks.

I didn't think about putting my navigation lights on when it got dark and had rather a rough reprimand from a boat which had nearly run me down!

4 December (Day 79)

I woke up full of the joys of spring. Today I would fix it – it felt right and I knew I could.

I was up the mast when I saw Peter arriving in a rubber dinghy with one of the people from the Royal Cape Yacht Club. With them was Cedric, who was also liaising with the BOC single-handed racing yachts who were setting off for their next leg to Australia. Cedric was very keen that I didn't stay long. He'd seen people relax back into the security of being within reach of civilisation until they found they didn't want to leave again. I could understand what he was saying but didn't feel it applied to me. Today, I was full of confidence – not even an inkling of wanting to give up.

The BBC came out to do more filming and happily I worked out how to get everything back together.

But by the end of the day I felt licked. The wind had shifted round and I was no longer sheltered. The swell was only about one and a half to two feet high but made everything so much more involved. Try as I might I couldn't hold things up the mast whilst controlling the bottom end to stop things sliding down and into the water. The more I tired, the more difficult everything became. I no longer had the strength to hold myself up the mast, let alone try and hold things in place.

I persevered until eventually I was stymied. I hadn't yet lost anything over the side but I had been lucky. Oh God, it just wasn't possible – the riggers were right. It just wasn't possible with one person.

I felt utterly forlorn. It was heartrending to see the look on Peter's face. I knew he would have loved to have been able to help me – two pairs of hands would have made it much easier – but all he could do was watch from his bobbing dinghy and shout encouragement. There was no point in them hanging around any more. Peter had put on a brave face, although it was obvious that he was feeling horribly seasick with the light swell bobbing him up and down, and I had passed the stage where I was thinking properly. As I waved goodbye, my eyes welled up with tears and I ran below to cry my heart out. What was the point? Just what was the point? I couldn't do it, I'd tried everything. Why didn't I just give up, go into port, get it fixed properly and join them all for a meal and an evening of laughter? If I did that then I might as well stay for a couple of weeks and have a look round South Africa. Having resolved that I could do so if I still felt the same in the morning, I happily went to bed.

I hadn't been there long before I realised that the whole boat was lit up and someone was calling me on a Tannoy. I rushed on deck to see the Navy and the Marine Police near by. They had come to wish me luck – how nice!

5 December (Day 80)

I jumped out of bed full of life. I was a little confused as to what time of day it was. It was still dark, and *Spirit* was riding well in the water, but I knew that within a few hours the sea would have built up again, so I needed to use it to my best advantage.

I had a decent breakfast of scrambled eggs tweaked up with onions, cheese and herbs, then leaving the washing-up till later, got everything together and suddenly the way forward was clear. Two hours later I was well on the way to fixing the furling gear and feeling pretty darned pleased with myself.

I radioed through to Peter's hotel and said that if there was a chance that someone could spend the day close by it would give me a lot of encouragement. Peter hadn't really planned to be coming out so much and nothing had been arranged, but luckily the Royal Cape Yacht Club eventually found someone. By the time Peter came out with his new helmsman Heggy I was in wonderful spirits. My confidence had been restored with gusto and I could see the relief on Peter's face. I felt guilty that I had slept so well as he didn't look as though he had slept a wink, and he admitted that he hadn't been able to bear the thought of joining the others for a meal. He had been so worried for me and had spent the night smoking numerous cigarettes and wondering whether he should get me towed into harbour for professional repairs.

6 December (Day 81)

The weather had worsened during the night and there really was no point now in hanging around except that I wasn't too keen to get going. I still had plenty of repairs left to do but they would probably be just as easy at sea as in the swell I was trying to ride. Also I had dragged my anchor during the night so I had to up sail anyway and move away from the rocks. We knew that if I didn't go soon I wouldn't. So as soon as Heggy and Peter arrived to keep an eye on me and make sure I didn't get into trouble I prepared to leave. The wind was quite strong and with sail up I crept forward towards the anchor. It was jammed. Trying to control the boat and bring in the anchor was just too much so I tied a float to it, and throwing the line over the side left my anchor as a souvenir for Heggy.

Then I was off.

They didn't follow me out, it wasn't what I wanted. I wanted to get away quickly, without looking back. I knew I had to be strong and that once I was under way again I would be OK, but I couldn't afford to get emotional and wimpish now. Only the seals kept me company for a couple of miles until the swell really built up and then they too disappeared for the last time. I felt horribly lonely and tried to cheer myself up with a drink and lunch on deck, but I needed more than that.

7 December (Day 82)

I've felt lousy all day today. I'm heading south-west back to where I was a week ago in a bid to pick up the westerly winds and still avoid the Agulhas Bank at the tip of South Africa.

There doesn't seem much that is positive today. This is sort of negative progress I am making as it is only taking me back where I have been before, but also I am feeling extremely lonely and low in spirits. Somehow having seen faces and been fairly close to people it is now much more difficult to be without. No doubt I will adapt to life again but I hope it doesn't take too long as I am really hating it at the moment.

To make matters worse I can't seem to communicate through the Goonhilly satellite any more, and I should be able to for another 1,000 miles or so yet. I tried to send through Sentosa but it wouldn't accept anything. The only alternative is to try and get a call through on the radio via Cape Town and hope to goodness it isn't a problem with the system that can't be rectified.

What a day not to be able to be in touch. God, I feel like I have entered outer space I feel so isolated. I yearn to go back to South Africa to see anybody, whether I know them or not, but I just have to content myself with the thought that once I'm back home I can spend as much time as I want with other people. I keep telling myself, 'I'm out here because I want to be,' but it doesn't feel very convincing.

8 December (Day 83)

It's grey, wet and horrible on deck and there's a gale blowing. However, I feel more relaxed today although the thought of the Roaring Forties is constantly at the back of my mind. I suppose it is only natural that I should feel this apprehension. I have never experienced the wrath of the Southern Ocean before so it is left to my imagination to conjure up just how bad it can be. *Spirit* is definitely at the lower end of the scale sizewise and quite heavy, which could mean that she is difficult to handle in large waves and swell. I won't know until I hit the first storm and then it's fingers crossed. In the meantime I am just spending my time checking everything so that whatever happens I have given myself the best chance of coming through it.

I can't help but look back to my adventures in the desert nearly four years ago. Setting off into the wilderness of the Sahara was equally dangerous in its own way. If anything went wrong we were on our own, far from help and civilisation, with no chance of outside help. That had been the appeal of course, the danger and excitement, the stories of how easy it was to get lost and never come out again – whole camel trains have gone missing. The constantly changing shape of the dunes can disorientate even the people who exist in the desert, and half a mile off course can mean an oasis missed, and a slow deathly thirsty walk into oblivion. But it was different. It was different because I wasn't on my own, I was with my friends, and any experience shared is easier to cope with. Now I am alone.

I've decided to forego the great circle track which cuts about 2,000 miles off the journey but would also take me way down into the Furious Fifties where conditions are much worse and the risk of icebergs much greater. Rather crazily I have been considering taking this track so that I can catch up on some time and get home quicker, but survival has to be my first thought, and after hearing that one of the BOC racing boats has just been dismasted in a vicious storm at 51°S, I've come to my senses and realised it isn't a sensible option. I had originally planned to stick to the recommended route which was above 40°S, but now I have decided to split the difference and have a go between 40° and 43°S. If it gets too bad I can always travel north a bit and get back to more steady conditions.

9 December (Day 84)

I'm still in 30 to 40 knots of wind and the seas have built up quite significantly since yesterday. *Spirit* is finding it hard work to climb these steep waves, and plummets down into the trough almost as though she needs a rest after all the exertion. The wind shifted slightly yesterday and although I had originally made some westing so as to avoid the frightening and notorious Agulhas Bank, the gale came from the south-west, not the north-west as predicted, and I was being pushed towards the very area I was desperate to avoid. However, the wind is now veering and I am at last able to head almost due south so with any luck will still be able to miss it. I am just 137 miles north of the Roaring Forties and wondering how much worse this weather would have been down there.

The deck is constantly awash with water and some small leaks are appearing so I'll have to deal with those. Occasionally there's an almighty crash as *Spirit* hits a large stopper wave and literally shudders to a halt. Closehauled at 40 knots the whole of the rigging and boat shake under the pressure and trying to do anything below takes a lot of effort. The violence of one of the knocks resulted in one of the cupboards opening and depositing the cleaning materials and liquids all over the cabin – what a slippery horrible mess.

I managed to jam my finger in the hatch and it's damned painful – how could I be so stupid?

The barometer's on the rise but rather too quickly for my liking which means there is probably worse to come.

I've put on some Vivaldi in an attempt to shut out the real world.

10 December (Day 85)

I've just clumsily bumped my head and realise I must be very tired.

I don't feel that I like *Spirit* today. I know it's rather disloyal of me but I can't help it some days and today is one of them. I suppose in certain conditions she seems so slow, and I find it unbearable – all I want to do is make good progress and get closer to home but she is finding these steep seas too much to climb.

I can't understand why I have no sense of achievement over what I have done to date. I felt marvellous when I crossed the Equator so why not now? But I don't, I feel nothing really. I hope I experience something when I get back, otherwise it will all be for nothing.

I guess I must originally have wanted to prove something to myself but at times like this I can't imagine what, and I certainly don't feel I need to any more. In fact I rather imagine that I am tempting fate at the moment – nothing tangible, just a sort of sinking feeling of foreboding. It's crazy really, the weather has improved, even the sun is out, but I can't seem to get rid of the nervousness in my stomach and the thought that I might not come back. It's ridiculous to be worried before I've really tried.

If I give up for no good reason I won't be able to live with myself. I've worked so hard for this opportunity. Imagine being home, and realising I'd thrown away my dream just because I had had a bad day! I'd lose all faith in myself if I showed such lack of staying power. I knew this wasn't going to be easy – I've always known that. God, how pathetic I can be. When things are bad they improve, so I should be looking forward to that instead. Gosh, I wish I had more to keep my mind occupied. I don't think I like myself when I look too deeply into my rather confused mind and see a cowering wimp overpowering the stronger person I would like to think I could be.

I wish I could make contact with home.

11 December (Day 86)

I have had a lousy bit of kip but surprisingly feel OK. In fact this morning I woke up thinking next time I shall have to use a faster boat!!! I have also been thinking, and I know this is slightly premature, but if I do manage to do this one, wouldn't it just be fantastic if Group 4 or someone with one of the British Steel type boats paid me to be the first woman to go the other way!

I guess however down I get, it's all part of it, and I shall always be looking for some exciting thing to do in my life.

12 December (Day 87)

Well, I've crossed the invisible line into the Roaring Forties, according to the fix from the satellites. It's ridiculous how something can have so much significance. I am only just a few miles below 40° and already I feel I have to be more alert – what difference can a few miles make? It's rather like having your fortieth birthday: many people treat it as a depressing day but in reality you are only another day older. What a crazy thing the mind is. At the moment I have light headwinds and am headed south-east instead of east, which is taking me down into higher latitudes. I am going to try and cross the Southern Ocean between the parallels of 40° and 43°S. It's undoubtedly safer to stay north of 40° but I am more likely to get variable winds, whereas I hope just that bit further south will give me more favourable though stronger winds. I don't particularly want to go further south than this if I can help it, except when I must, such as passing Tasmania when I will have to go to between 45° and 47° and then south again to clear New Zealand. I might then try and return to the latitudes of my current track before dropping way down to the Furious Fifties to round Cape Horn at about 57°S.

Passing all of these Capes I shall be in very high latitudes and an extract from *Ocean Passages* produced by the UK Hydrographic Office makes frightening reading:

Tempestuous gales, sudden violent and fitful shifts of wind, accompanied by hail or snow, and terrific and irregular seas are often encountered in the higher latitudes; moreover the islands in the higher latitudes are so frequently shrouded in fog that often the first sign of their vicinity is the sound of the surf beating against them.

I hope my passage across the Southern Ocean isn't too slow as I'm already concerned that I shall be late trying to round the Horn. I really had hoped to be rounding it late February early March as the conditions will get worse every day I'm delayed after that.

There's little point in worrying about that now, otherwise I shall be turning round and heading back for Cape Town! So, for the time being I'll just try and make the best progress I can and face each day as it comes.

I caught my finger again today but at least it has burst the blood blister that was there before, so it is probably a good thing.

I've done quite a few useful jobs today including replacing the impellor. This is a tiny plastic instrument that spins round under the boat and tells you how fast you are going. To replace it means bringing the connection up into the boat. Of course as soon as the impellor is out it leaves a hole in the hull and the sea comes rushing in so it's essential to bung it up as quickly as possible. I'd done it before on *Zany Lady* so I knew what to expect and managed to do it without letting too much water into the boat.

I've fixed the kitchen timer, which is by far the best alarm clock I have on board as it is the loudest. I was starting to find that when I did get to sleep I was so tired that I didn't hear the normal alarms, and had been resorting to sleeping on the bunk without a lee cloth so that if anything did go wrong I would be tipped on to the floor – which is surely the best alarm ever, but slightly abrupt to say the least! However, now the timer is fixed I can rely on a more gentle nudge to bring me round. I've also cleared up numerous other little things that had been getting on my nerves, and I've made a fantastic curry which I have had for lunch and shall finish for dinner tonight. And I shall need it. I reckon I have had to correct the helm over thirty times to put us back on course during the last few hours, as the wind seems to have become totally erratic in direction. I wonder what is afoot?

I think I had better go and get some sleep as last night was yet another with only a couple of hours, and tiredness leads to silly mistakes which I simply can't afford.

13 December (Day 88)

All through the night I was like a yo-yo. Up down, up down. I had based myself in the navigation area. Sitting on my captain's chair with my pillow on the chart table, I would wriggle into my sleeping bag, set my kitchen timer for half an hour and lay my head down. But as soon as I was comfortable, and my feet started to thaw out, the boat went off course and I was once again struggling to get out of my warm cocoon and back into my sea boots so I could go on deck and put us right again.

Because it was such a fiddle I was half tempted to move my sleeping bag back to the bunk where it belongs and where I knew I would be able to relax properly. But, of course, I couldn't. Knowing that I might be headed in the wrong direction for even an hour seemed to compel me to stay cramped up in the navigation area keeping a constant watch on the instruments and course indicators.

It seems ridiculous to worry about going the wrong way for one hour but I guess my real fear is that if I lie down and get too comfortable I might fall heavily asleep and be out for hours, and wake up to find I am further away than ever, and that would really depress me.

Although progress and rest overnight weren't brilliant I feel in a good frame of mind today. I suppose it must be the colder weather, but my mind keeps whisking me off to the ski slopes. I don't even know exactly what is causing it but today I am feeling something that is synonymous with being in the mountains, and it's difficult to believe I am here and not there.

Whilst the weather is relatively light I think I will have a go at the rigging and check the tensioning. Once the weather gets stormy the load on the rig will make it much more difficult. Looking at the mast I think it is fairly evenly balanced so I must make a note of every turn I make so that I can equally adjust the other side. I don't want to cause additional problems by creating stress areas. Then I think I will grease the runners on the main hatch. Dad has this mortal fear that they will freeze up and I will be impri-soned down below. I wouldn't of course because I could always get out of one of the other hatches, but I might as well do it and save myself any potential inconvenience and relieve Dad's anxiety a little at the same time.

14 December (Day 89)

This morning there was a blue sky and just 6 knots of wind. I was tempted to put the spinnaker up but decided to watch the situation for a while – somehow the thought of the spinnaker in the Southern Ocean didn't feel right. So I poled out the biggest other sail I have and decided to wash my hair and do some laundry.

No sooner had I gone back down below, stripped off and got the soap in my hair than I could feel that the wind had suddenly come up, and by the time I managed to wipe the soap from my eyes, throw some foul-weather gear on over my wet shivering body and clamber on deck the sky was grey and the sea was already whipped up. It's frightening how conditions can change so very rapidly.

I managed to get the large genoa and pole down OK but couldn't get the staysail in. It was just completely jammed. I eased the sheets off and let it out again but each time I tried to wind it in it got stuck after a few turns. I checked the drum but it all looked OK. I was beginning to despair. The water washing over the boat was washing the soap out of my hair and it was running into my eyes. The salt and the shampoo were a vicious mixture and my eyes smarted from the invasion. I had to sort out the staysail – if I didn't the sail would be torn to shreds in no time. But somebody was looking kindly on me. The wind was moving round and fairly quickly dropped to a force 7 which made it slightly easier to spend time on deck to see what the options were for fixing the problem.

After what seemed like hours but was in fact only just over one and a half, I managed to release the sail so that I could use it. It was damaged though, so some time I will have to see if I can put it right otherwise it might cause other problems, but the main worry was gone. I could now put the sail out and take it in again. I came down below wet and exhausted but relieved. There's nothing worse than having an unsolved dilemma on your mind, and at least now I could concentrate on just sailing the boat. There was no need to put any more water on my hair either as all the soap had been washed off with seawater!

15 December (Day 90)

The wind is now coming from the very direction I want to go in which is thoroughly disappointing as it means I can't make course, and what's worse it's almost died – at least it keeps dropping to just 4 to 5 knots. As soon as I think of getting one of the fair-weather sails up it suddenly rises to over 20 and shortly after dies again. The sky still looks rather ominous so I think I have just got to try and put up with this fickle and frustrating weather. It's tiring and demanding, for when the wind suddenly lapses, *Spirit* loses all way, and on the top of a swell just turns 90° off course, so I have to rush on deck, grab the wheel and bring her back. Progress is quite frankly lousy. I seem to be expending a lot of energy for little reward, and it all seems rather depressing. The self steering can't cope with this sort of instability so I am having to use the autopilot, but that is using power that I can't really spare.

However, there is little option. I can't stay on the wheel all day, it's too damned cold. Even with balaclava and gloves, my hands and face are painful within minutes of being up on deck.

The instruments down below have been having a fit. The wind indicator looks as though it's being zapped with a series of electric shocks as the wind rises and drops and comes from literally every direction on the compass. When it's not doing that it's sweeping round in circles. The sails are slapping and banging as the wind attacks them from one side then the other, and everything inside the boat is being thrown around in the confusion. I've never seen anything like it – and I don't particularly want to again. I became transfixed to the wind indicator needle but in the end I have had to force myself to stop watching as it was making me feel quite ill.

16 December (Day 91)

Oh God, this is awful. I'm finding it all quite stressful. My nerves seem to be constantly on edge and I am just praying that a constant wind will soon be helping me on my way. This is not what I expected down here. It's supposed to be constant winds, not this.

I am absolutely shattered and demoralised. I've now in desperation put up the biggest sail I have in the hope it will help me to make some progress. I hate not getting anywhere – it's really driving me mad and I just feel like crying my heart out. Hopefully I'll feel better after a rest. I feel rock bottom – never have I felt so low. I wondered before I set off how I would cope with these sort of negative feelings, and still the answer is that I don't know. I have no idea how well I am or am not coping. I've never experienced this sort of despair before and for the first time can understand why people just step off the side. I don't feel tempted to do that – I think it is a natural instinct to survive and not be beaten – but I'm also sure this is easier when one is battling with physical dangers rather than psychological ones. I'm really not sure how to break myself out of it. I suppose I have just got to dig deep and wait for better times. Perhaps I should try and get further south. Stronger winds seem a great option at the present regardless of all the recommendations of staying north.

I am dreadfully envious of everyone back home who can just go to sleep in the evening and get up in the morning. How I would love to be able to jump in my car and go wherever I liked and be with people – God, how I am missing it. When I get home am I going to have some fun or what!!!

In the meantime I have decided to try and get some rest. I know that lack of sleep is the root of many things, and I will feel more practical in my approach if I can think clearly.

17 December (Day 92)

I feel much more my old self, possibly because at last we have some decent winds. It's grey and damp up on deck but I feel quite chirpy and full of energy. I've even ventured to experiment poling out both foresails, to keep the sails stretched out and catch the most wind. It took me about an hour and a half to get it all set up and I found it was extremely tricky to handle the second pole, which is about eighteen feet long and unwieldy in the slightest swell. I only managed to get it into its retainer by climbing the mast and hauling it with me.

Of course my main concern now is how on earth I am going to get it down when the weather deteriorates. Still, for now it is occasionally giving me 6–7 knots so it is worth it! This is the most tremendous sailing I have ever experienced. It's as much fun as driving a really fast car as we surf down these waves. I haven't felt so exhilarated for ages.

18 December (Day 93)

18 DECEMBER (DAY 93)

....

18 DEC   FROM: BT INMARSAT-C FAX   TO: PETER HARDING

....

Hi Peter,

I am down at 42° but still only south of Maputo on the coast of Mozambique. I've travelled 1,060 miles since Cape Town but as the crow flies I am still just 840 from Cape Town. I really need to make a better average speed otherwise I shall be rounding the Horn very late, which won't be too clever.

The wind is still from the south-west and quite strong but is veering round to the north again. I hope another low comes through soon. *Spirit* and I have decided that we would prefer weeks of gales than to be left drifting around again in light winds. It's just not good for the sense of humour!

I've analysed that there is a problem with the self-steering gear which might partly explain why we so easily slewed off course. The pendulum rudder seems only to be wanting to go one way. According to the manual I need to remove the whole frame to correct it but that is a Herculean task and I can't bear the thought. If it were situated above the deck I would have a go, but hanging off the stern of the boat like that there's more than a strong likelihood that one of us would end up in the drink. I've been able to make some sort of repair from on deck – it would be great if it would last the next ten weeks to the Horn, but I doubt it. I'll actually be glad if it lasts a few days! Could you please do me a favour and have a quick chat with the manufacturers to see if they have any ideas.

It's incredible to think that I have so far experienced very little strong wind in an area which averages one in three days of gale force 8 or higher. Still, today isn't a day to be groaning. Over the last seven hours I have ticked off a fantastic 61 miles which means an average of 8.7 knots. I'm occasionally surfing at 10 knots, which is crazy, but it's so exhilarating and I keep thinking of all the time I am making up.

We are yawing around quite a bit at the moment and the barometer is dropping again.

Don't worry, I shall reduce sail before dark!!!!

Ciao,
Lisa.

....

....

18 DEC   **FAX TO LISA**   **FROM: PETER HARDING**
....

Hi Lisa,
Yes OK will have a word with the manufacturers. Great to hear that you are having a good sail but please don't take any risks! I know you want to make good progress but don't go and blow everything by making a mistake and getting into trouble.

Some wonderful news by the way: you have been voted BBC Radio West Midlands Woman of the Year. Isn't that marvellous? Your parents were listening to it as well. We all felt quite emotional and very proud of you. You can't imagine the amount of support you are getting from the people of Birmingham – it's really wonderful. Anyway, have a good sail now and remember to be more careful when it gets dark.

Will be in touch again tomorrow, and as soon as I get any useful information to help with the steering I will send it.

Take care, crazy lady!
Peter.

....

19 December (Day 94)

Last night was beautiful. A full moon was shining clear and at midnight it was almost like daylight and the sea was glistening. I saw a small corona around the moon and then I realised that was just the inner circle of a humungous halo that filled the whole sky – it was incredible, but also got me slightly concerned about the bad weather it might be foretelling.

At 0230 this morning we once again went off course as the steering gear couldn't cope. I put the automatic pilot on until daylight when I was hoping to be able to fix the steering gear again. But I wasn't too relaxed as the winds were gale force and the automatic pilot was really struggling over force 6–7.

Still, we've been sailing along well and although I know I should shorten sail I am enjoying it too much to be totally sensible, so I'll give it another hour or two – it's just too good to miss.

2300 hours: Conditions stayed much the same and the autopilot kept cutting out because it couldn't cope with the surge of the seas. It was impossible to do anything but sit at the chart table doing some embroidery or reading and keeping an eye on everything, because as soon as the autopilot cut out we lost control and I had to dash on deck and put us back on course again.

I was going to try the self steering again but when I went to link it up I saw that the gears are no longer meshed. The top set has turned 180° and isn't meshing at all. I don't know how the hell I am going to fix that but it is impossible even to try until I get some calmer conditions.

20 December (Day 95)

I went on deck at first light to make my inspection and there was quite a mess. Some of the ropes had come partially uncoiled and were dragging in the sea. Also the boom vang which controls the set of the mainsail had sheared off. I crawled along the deck in my safety harness for security and managed to disconnect the part still attached. The seas made life very difficult and at one point I found myself thrown across the deck. Luckily my safety harness yanked me to a stop. Thank goodness I was wearing the shorter-length one and not the one I normally use, which is twice the length.

Returning down below with the offending boom vang I pushed the hatch back and a wave broke over the boat and spilled down below right over my sleeping bag. As if conditions aren't uncomfortable enough, without anything else to make it worse. I was really fed up. I have got a spare one, but how I am going to dry this one out I don't know, and the thought of a wet pillow for my weary head is not one to relish. What bloody awful weather. To cheer myself up I sent a fax to Peter and he wrote straight back with lots of encouraging words. We've been writing to each other daily and got to know each other really well. What a tremendous support he is to me.

21 December (Day 96)

Conditions are still not good but I spent hours today making a brilliant repair to the boom vang. I was really pleased with myself and anxious to put it back. I got together everything I needed and made two trips on to the deck. I carefully wedged the boom vang so that my hands were free to get the rivet gun and rivets. At that moment the boat was thrown over to one side. Luckily I was OK but watched in horror as the boom vang slid over the side and quickly sank. I couldn't believe it. After all my hard work. Having achieved such a good repair how could I have been so damned careless?

I retired below and decided to have a coffee and something hot to eat before even attempting anything else. There was no point in spending time and energy on things if I was going to throw it all away at the last minute.

I eventually returned on deck and rigged up a rope and tackle to replace the vang, which was the best I could do in the circumstances.

22 December (Day 97)

Not good progress in the night as I went slightly north, but I couldn't get up the energy to gybe the boat.

I've just attached a proper safety belt to the navigator's chair, since I seem to live here amongst the instruments these days!

Although the wind is strong the sun has come out and whilst it is bitterly cold it is a truly wonderful sight. When everything is grey it all looks more frightening, but with the sun it looks exciting. The barometer has also risen a bit so I hope it is a good sign. It would be great if the wind would die right down for a day and give the sea a chance to flatten a little. This would make repairs much easier, and after my fiasco yesterday I don't feel I ought to try too much.

The comforting thing is that *Spirit* has so far looked after me well and seems to be coping with conditions even better than I had hoped.

23 December (Day 98)

I'm dreading the thought of Christmas and New Year on my own. I hate the thought that everyone at home is busily rushing around getting into the spirit of things.

My neighbours Jane and Roger will be preparing for their Christmas Eve champagne party, my friends Ricky and Roundy will be organising smoked salmon and champagne for Christmas Day breakfast which will continue the same without me, and my parents will be all set for an extravagant and bubbly few days. They'll probably drink more than normal because they will be missing me!

I don't think Peter will have much of a Christmas. Thank goodness his family are so understanding! I have this horrible feeling that he won't relax enough. I don't think he'll feel free to enjoy the festivities, which is crazy really. He seems to spend every waking hour on call for me and I know he won't want to be away from the fax machine which he takes with him everywhere he goes.

I've been composing poems to send back, which is about as much as I can do.

The nicest Christmas present I could have right now is better conditions!

24 December (Day 99)

Hi there,
Let's hope that we all get through tomorrow, but anyway, know that we are all missing you too and our thoughts will be with you.

I learn from Peter that you are having problems with the heating. I'm sure you already know that thirty per cent of body heat is lost through one's head (if you see what I mean!).

I feel very frustrated at times, wanting to help you and knowing I can't, just hoping that you have your fair share of luck to offset your problems; this is in no way doubting your ability, but I am thinking of luck as being the opposite of unluck!

If you ever pray I am sure that God will forgive you if you keep your hat on!

Merry Xmas, darling, and remember – we all love you and pray for your wellbeing all the time.

Mum, Dad et al.

xxxxxxxxxxxxxxxx

....

Spirit and I have decided to give each other a Christmas present, and head slightly north in the hope we will get slightly lighter conditions.

I'm still not looking forward to tomorrow. Christmas is about being with the people you love, not being stuck on your own. The thought that everyone else is together is something I would really like to be unaware of, but of course it's impossible.

None of this has been helped by one of the Christmas greetings faxes I received today. Ken's fax informed me that *The Times* had reported that a nasty cold front is due to come through tomorrow with a ton of wind behind it, and it must be something big if they have bothered to report it.

I've put extra thermals on today – I'm now wearing three sets – very sexy! I've poured myself a glass of wine and shall soon try and get some sleep. At midnight UK time Peter and his son Daniel are going to Birmingham cathedral to light a candle and read out a prayer for me.

25 December (Day 100)

Christmas Day.

Woke up feeling wonderful. There was still about 30 knots of wind and we were sailing well. I was incredibly cold.

I decided to make a real effort and get all dressed up in the hope I would soon get into the spirit of things. The boat was horribly cold and damp and the thought of having a shower and then coming out into such beastly clammy conditions was almost enough to put me off. I still haven't managed to get the heating to work properly so decided to treat myself by putting the oven on and warming the boat. Whilst the boat was getting warmer I dragged Santa Claus's sack out from the engine room and into the snug.

I ran the engine so I could get some hot water and eventually plucked up enough courage to peel off my layers of clothing. I had a shower and washed my hair and suddenly felt much nicer. Then I selected some brighter-looking clothes – a lovely purple fleece, purple and blue scarf, two clean sets of thermal underwear, bright pink thick woolly socks – and hurriedly got dressed again.

My hair was still horribly wet and even with the oven on everywhere was icy cold. I put the engine on again so that I could use my 12-volt hairdryer. That really warmed me up and I suddenly felt really Christmassy. I put some make-up on and chose a few bits of jewellery to add the finishing touches. Then I made myself a hearty breakfast and large mug of steaming black coffee.

I was dying to open my presents but knew that once I had done that there would be nothing left to do so I held off for a while. I really wanted to say Happy Christmas to someone but with the time difference they were all still fast asleep at home. I decided that I could get away with sending my sister Sara and her family a fax in America even if it was still only 0430 their time. Having done that I felt slightly naughty but not guilty and it put me in the right frame of mind for the day.

The champagne was nicely chilled so I poured myself a glass, cloaked myself in the driest sleeping bag and started to go through my sack. So many presents and cards. Like a child I ripped off the wrapping and tossed it to one side. Lovely perfume from my parents, so I smothered myself with that; lots of silly puzzles to keep me occupied; a pearl necklace from Peter, and I put that on as well. What chaos everywhere. All the presents heaped up on the floor and a mass of envelopes and paper littered throughout the cabin.

I gathered all the cards together and once more started to read the lovely messages inside. I put on the tape of Christmas carols and sang along to them for a while, but by this time I was starting to feel emotional and a bit tearful.

What else could I do to keep feeling in the right frame of mind? Nobody else had started their Christmas Day and I'd already done all the things that would make it different from any other day.

In a crazy bid to keep happy I put on some Spanish sevillana music and tried to dance a bit of flamenco. The boat was rolling around wildly and I quickly lost my balance and fell on to the bunk where I collapsed in a heap of laughter.

I cleared up a lot of the mess and strung the cards up around the cabin. I chose a new book to read and slipped into my sleeping bag to read the day away until it was time to try and contact my parents at 1400 hours UK time.

I started trying to contact them via Portishead Radio well in advance of time as I knew that everyone would be wanting to speak to loved ones on Christmas Day. I spent hours trying to get through, but Portishead Radio and I kept losing each other. Eventually I got through at about 1500 hours but although I could just about hear them they couldn't make out what I was saying. Then I chatted to Peter and the line went much clearer so Portishead got hold of my parents again. When Dad realised it was me again he couldn't speak so I had a quick word with my mum and my brother Paul. But it was awful, we were all so emotional that by the time I had finished I was too choked to manage to thank Portishead for their fantastic efforts in linking us up.

My sister sent me a fax from California telling me that she had spoken to Mum and Dad and learnt that nobody had been able to eat any Christmas lunch at all. I felt lousy and just couldn't wait for the day to end. *Spirit* was sailing along just fine so I curled back up in my sleeping bag and tried to escape from it all by reading a book and gorging myself on an oversized piece of Mum's delicious Christmas cake.

The barometer had plummeted and the wind was soon at force 9 gusting occasional 10. I could feel the whole of the rigging vibrating under the pressure. I dragged myself back out of the warmth of the cabin to the horrific world outside and sheeted the storm jib flat again. Then I retreated back down below and settled into the navigation area for the night.

26 December (Day 101)

Boxing Day.

We survived the night but the winds went up to over 55 knots and today I have spent some time putting everything in order again. I really could do with a break from it all. I am so cold and so so tired. I am also emotionally drained after getting upset yesterday. I know it's a bit pathetic but that's rather how I feel.

27 December (Day 102)

Well, the wind has dropped to just a force 8 but I need a rest. It's tiring being thrown around like this and makes every simple task such an effort. The seas are still huge and incessantly throwing *Spirit* on to her side, with the next wave catching her before she's recovered, and breaking over the deck. It's totally miserable up there, and very unstable. I seem to be perpetually cold. How I would love to able to get off, to be at home immersed in a tub of hot water with heaps of bubbles and nothing to worry about except what I'll do when I get out.

But I'm not there. I'm here – imprisoned in this damp and uncomfortable excuse for a home, feeling worse than yesterday with a raging temperature and sick headache. Trying to live with today and not think beyond. Just praying that conditions will improve and life will become a little more normal. I am making myself eat hot food but I really am having to force it down.

28 December (Day 103)

I don't know what happened but I went on deck early this morning to see that the topping lift halyard which connects from the outward end of the boom to the top of the mast had come loose and was swinging around violently. Seeing as conditions were so bad and I couldn't catch it, I decided to cut my losses and just haul it up to the top of the mast where at least it would not do any damage. But as I hauled it up it swung round the top crosstrees and wrapped itself round and round. I looked at it in dismay. It wasn't doing any harm now, but now long would it be before another roll of the boat unwrapped it and it was again a hazard?

I decided I had to get it down. I would have loved to leave it but knew it could cause other problems. So I took a deep breath and started to climb. I never use my safety harness when doing this as it is actually more difficult to attach and undo the safety harness than to just get on and do it. So up I went. She was swaying around horribly and I was finding it tremendously difficult. I decided to stop for a minute and see if I could gauge some sort of pattern to the waves. If I could judge when the smaller ones were coming I would climb then hold on for dear life when a big one was approaching. What a mistake. I was only about fifteen feet above the deck but the sight of the sea from up there was more horrific and I was

143

completely mesmerised by it. My legs had been wobbly before I started up but now they were shaking violently. All I wanted to do was go down again to the relative safety of the deck, but I knew I would only have to start all over again. So, telling myself to stay calm and just take it one step at a time, I forced myself to carry on up the next thirty feet or so.

There is one extra tricky bit where obstructions on the mast mean you have to swing out, grab the other side blind and quickly find the foothold in the maststep, but I couldn't find it. Half of me was screaming in sheer panic, the other half was telling me to keep calm. It must be there, it must be there. But I couldn't locate it and had to risk swinging back. I made three attempts and finally discovered something was blocking it. I eventually managed to clear it and swung over. By now I was shaking so much I had difficulty doing anything, but bit by bit I progressed up. I could see the wayward halyard wrapped around the outside of the crosstrees.

Now I was wishing I had a halyard with me to swing on, but I hadn't and I definitely wasn't going down forty-five feet to come up again. It looked so far away. I knew what I would have to try but my mind didn't want to accept it. I was desperate to be sick but forced myself to stop. There was no other way. I waited for the right motion of the boat and then holding on with one hand used the roll of the sea to throw myself towards the halyard with my fingers outstretched. I pushed it and it unwrapped itself and came towards the mast, luckily the side I was on. I was a complete nervous wreck. Now I had to pull it down, but needing both hands to get down knew I would have to tie it to me somehow. I put one of my arms through the foothold and tried to wrap the halyard around me with the other. Four times I lost it because my fingers were shaking so much, but telling myself to keep calm I eventually had it secured.

Somehow I got down to the deck and stumbled into the cockpit, shaking uncontrollably and feeling extremely weak and frightened. My nerves were completely shot to pieces and I had a cigarette and a sip of brandy to try and pull myself together. The job wasn't finished yet but the rest would be from deck level. As I started to move forward the reaction set in and I was violently sick over the side.

29 December (Day 104)

We got knocked flat during the night. One minute we were upright, the next on our ear, but *Spirit* ricocheted back up again, recovered very quickly and carried on sailing. Maybe it all happened too quickly, but even afterwards I didn't feel too concerned, just went on deck and spent some considerable time tidying up. What a boat she has turned out to be. I can't imagine many boats would have bounced back so well, and surprisingly I wasn't scared. I feel safe in her and in fact now I am enjoying myself again. I guess it is partly because I feel more my old self again today.

Even though I am enjoying the sailing today, I still wish the wind would die a bit. The rigging seems to be vibrating an awful lot which must mean that there is something wrong with the tensioning of the stays. The shock reverberates right through the rigging and into the hull when we get walloped by the seas. If it is causing so much reaction the stress must be terrible. I hope it all holds out.

30 December (Day 105)

My birthday today – thirty-six years old already, and I feel I've hardly started my life.

I am due north of the Iles Kerguelen in the middle of nowhere – what a place to spend it! Still, when I look back over the last few years I have usually spent my birthday preparing masses of food for a five-course New Year's Eve dinner party for sixteen people, so I guess I'm not missing too much! It's an awful time to have a birthday and for years I've been joking about swapping it for an official birthday in the summer – maybe it's not such a bad idea after all. Perhaps I'll take the day I eventually return home as my birthday in future.

I'm apparently having a birthday party at home – well, at least everyone else is going. I know Mum's cooked some delicious food and Dad has got in tons of champagne. I've made myself the same salmon pasta meal as Mum and I've got some champagne too. I've opened my presents and my cards and have had a horrendous few hours trying to get through but I can't. Portishead have contacted my parents to say it is hopeless.

2250 hours: I sent them a fax in the end but I felt as miserable as sin. I knew it just wasn't the same. They were all expecting my call and Dad had even rigged up speakers so that everyone could hear me. How bloody unlucky. Still, a fax was better than nothing.

145

31 December (Day 106)

New Year's Eve.

Had a terrible night and was rudely awoken by the gas alarm going off. But whilst I was trying to find the leak it stopped and hasn't gone off again. I feel a total wreck today. I wish something nice would happen.

Still sailing reasonably well, but for some reason I am sick of it all today. I really don't want to be here. I want to be doing something different. Anything really. Go out for a nice walk all wrapped up in colourful winter clothes and then come home to a merrily roaring fire and enjoy a warming pot of tea with toasted crumpets dripping in a plethora of fresh butter. Or be skiing in the mountains, with freshly fallen snow, blue skies and the wonderful backdrop of the mountains. Down to the log cabin surrounded by discarded skis. And inside to the glorious intoxicating aroma of hot mulled wine, and a host of blooming humanity. The buzz of chatter in the air, everyone heartily encouraged to join in and add to the jollity of the *après-ski*. To be free, free on the mountains, oh how I would love that.

I've done little today except what is necessary on deck and dreaming. I looked through the list and didn't see anything I felt in the right frame of mind to tackle, so I didn't. Naughty, I suppose, but it's only one day.

1 January 1995 (Day 107)

....

01 JAN   FROM: BT INMARSAT-C FAX   TO: PETER HARDING

....

Hi Peter,

Happy New Year to you too!

Didn't expect you to be in the office, but since you are . . .

I am still having trouble with the self steering. It seems to have got less responsive again, but this time I think it is related to friction on the main steering. I can hear the arm of the autopilot moaning even though it is not switched on and I am wondering if it is dragging. It might need oiling, I suppose, but I haven't used it that much, so I would be surprised. I expect the sensible thing, seeing as the autopilot is currently not usable, would be to disconnect the steering rod on the autopilot and see if it eases it. The trouble is, if I do and it isn't the problem, will I be able to put it back? It'll mean crawling through everything in the engine room, over the engine itself and then dragging myself on my stomach to the connection point on the quadrant. It's not going to be an easy job but at least at the moment there is very little wind. I've got to make my mind up quickly as the forecast is for another gale by tonight/tomorrow with rough to very rough seas, and then my task will be much more complicated.

Any ideas?

Thanks,
Lisa.

....

In spite of all the problems today I have a great psychological boost. Today is New Year's Day and this year it has meant more than ever. Not that I have made any New Year's resolutions because I never keep those anyway. No, this New Year it is the day itself that is important. Why? Because for the first time I can say, 'I shall be home this summer, I shall be home this year.' Not next year, which sounds so horrible and almost incomprehensibly far away, but *this* year. I suddenly feel much closer already and more positive. I really feel that it's within my grasp and that I can make it! It's a wonderful wonderful feeling.

2 January (Day 108)

Unbelievably the wind has just died. I am rolling about in a leftover sea and going absolutely nowhere. I don't know how this can be happening when such strong winds are forecast. I've spent the day doing various repairs and preventative maintenance, but otherwise it has been totally frustrating.

It's getting dark now and I am still unhappy with the steering. I have a horrible feeling it might be the main rudder which is at fault now. Still, I can do no more for the time being and will just have to hope that it works OK when I need it most.

I'm really hating every minute at the moment. I just don't seem to feel any enjoyment about anything today and it's taking everything I have got just to keep going.

3 January (Day 109)

Christ! Still no wind. I've actually taken all the sails down today. It's the first time I've had nothing up at all, but the violent slapping of the wind which is just occasionally blowing from various directions was driving me mad. It was impossible to make way and now I have taken them down the relief is enormous. I knew it was getting on my nerves but it is only now that I realise how pent up I had become. The quiet and peace is like a balm.

I felt relaxed enough then to bake some fresh bread and make myself a tasty pasta dish.

Then I tried to fix the compass again but didn't succeed.

I feel as though I am a bit of a failure. I don't know why. I've felt this at various stages over the last few years. I guess now it might be caused by the fact that *Spirit* is a bit of a lump and we are making embarrassingly slow time. It makes me feel very second rate somehow. I guess that is what's brought on these thoughts of 'Is it all worth it? Should I be bothering to carry on?'

Hopefully the wind will come soon then maybe I will come to my senses.

4 January (Day 110)

I spent the day working hard to keep myself occupied and prevent myself from getting down.

I analysed a slight software problem on the navigation instruments. It is impossible to put in 90–99°E so I faxed Peter with instructions on how it could probably be solved.

I spent a few more hours on the heating system and whilst I am fixing it bit by bit, it is nowhere near ready to be used. I spent a lot of time on deck and rerouted the control lines for the furling gear so they are all controlled through the sprayhood instead of running along the guard rails. In addition I also perfected many things that had been irritating me.

There is only about 10 knots of wind which is hopelessly light but at least we are making some way again.

Despite all my efforts I feel depressed. I need to be with people. I've had enough of being on my own. Enough sailing, enough pressure, enough disturbed sleep and enough tinned food. I'm desperate to be home! What on earth am I doing out here?

5 January (Day 111)

God, what on earth is the matter with me? This is pathetic. The weather is OK and there's simply no good reason to feel like this. One minute I'm fine and then for absolutely no reason and without warning I can feel panic welling up inside me and it's taking all my control not to flip.

I've tried doing things on deck but I'm aware that I am working at an almost frantic pace. It's not that I am doing anything wrong, in fact I am working extremely quickly and very effectively. I've seen solutions to things that before I couldn't remedy. But my brain seems to be working at twice its normal speed, almost as though it is racing and I can't slow it down. But why? There is nothing I can put it down to. I just don't feel in control of my inner self and it's a frightening experience.

I am better if I lie down and just try and compose myself but I can't stay there for ever like a zombie. I've taken a Prozac tablet, which is supposed to make you happy, but it doesn't seem to be helping. Maybe I need to take more before they will have any effect. But what if they are addictive? I only have thirty and I've got months at sea yet. And anyway the thought of relying on something like that is worrying me in itself.

Maybe sleep is the answer. Or lack of it. I haven't had more than a couple of hours over the last few days and this could be causing it. I've also been on tenterhooks waiting for this gale that hasn't yet arrived.

It seems such a long time until I will be home, so I've told myself that if I don't want to go on I don't have to. I can stop in Australia, and that's not too far away.

I guess the best thing to do is try and get as much rest as possible, not cramped up in the chair but lying on the bunk in a more relaxed position. Whatever I decide to do I've got to be more rational and in control.

6 January (Day 112)

***

***

Hi,

I am at 42.28°S and 82.27°E on a course just south of east. The wind is up to force 9 now and we are batting along at between 6 and 7 knots though occasionally surfing at over 10. I still don't feel very relaxed even now the bad weather has arrived but I think it is partly that I am having a bad reaction to those happy pills. I've stopped taking them now and whether it is just psychological or not I don't know. I really don't care as I am feeling less panicky.

I am sure it was partly helped by reading Chichester's book *The Lonely Sea and the Sky*. I feel a certain empathy with him. He says he used to get an idea that he had to carry on till he could prove something was possible, even though he suffered from panic attacks too. One of the lovely bits I was reading this morning was just after pages of misery, and he has written in his log, 'I feel very happy again tonight. I have not enjoyed myself so much since I was preparing to fly out alone to Australia in 1929. I was thinking the old query, "is fate too strong for man's self-will?" Am I so happy because I am doing the sort of thing I was destined for? How I enjoyed it – no, that's not right because I hated a lot of it, always scared stiff – my flying. No, I should say how it satisfied me!'

Many times in his book he says that he had to use all his effort to control himself and stop a fit of abject panic, so at least I am not the only one. Perhaps it is OK to panic. Perhaps it is only natural. It certainly makes me feel better to believe that.

Anyway how are you?

***

7 January (Day 113)

Still travelling along at about 7 knots, which is great, but I hope they are right when they only forecast snow south of me. I really don't fancy being caught out in that, and conditions here are bad enough anyway. It's force 10 and *Spirit* seems to be handling it fairly well. We are just under the storm jib at present and I have got my huge heavy Channel Islands warp ready to stream out over the stern to slow us down more if necessary. I can hardly believe that I am still underway in such awful seas but I can't bear the thought of just lying there sideways on and feeling the full impact of all that water. The sea state is very high; the waves look as high as houses before they crest and tumble into a torrent of foam.

I had a really disturbed sleep last night, but didn't feel too bad this morning so have spent the day carefully reattaching things that had come adrift or actually broken during the hours of darkness.

Now I have good reason to panic, I am not. I seem to have regained my sanity today, which is wonderful. I'll never resort to taking pills again – they obviously don't suit me. I think I am better off suffering bouts of depression than losing my self-esteem by giving up the control of my mind and body to some alien chemical.

8 January (Day 114)

Conditions are still bad although the wind has dropped slightly to force 9. The sea state is very rough and the waves huge. *Spirit* is just being lost between the height of each one. They must be fifty feet or more.

I keep thinking I ought to be capturing it on film but the thought of taking everything on deck and rigging it is too much. Anyway, I would probably lose everything over the side so I think I'm doing the best thing by just sticking to what has to be done and nothing else.

I'm really appreciating the fax machine. What an amazing thing satellites are. It's so good to stay in touch with the outside world. I know I'm being quite irresponsible with the amount of faxes I'm sending but it seems important to keep that link, regardless of battery power and cost!

9 January (Day 115)

09 JAN   **FROM: BT INMARSAT-C FAX**   **TO: PETER HARDING**

Hi there,

The wind has dropped right down to between 20 and 30 knots, which is great, and hopefully the sea will gradually subside as well.

For some reason the instruments have all frozen. I have checked all the wiring and reconnected some but still can't get it to work properly, in fact I now can't reconnect the illumination wire without cutting everything out. It's really tricky working on such a fiddly job. I've tried working behind the displays in the engine room but trying to hold myself clear of the batteries, hold the torch and work with tiny screwdrivers and thin short wires requires more than one pair of hands. I guess I'll have to leave it till I get quieter conditions but in the meantime it means I have no instruments to tell me exactly where the wind is coming from and it makes it extremely difficult gybing the boat in a controlled manner.

My current position is 42.23°S 92.58°E and another gale is forecast. What lovely weather!

Hope all is OK with you.
Ciao for now,
Lisa.

10 January (Day 116)

The boat is still rolling from side to side and is bloody uncomfortable but should settle down a bit soon as the wind has suddenly dropped from over 40 knots to just under 20. It's also shifted 90° so I have just swapped all the sails over to the other side.

I seem to have collected a lot of forecasts today – South Africa, Perth and the Antarctic Met Centre – but that is probably due to the warning of

Tropical Storm Christelle. It is quite a way from me at the moment but heading in this direction. I feel almost sure its path should keep it clear of me but I need to be a couple of hundred miles away from its centre to survive. It's incredible how much more scary and threatening it seems when they actually give it a name.

11 January (Day 117)

The return of strong winds has really brought with it a return of my spirits. Looking back at all the contributing factors I am now not really surprised that I reached such a low ebb, but it was certainly a feeling that I wouldn't like to have again. When you get that low it just seems that you will never come out of it. I kept saying to myself, 'This too will pass ...' but it honestly didn't feel as though it would. However, now I am once again my normal self and battling with the elements.

To be honest the weather is lousy: cold, wet, grey, and a constant stream of depressions bringing strong winds which veer and back as the fronts pass through, creating confused very rough to high seas.

Spirit is sailing beautifully, however, and seems to love surfing down the waves, though we tend to yaw from side to side and our speed over the ground is quite a bit less than the speed at which we're helterskeltering along.

12 January (Day 118)

Woke up this morning determined to spend the day fixing things. How I hate to be surrounded by things that are not working. I used to feel confident that I could fix almost anything if I really wanted to, but when I look at the list of outstanding jobs I can't help but feel that I am losing the battle to keep on top. It doesn't help psychologically either, to know there are several unfinished jobs, the pieces for which are just in boxes hidden away in cupboards and waiting to be fixed. Everywhere looks deceptively tidy but I know in my mind what isn't visible to the eye. I am getting behind and in a bit of a mess.

So I started off by stripping the heater motor again, then through numerous faxes with Peter checked every single thing. I cleaned everything until it was smooth and clean but when I started to put it back I remembered that this was one box of bits that wasn't complete. I had lost all of the screws, washers and bearings in the bilges. Painstakingly and with a certain degree of inventiveness I made replacement parts and eventually rebuilt it. It had all been worth it when I heard it start up. My feeling of euphoria vanished shortly after when it spluttered and died – I could have screamed.

Everywhere is so bitterly bitterly cold and it's all my fault. If only I had had the sense to look after the motor earlier on then it wouldn't have corroded, and I wouldn't be spending hours and hours trying to fix it. How bloody stupid!

Anyway, since I couldn't face the thought of stripping it again I got on with some general resorting and more simple jobs that at least I knew I could achieve.

13 January (Day 119)

Optimism is a wonderful thing. The forecast had been for imminent force 8–9, but when it hadn't arrived, the barometer was steady, the ominous-looking sky had seemed to lighten, and the wind had dropped to under 20 knots, I was quite happily convinced that maybe it had somehow passed me by. But four hours later it was the top end of gale force 8, and soon after severe gale force 9 gusting storm force 10 (50–60 mph winds). The barometer plummeted 10 mbs in just a few hours, which was bad news, and I was beginning to feel it was going to be a typical Friday the 13th, full of bad luck, and bad omens.

The waves looked over forty-five feet and there was a high swell. Visibility dropped down to about half a mile and the force of the wind was blowing the tops off the waves in streaks – quite a sight. Unfortunately there seemed to be some fault on the camera so once again I didn't manage to catch it on film. I decided to wait until the weather improved before I tried to fix it – I was sure there was going to be no shortage of good footage in the weeks ahead.

Despite my concerns, *Spirit* raced along under just the storm jib and coped extremely well, but I was concerned again about the rigging. The forestay was shaking violently and causing exceptional stress on the terminals.

As a temporary measure I raked the mast back as far as possible by tightening the backstays in an attempt to take out some of the slack. It wasn't really enough, although there was nothing else I could do but pray for some calmer conditions soon so I can dismantle the furling forestays and tighten them up. My real concern is that I am gradually moving further south where chances of calm weather are decreasing. It's a job that can't be tackled unless I am sure that I can finish it before the bad weather returns – to be caught out halfway through doesn't even bear thinking about.

14 January (Day 120)

I am having a horrible day today. I feel tired and upset.

The wind has dropped to about 20 knots but the sea is still high and the forestay seems to be bowing badly. I've had to take it in today as it was shaking so violently. There must be twelve to eighteen inches' arc at times, which can't be right, and certainly the vibrations it's sending through the hull cannot be good news.

I'm really torn about whether to try taking it down. I've been on deck and removed all the protective tape from the bottle screws connecting the stays to the chainplates on the deck, but there looks to be very little adjustment room left. I might manage two turns, but to do that I shall probably have to disconnect the furling gear so that I can hold the stay and prevent it twisting as I tighten.

1600 hours: I kept going on deck and then back down below. God, I felt so tired and unable to decide what to do. Three or four times I got all my tools together, crawled up to the bow and started. Then it would feel like the wind was gusting a bit stronger and I would chicken out. The thought of dismantling it and then not being able to put it back quickly had my mind racing. What should I do? Try it or leave it?

Oh God, I don't feel able to make this decision today. I just want to sit down and cry. I don't want to be here.

15 January (Day 121)

My dad's birthday today! I have sent him a poem and permission to have my share of the champagne. I would love to be there too but I can't. Peter has been great and organised a card, a bar of Fry's chocolate and a bottle of something from me.

The good news is that I am only 250 miles from a point south of Western Australia. There is still only 20 knots of wind and the sea has flattened quite a bit so I have been able to have another go at the furling gear.

I managed to tighten the bottle screw up a couple of turns but it still wasn't enough. So then I set about disconnecting the telescopic section of the foil so that I could raise it, shorten the stay and hence give more adjustment space on the bottle screw. But one of the Allen screws had a messed-up head and I couldn't undo it. The only option seemed to be to drill it out, but I wasn't sure I would be able to resecure it again so for the time being I put it all back together.

With a small crow bar I managed to take a couple more turns on the twin backstays. It still didn't seem tensioned enough but the mast was beginning to look very raked back. I decided to get some advice before doing any more.

I felt positive there should be something better I could do but my mind seemed to be all confused with it and unable to analyse the problem properly.

However, I did seem able to work well at other things so spent the rest of the day restripping the motor for the heater, which is now working fine. I've tested it by taking some power from one of my 12-volt sockets, but haven't tried to put it back in its casing as I decided instead to fix the motor pump for the water system, also successfully. These motors are dead simple when you get the hang of them.

I celebrated the day by having a glorious hot shower. Then squeaky clean for the first time in ages I treated myself to a glass of wine and got out the tapes that I had been given to watch. There were three which had been transferred to Hi-8 so that I could play them back through my video camera on to a separate mini screen. I had been given a choice of *When Harry Met Sally, Father of the Bride* and one just marked *?*. I had already seen *When Harry Met Sally* on the television at home and although I enjoyed it, decided to watch something new instead. I was naturally intrigued with the mystery tape so set it up to play. With my glass of wine I got comfortable in my navigator's chair where I could both watch the video and keep a watch on the instruments as well. I couldn't believe my eyes, what on earth was I watching? Like a naughty schoolgirl I switched it off, and then couldn't help but giggle. A blue movie! I remember opening up to some friends before I left that I'd never seen one – but I don't think

I want to watch one here like this, not tonight anyway. I took it out and replaced it with *Father of the Bride*, but my curiosity has been aroused and I think that at some stage in the future I'll have to have another peek!

16 January (Day 122)

I woke up feeling most uneasy after having disturbed dreams again. *Spirit* and I were racing along at breakneck speed towards the shore. I was driving her like I would a car, looking through the windscreen in horror and trying to put the brakes on. One huge wave picked us up and sent us slewing up the sandy beach. A woman came over, started to shake my hand and said I'd arrived a little early, the Women's Institute didn't meet until 12 o'clock and perhaps I'd like to use that time to have a wash, and then I could phone Peter, who wanted to be informed I had arrived safely. I grappled round trying to find 10p for the phonebox only to realise I hadn't got any money. I turned round to ask the woman but she'd gone.

A ridiculous dream – totally absurd, but how I hate it. I never used to suffer this at home and I always feel a sense of foreboding when I get dreams now. I wish I had never seen that book on the meaning of them as I feel sure they are warnings of things to come. To bring myself out of it I made a large black coffee and had a feast of boiled eggs with freshly baked bread.

All night I'd been aware of a clunking sound again, and although I tried to investigate, I wasn't able to determine what it was. As I sat there deciding what to work on, the clunking started again. I raced on deck but everything looked OK so I went below to the engine room and dragged myself over the stores to where it appeared to be coming from. I couldn't see anything but it was still there. I went back on deck and listened again for the sound. Then I noticed that the frame holding the self-steering gear was just slightly out of line. The whole lot had shifted and the nut securing one of the outer legs was just about to come off. This was causing all of it to move slightly under pressure.

I went below for my spanners and returned on deck. I secured myself with a couple of harnesses, and gripping with my toes leant down over the stern to start working. There's no doubt that working upside down makes life exceptionally difficult, and I was almost finished when I strained my shoulder. I managed to pull myself back on deck, relieved that I had finished but cursing that I had hurt myself.

I retired below and smothered it in Deep Heat.

17 January (Day 123)

My shoulder feels worse today, but according to Joe Jordan who is advising me (via Peter) on any medical problems, I made it worse by putting Deep Heat on it so quickly. I wasn't aware that you should wait twenty-four hours before putting it on, otherwise it actually exaggerates the problem. Still, there isn't much I can do about it now, except use it as little as possible and hope I don't have to do any major work on deck. I've limited myself to working on light easy things which won't do any harm.

People often think you get bored on a boat. They seem to visualise sailing as just sitting there and watching the sea go by, but it's not like that at all. Not if, that is, you want to keep everything in tiptop condition. You can adopt the view that you only tackle problems which arise, but personally I wouldn't dream of it. I very much believe that preventative maintenance is essential to minimising the risks of being on board. And even so, there is a list as long as my arm!

I've pottered all day, and feel quite pleased with myself. In fact I feel more than pleased, as I have reached another milestone.

....

17 JAN 14.28   FROM: SENTOSA C LES   TO: PETER HARDING

....

I am now south of Cape Leeuwin, Australia!

....

18 January (Day 124)

My shoulder is still making some tasks difficult, especially things on deck. I am having to do as much of the more strenuous work as I can with my left hand, which isn't easy.

I really shouldn't have tackled the heater but the thought of a little discomfort and a warm cabin later persuaded me to have a go. I managed to put the motor back and with all my newfangled pieces rebuilt it. I said a quick prayer then turned it on. I couldn't believe it – it worked! The fan was spinning round, I rushed on deck and the exhaust was emitting smoke. *Yes yes yes!* I couldn't help but jump up and down with joy. After about ten minutes of jigging around I partially slid back the hatch so I could go down into the nice warm cabin. But it wasn't. The fan was still working, but it was now pumping out cold air!

After a lot of deliberation I came to the conclusion that when I had originally kept trying to run it I had damaged other parts too. I could remember it well – feeling so damned sure that positive thinking alone would get it to work.

So I faxed Peter and between us we discussed all the options. I spent hours replacing flame detectors, glow plugs, electrical control units, etc. on the heater. I checked all the wiring with the circuit tester and finally had to admit defeat. I'd completely run out of ideas and inspiration and knew that there was no point in doing the same things again.

Great! Here I am freezing to death in a nasty damp boat and instead of getting the heating fixed I have got myself air conditioning!

It was whilst trying to bring back some order to the workshop that I noticed that the sole of the cabin was wet. At first I presumed it was the air vent again and was taking that apart when I realised that this water had an unusually strong smell. I dipped my finger in it and warily licked it. Mmmm, lovely. *Oh no!* My last box of wine. The foil inside had obviously rotted or ripped and the contents had either been absorbed into the wood or drained into the bilges. What a waste!

Crikey, what a day. Well, it's certainly character forming (or is it *re*forming!).

19 January (Day 125)

It was lovely on deck last night. I watched the moon rise. It was a full moon, huge and bright and yellow – absolutely magnificent. I haven't seen any shipping but I guess that is because I am so far south of Australia. But just in case, I put the navigation lights on and also the radar. I was producing a lot of power as both the towgen and the generator taking power from the prop shaft were spinning well, so I could afford to be a bit extravagant, but I also got some enjoyment from watching the radar signal go round and round and kept switching it from one range to another. There was nothing to be seen except the state of the seas but it kept me amused for a while.

After an enjoyable couple of hours listening to some CDs I decided to get some sleep in my bunk but woke up lying on my front with my shoulder trapped beneath me. I was in agony and stuck. How I managed to get into that position when I was in a cot surrounded by all my teddies I can't imagine. It got better during the day, I suppose movement must help it, but it certainly put me in a poor frame of mind.

The weather is now awful, with the wind going up and down like a yo-yo, from 18 to 35 knots; the sea is lumpy and very uncomfortable and I am even having to hold myself rigid in my navigator's chair.

There's a four-foot rip in the foresail so I've taken it in more. It's so darned difficult to have the right amount up when it keeps changing like this. Not enough canvas up and the boat can't make way; too much up and it rips!

There's simply no way I can repair it in this weather. Were it a hank-on sail I could just lower it, unhank it and bring it below to repair. But being a furling sail, to take it off I would have to unfurl it all before I could even attempt to pull it down. It's not only the worry of having all that sail flying, it's also the concern of what happens if it gets stuck halfway – it would be torn to shreds in no time. No, I'll just have to leave it until I get calmer weather.

I feel low, lonely, exhausted and tired of being thrown about. I've had enough of it today.

20 January (Day 126)

....

20 JAN   **FROM: SENTOSA C LES**   **TO: PETER HARDING**

....

Hi Peter,

Well the wind has dropped even more today but there is still a tremendous swell. It doesn't know quite what it is doing today. I guess I must be in a trough of some sort as the wind is very erratic – coming from all around the compass and ranging from 10 to 30 knots. It's awful when it is like this, impossible to make any decent progress and yet not calm enough to do some of the more urgent jobs. Still, I have had a productive day and seem to be whipping through the list of slightly less major jobs. It had got to the stage where I felt I couldn't keep up but now if I can get a patch of calm weather I shall be able to get on top of everything again.

Hope everything is OK with you. Will be in touch again soon.

Take care,
Lisa.

....

....

20 JAN   **FAX TO LISA**   **FROM: PETER HARDING**

....

Hi Lisa,

Well, sorry to hear that the wind is playing up but at least you are getting the chance to sort out some of your problems, which will make you feel more confident when it picks up again. Don't worry about time – you are doing really well now. Just stick with it.

If I can do anything for you just let me know.

Peter.

....

I ran the engine to top up the batteries and make water, but soon discovered that the casing on the engine was very hot. I checked everything, including the seacock and the water impellor, but all seemed OK. The engine casing also appeared to be vibrating more, and although I tried everything I wasn't able to secure it better. It was probably this shaking that caused the watermaker to burst a leak on the high pressure side. I managed to cut the copper pipe down and put on a new fitting and then it was working again. This marvellous piece of equipment can take loads of seawater, push it through filters, and then through membranes at high pressure where, by a process of reverse osmosis, it produces pure water. I had been a bit careless really by letting my water supplies run right down, and if I hadn't been able to fix it I would now be in a hopeless situation, indeed one which could have jeopardised the whole trip. Without water I couldn't possibly survive for long and I couldn't expect to be able to catch rainwater until I hit the squalls up on the Equator, which is months away.

I've also been trying to find out why so much water was getting into the engine room. It was starting to corrode quite a few things which would give me more problems later. One was the water injection tube coming out of the deep sea seal, which seals up where the propeller shaft goes through the bottom of the boat. Apart from keeping the sea out it needs to give freedom of movement for the propeller shaft to turn. A small amount of water helps lubricate it and to stop that water coming straight into the boat, a small tube travels up above the normal water level. However, because we were sometimes heeled over so far, the waterline was higher, so I made an extension to raise it to a higher point.

There was also water coming in through some of the deck fittings. I did consider trying to remove and refit them with a seal of Sekaflex but it was impossible to hold the nut on deck and unscrew below at the same time. So instead I plastered everything with a thick coat of sealant. This might sound easy but in a rolly sea was almost impossible and when I reached up over my head, the inevitable happened.

I am covered in sealant. It's in my hair, all over my sailing gear, and of course splattered on my face and hands. I tried to wash it off but it just seems to smear so I will just have to wait till it dries and hope that it will then peel off. In fact I look rather like I do when I am decorating – like a child who's been at the paint pot. But I've really enjoyed today. In fact I have just realised I am starving – I've been working for eleven solid hours and not yet eaten!

....

20 JAN   **FROM: SENTOSA C LES**   **TO: PETER HARDING**

....

Hi there,
I am at 44.19°S 124.10°E and with any luck will be south of the western tip of Tasmania in a week – YES!

....

21 January (Day 127)

The printer has developed problems on the screen. I have a large orange stripe right down it which might of course be caused by the damp atmosphere everywhere. Also the printer side of the PC won't take the paper. I've opened it up and tried to push through some feeler gauges to make sure it has a clear run for the paper feed but it hasn't made any difference. In fact the only thing I have done is to razor my fingers to pieces, which was particularly foolhardy. I've covered them with antiseptic and they feel so cold I can't feel anything else.

There also seems to be a squeaking on the main steering but although I have taken that apart I cannot see why it is happening so have just poured some oil down for now and hope that will stop it.

22 January (Day 128)

The wind is still from the north but has dropped right down to a fickle 12–20 knots which isn't really settled enough to do the rigging, so in a bid to get some fresh air I went on deck and helmed for most of the day. It was biting cold up there and even with inner and outer gloves my hands were terribly swollen and red.

Apart from that I did very little except some cleaning down below and made myself spaghetti carbonara. I felt a little guilty about the fact that I kept choosing what to eat instead of sticking to Bill Jermey's recommended menu. He'd gone to a great deal of trouble to make sure it was a well-balanced diet but I was eating what I felt like instead. Still, much of what he had done was appreciated. Many things were in individual portions, such as cheeses, chutneys and rice. There was also an abundance of fresh eggs and onions, a wonderful selection of herbs and spices, and many other delicacies. I've never enjoyed sticking to recipes, and being an inventive cook is a tremendous asset on a boat where you can't go and shop for ingredients.

23 January (Day 129)

23 JAN **FAX TO LISA** **FROM: PETER HARDING**

Yes, if you are in the mood I can certainly work with you to fix the heater. Just let me know what the current status is when you are ready.

Speak to you soon,
Peter.

We worked on it for ages but still didn't manage to sort it. I was starting to worry about what else the lack of heat was affecting, apart from me. The computer was looking worse. I left it switched on, but with the lid down, hoping that its internal heater would dry it out, but it made no apparent difference. I made up a hot-water bottle which I wrapped up to make sure it didn't give out any moist air then placed it on the computer to see if it would help to dry it out.

24 January (Day 130)

The hot-water bottle doesn't seem to have done any good at all but the advice is to keep trying, although I'm not sure it isn't making it worse. I've tried to dry it out with my little 12-volt hairdryer, but apart from using up a lot of power I don't think it's done much good. I really do need to get this heating fixed, otherwise I could soon lose the screen altogether and then I will really be on my own. Mind you, there could be advantages to this: I could just potter on at my own pace without worrying about what people think of my progress. I'm sure I would enjoy myself more. It would certainly give me a certain sense of freedom which I don't really feel I have at the moment. All I feel now is a strong obligation to be doing better than I am. But that is selfish. So many people have helped to put me out here and I shouldn't be whingeing about letting them know how I am doing. So I've decided today to just keep at it and I am not going to stop until I have a nice warm dry boat. I have prematurely lost contact through the Indian Ocean but I think I am not in range of the right satellites.

24 JAN 22:55 HOURS   FROM: SENTOSA C LES   TO: PETER HARDING

Hi, this is just a test file. I have lost the Indian Ocean and it has swapped to Pacific – I am trying Land Earth Station 210.

Lisa.

25 January (Day 131)

| 25 JAN | FROM: SENTOSA C LES | TO: PETER HARDING |

25 JAN **FROM: SENTOSA C LES** **TO: PETER HARDING**

WE HAVE BLAST OFF!!!!!
YES YES YES!

After numerous faxes to Peter (which kept him up all night) and continually testing and replacing every single part of the heating system, I have fixed the heater.

I feel really good today. I've got a lovely warm boat and for the first time I am beginning to thaw out. I've put the computer and cameras into my 'hot locker'. This is a specially designed locker that was meant to be for hanging clothes to dry, but I've just used it as a normal hanging locker. Now it is invaluable. I just hope it will do the trick and clear up the problem with the computer screen. I'm not hopeful that it will get rid of the lines already there but I'm keeping my fingers crossed that it'll prevent any more appearing.

Unfortunately I still haven't had much luck with dismantling the yankee furler part of the rigging. I just can't get that all-important Allen screw out even though I tried to knock it with a punch and tap a new groove to take a screwdriver. I really need to find a way of getting this off.

I am just south of Kangaroo Island now, not brilliant progress over the last few days although at the moment I am not too bothered.

26 January (Day 132)

Yesterday I felt as though I could achieve anything, and in the evening celebrated the luxury of a warm cabin with a half bottle of champagne.

Today has sent me plummeting to the very lowest ebb.

I woke up feeling good and thinking how lucky I was to get that much-needed calm weather to tackle the most major problems on the boat – repairing the torn sail and fixing the furling gear.

I managed to lower the sail but for some reason it wouldn't come all the way down and I had to repair it standing up and trying to hold the sail flat. It was jolly difficult trying to sew something so big when the wind kept catching it and it took an exhausting couple of hours. It wasn't a work of art but it didn't look too bad, as it was actually only the seam that had come undone. However, when it came to that blasted Allen screw I tried everything and in desperation started to drill it out.

I'd successfully done this before in the quiet waters of Cape Town, but trying to keep my balance and drill at the same time resulted in a complete botch. The hole got bigger and bigger but it still held together. So I decided that if I undid the remaining Allen screw then I could maybe knock it apart. Then I found the second one was the same. Determined as I was, I knew I couldn't afford to have no way of securing that bottom end. After a cup of coffee and a lot of thinking I decided that I would have to put back everything that I had painstakingly taken apart and rehoist the sail.

The sail wouldn't go up. I thought it might be the pressure of the wind but eventually saw that there was a loose screw about thirty feet up the foil. I got out the binoculars and on closer inspection could see that there are other loose screws and some completely missing.

How bloody ironical! The screws I can reach I can't shift and the ones I can't reach are falling out! Instead of being a continuous foil, the link plates are no longer doing their job and it is now in sections. I couldn't think of a way to get any way near the problem. Every time I tried to raise the sail it took the top sections with it, so I had to let it drop again until they were at least sitting together.

Was it my imagination, or was the wind starting to gust stronger? What the hell was I going to do with a half-hoisted big sail? I decided that if I couldn't take it up I would reluctantly have to bring it down and try again in better conditions – but it wouldn't come.

I was left with no option but to stand there and try and tease it up. I secured the drum with lines so that the runner was facing directly towards the mast, and half-inch by half-inch tried to hoist it. Up half an inch, down a quarter; up half an inch, down a quarter; up half an inch ... Oh damn, down half an inch. Up half an inch, and so on.

The wind was definitely picking up and I could feel stirrings of panic inside. Keep calm, don't rush it, it will go up eventually.

After a couple of hours it was up and with relief I untied my tool box and took it back to the cockpit, unfurled the sail and once again we were off.

I feel relieved in one sense but not in another. How am I going to replace the halyard or repair any rips if I can't get it down? And what about the main problem which I already had? It is still too slack and damaging the rig. If I can't fix it I could lose the use of it altogether.

God, I feel as sick as a parrot. I've made no progress through the water, and whilst I have fixed the tear, I have discovered other more serious problems.

I feel totally and utterly defeated.

....

26 JAN   TO: LISA   FROM: PETER HARDING

....

Hi Lisa,
Thought I would send you something that I know will cheer you up! A special personal fax arrived at the office this morning and I have a feeling you would like to see it!

10 Downing Street
London SW1A 2AA

THE PRIME MINISTER   26th January, 1995

Dear Lisa (handwritten)
    I wanted to send you my best wishes on your world trip. The courage, determination and endurance that are needed for such a venture can only be admired and I know how well you have coped with the challenges you have already met.
    I wish you every success with the rest of your trip.

Yours sincerely
John Major

You deserve it, Lisa. Isn't it great! Write back as soon as you can, and then I'll write again.
    Peter.

....

10 DOWNING STREET
LONDON SW1A 2AA

THE PRIME MINISTER

26th January, 1995

Dear Lisa,

I wanted to send you my best wishes on your world trip.

The courage, determination and endurance that are needed for such a venture can only be admired and I know how well you have coped with the challenges you have already met.

I wish you every success with the rest of your trip.

Yours sincerely,

John Major

Miss Lisa Clayton

27 January (Day 133)

It's surprising how a few hours' decent sleep, combined with the lovely fax I received last night, can make everything look brighter. I've woken up this morning feeling positive again, and determined to relook at yesterday's problem from a completely new start. The wind has arrived so I can't actually do much on it today but this is probably a good thing. I need to stand back and look at it afresh. Sometimes when there are so many problems inside your head it is easy to get too wrapped up in them and not see solutions. I am going to spend the day pottering doing little jobs and not try to rack my brains trying to find a solution.

I have always been a firm believer that with the right attitude and approach nearly everything can be solved or improved. I think what shook me yesterday was that I had felt right, I had been determined and was actually looking forward to the challenge, so I was rather shattered when I couldn't remedy it.

Later I shall sit down and write things down in black and white and discuss it with Peter and the riggers. I feel so sure there must be some way of at least improving things even if I can't completely remedy the problem. As they say, necessity is the mother of invention, but I have looked at the problem for so long now that my mind has become cluttered. I need to clear it and reassess the possibilities – however unlikely some of them may at first seem.

My father always says I wake up with a smile on my face, so I guess I am basically lucky that I am an optimist – or as Robin Knox Johnston would say, a realistic optimist.

28 January (Day 134)

I've felt lethargic all day. My shoulder seems to be worse than ever, which I suppose is hardly surprising – I've not given it the rest I intended to and it is screaming in protest. My poor old fingers are horribly swollen, cut, and plastered in blood blisters from when I caught them in the hatch during the night.

I suppose I should just be glad I don't wear rings otherwise they would have been a worse mess. Even so, I can't move them at all without being in pain. What a wreck!

The weather is much the same, still heading me and forcing me further south. I'm already down at 49° but not yet south of Tasmania.

What lousy progress. It's very grey everywhere and pretty dismal, and reflects my mood to a T.

29 January (Day 135)

The weather is still up and down, and every time I need to change the sail area I have to use my shoulder, which is really draining me.

To try and take my mind off this exasperating weather I have spent the day looking back over the last few years and realising just how lucky I am. So today is a horrid day for me, but it isn't that bad, it is just that I am feeling down.

I am so lucky to have had this opportunity, to be here. Lucky to have read Naomi's book, lucky to have found a rusty shell I could afford, lucky to have got all the support I did, lucky to have met Peter who really pushed the project forward. Lucky to have such wonderful parents. I am just lucky lucky lucky. So why do I sometimes forget?

30 January (Day 136)

At last I've reached a point south of Tasmania. The last few days have driven me to distraction with variable headwinds which shifted between 100° and pushed me south down to the border of the Furious Fifties. There is nothing worse than not being able to make progress towards where you want to be – especially when the prevailing winds should be westerly. I've lost yet another few days.

I've found it very difficult to get on with anything else. Instead I've just lost the day, almost hypnotised by the dials on the navigation equipment, and willing the wind to at least stay in one direction.

Normally if I can't do anything about a situation I manage to get on with something else but on this voyage it is somehow more difficult. Nothing else seems to matter except making progress – it's the be-all and end-all of my existence.

It would probably help if I could feel some sense of achievement for what I have done so far, but for some reason I don't. Maybe it's because I am tired, maybe it's because there is so much to do, or maybe if I had actually seen Australia it would seem more real. But since Cape Town the only thing I have seen is sea, sea and sea. The only thing

I really feel is that I still have such a long long way to go till I am home.

31 January (Day 137)

The wind suddenly rose during the night to gale force and I was forced to go on deck to take down the large genoa. With the decklights on, it was well lit, but elsewhere it was pitch black, broken only by the white of the crests of the waves close by. I tried to bring the sail down in a controlled manner without it going into the water and had managed to get it about halfway when I felt it wouldn't come down any more. I realised that the halyard must be stuck on the winch but just as I let go to release it the wind billowed out the sail and I found myself strapped against the forestay by one of the ropes.

After a terrible struggle I managed to get free. Ridiculously I continued to try and haul the sail down, but after four attempts lost it again when the wind once more set the sail flying. Because of the lack of driving force, *Spirit* went off course and I rushed to the helm to put her back on a better course. I eased off the sheets a little in the cockpit, released where the halyard had knotted at the mast and went back to the bow. There was so much wind in the sail that it was a battle to start hauling it down. Then suddenly I was hoisted into the air. I was soon back down on the deck, but before I had time to come to my senses and let go I was hoisted up again, and with the roll of a wave I was suspended out over the water.

I was holding on for dear life and my shoulder was screaming in pain. Safety harness, where was my safety harness? My legs were flailing around in a desperate attempt to get a grip on something. My feet found the guard rail and the next thing I knew I was unceremoniously dumped on the deck. The sheets were snatching about violently in the wind and one whipped me across my face. I didn't feel I could move but knew I had to get things under control. Ignoring the pain in my shoulder I got on to my knees and elbows, and using my hands to protect my face slowly made my way to the mast. Once there I just let the halyard drop. I didn't care any more if it went in the water, I just wanted it down as quickly as possible, to be free from the danger and slapping of the sails which seemed to be pounding my ears.

Bit by bit I hauled it out of the sea and on to the deck. I was hot and exhausted with the effort of trying to pull against the drag of the sail in the water, but eventually it was there. I needed to put the storm jib up but didn't feel I was capable of unhanking the large sail from the forestay, carrying up the storm jib and rigging, so I let out a tiny bit of the roller furling sail instead. It wasn't very satisfactory – it isn't really designed for this sort of weather and if it ripped I knew I would curse myself – but I'd had it. I just didn't have the energy to do anything else, so I sluggishly went below and collapsed into my chair, dry mouthed, exhausted and feeling totally wrecked.

My face was smarting and when I looked in my mirror in the heads I saw a lovely weal across a pale face. I got a portion of butter out of the cupboard and plastered it on.

1 February (Day 138)

....

01 FEB   FROM: SENTOSA C LES   TO: PETER HARDING

....

Good morning, Peter,
This is your early morning call. The time is 0530 precisely . . . pip pip pip.
   Hope you are not feeling as bad today.
   Speak soon,

   From your BT Personal Alarm Service, Southern Ocean

....

I've been worrying about Peter for some time now. He has taken on so much. Setting up his new business has taken second place to what I am doing. It's not just the amount of work as much as the psychological pressure. He keeps saying he's responsible for me, which isn't true. I can understand he feels that but I keep trying to tell him that what he did was to make sure I set off with the best of everything. I would have done it anyway. I would have done it without this wonderful satellite system and some of the more expensive items.

Sometimes I wish I hadn't got this facility that keeps him up to date with everything. It's great being able to talk my feelings through and I can let everyone know where I am, but at the same time I am aware of the fact he is finding it difficult to cope. It seems so unfair on him, as it's all turned out to be so much bigger than he could ever have imagined and has completely taken over his life. He hasn't even been out since I set off because he feels he has to be there for me, and I bet he won't go out until I am back either. He's trying to shoulder everything on his own. Because of me he is suffering from his nerves. I keep telling him not to worry, to try and live some sort of a normal life. I really wish he would, but he isn't like that, and he's going through hell. Oh God, what a mess.

As I'm currently using radar and navigation lights at night, I've been using more battery power than normal. Even so, with all my natural sources I shouldn't be needing to run the engine to keep the battery topped up, but I am. On checking all my natural power sources I found that the alternator belt that was running off the spinning propeller shaft was a bit loose. Should I tighten it up? I wasn't sure. What if it made the engine vibrate more? If I didn't I was going to have to choose between either using precious fuel or not using navigation lights. I decided I had better try and sort it. I was closer to land now than I had ever been and I didn't want to be run down by an unsuspecting ship. So I decided to have a look at it before lunch.

The alternator belt was horribly black and mucky and within no time at all I was covered in an oily mess. We'd carefully placed some spare belts near by, so instead of repairing this fairly well worn one I decided to do a proper job and put a new one on. Cutting the old one off was no problem, but when I came to slide the new one on, it wouldn't come. I remembered then that some slight amendment had been made since they were originally put there and now there wasn't enough space under the prop shaft to pull it forward. I could have kicked myself. Now I was even worse off than I had been before.

I thought of the implications of trying to manage without it and knew I couldn't. Well, I'd just have to force it through. I pulled and pushed and pulled, but it just wouldn't go. It's a fiddly place to work and impossible to see what you're doing, but obviously there had to be a slight gap there or the propeller shaft wouldn't be free to spin. I couldn't do without it, therefore I had to fix it. So I just kept at it, yanking away with all my might. Then it seemed to move. I felt down with my fingers and was suddenly aware of two things at once: the sound of water running and an awareness of water cascading over my hand.

It's a nightmare of any sailor and I immediately jumped to the conclusion that I had split the deep sea seal. My mind raced over the possible ways to stop it flooding. Tape? Sealant? Rags? Rags soaked in porridge? How long did I have?

Since I had got the fanbelt this far I might as well pull it the rest of the way then quickly find a way to make us watertight again. Eventually the fanbelt was on the right side and I turned to the more immediate problem. I soon realised that I had in fact rolled the seal back so I pulled it into place again. I was hoping that it would be OK again, although not really believing it. There was so much water swilling around in the bilges it was now impossible to tell if it was still coming in, so I wiped my hands and pumped it dry. I was relieved that it seemed to be OK, so with fingers crossed I said a quick prayer and vowed to keep an eye on it.

Back to the fanbelt. The adjustment stanchion was too close to the alternator to be able to drop it down enough and slip the belt over the pulley on the prop shaft. So out with the WD40 to ease the rust, then down to work with the spanners to move the adjustment pulley. Bloody hell. What a damned stupid idea, positioning it like this! As I started to make progress my mood was improving. All I had to do now was to tighten the alternator back up and tension the belt. Two of the nuts promptly sheared off in my hand, with the other ends still stuck. God give me strength. Surely stainless steel didn't rot – unless they weren't stainless!

I fetched my selection of spare nuts and bolts from the workshop and went back to the cramped engine room. Finally the job was done.

Aching in every limb, my hands and fingers red and cut from slipped spanners, I stretched myself and went on deck to move about a bit and get some air. All I had to do now was to put the prop shaft out of gear and hey presto it would all have been worth it. But I couldn't believe it, it was jammed!

I didn't react. I was so worn down by it all. Like an automaton I went below, crawled over the engine and started to strip the linkage system on the gears. It took five attempts to free it all.

Three and a half hours. Jesus. Why is it that whenever you go to do a job on a boat it's never as simple as you anticipate? I was filthy, dead beat, and past being hungry. I just flopped into my navigator's chair and rewarded myself by staring mindlessly at the needle and watching the batteries slowly rise again.

2 February (Day 139)

How unlucky can you be? Up to 40 knots of wind right from where I want to go. *Spirit* is really not at her best closehauled and we are having a very bumpy and slow ride.

I've asked Peter to start getting ice reports as I may need to go north just past New Zealand to avoid the hazard of ice or icebergs. Certainly I need to get some idea for crossing the next bit of the Southern Ocean and rounding the Horn.

It's funny how everyone thinks that because I am near to Australia and New Zealand that I am in warm weather. If only they knew. I am sure it is lovely further north but down here is by far the coldest sailing I have ever done – it's cruelly raw and biting.

I've got the heater on again today for odd spurts but the heat seems to disappear very quickly, so I have taken down the shower curtain and pinned it up around the navigation area. If I shut up all the other valves except that in the hot locker I am hoping that it will keep it reasonably warm. I might even be able to dry out my sleeping bag and pillow which would be luxury indeed!

3 February (Day 140)

Apparently an update of my voyage is going to get weekly coverage on BBC television, which is exciting.

I need some good news. The wind has died altogether and we are going nowhere, just drifting round in circles. If I could just get some decent weather I would be south of Snares Islands off New Zealand within two days, but all I seem to be getting is either strong headwinds or nothing. Oh wind, come on!! You are driving me crazy!!

4 February (Day 141)

According to the forecasts I'm surrounded by westerly gales but stuck in an area of bloody easterly variables and it's driving me demented. Considering at one stage I was at 50°S I will now be lucky if I can clear Snares Islands without having to tack! Also, because it's so fickle the steering can't cope with it. I'll have to steer again during the night to make any headway.

5 February (Day 142)

Despite being up most of the night we only managed a total of 50 miles, which is pathetic. The wind since dawn has really got up and I am now heading into a gale, and the seas are almost forbidding any progress at all.

Come on, wind, give me a break – go round to the south-west!

I've spent the day sitting in the navigation area wrapped up in my sleeping bag to try and keep warm. I seem to be cold to the bone today. I'm wearing a balaclava and a hat on top of that, plus gloves and quilted jackets – I look like the abominable snowman.

It's too horrid to be on deck so I have been doing some embroidery. It's something I would never think of doing at home but it was a surprise present I found from Peter and I'm really enjoying it, despite the fact that it is extremely difficult to get the needle into the right hole! It's also very dark down here today and not easy to focus. I don't feel I can afford to use the lights during the daytime as well, as they take up so much power.

Peter has told me that Richard Cariss, who is a very good friend of mine, is going to buy the equipment required to be able to communicate with me directly. Richard and I have enjoyed a few laughs in the past. I just hope the system keeps working for the rest of the trip!

6 February (Day 143)

The computer is having a few problems with this damp atmosphere and being knocked around so much. Peter's last fax came through as a fax from Richard Uridge saying 'Congratulations on crossing the Equator', which is obviously an old file.

How I hate this weather. Nothing but headwinds for days now, making it impossible to sail in the direction I want to. I am not sure which I hate most – the fickle variable headwinds which mean one minute you're heading just south of north-east and the next you find yourself travelling just west of south; or the weather as it is now, battling into a force 9 with stopper waves that literally stop *Spirit* dead in her tracks, so she has to start to regain her momentum all over again. The noise when we get walloped by these waves reverberates throughout the hull and then she shudders and you can feel her start to go off course. It's impossible to run up on deck every time this happens in order to pull her back; instead I pause in whatever I am doing and wait to sense that she has started to recover speed and correct point of sail. The motion is quite different if she doesn't and then I have to don my waterproofs (which isn't easy with all the layers of clothes underneath) and rush on deck.

It's hardly relaxing when it's like this and not helped by knowing that progress is lousy. It means it is mentally as well as physically tiring and makes it difficult to fight off a feeling of despair. I seem to be going up and down the chart but not along it. I have been down as far as 50°S, back up to 47°, and am back down at 50° again, and I have hardly crossed off many miles. I've just reached the most western part of New Zealand but I should have been way past here by now. These headwinds have tripled the distance I have had to travel. If I get too much more of this I shall go perfectly crazy. I had timed this leg with mostly favourable winds and shall be really hacked off if things don't improve soon.

Peter has sent me what information there is available on ice but it really isn't much. The satellites pick up large icebergs but not the break-offs from these or indeed drift ice. There's no shipping down here either which means there aren't any observation reports available. I think I shall stick to my original thoughts and try and stay between 47° and 50° until I get nearer the Horn when I shall drop south. The recommendation is that I go back up to 40° but I can't bear the thought of the extra days that this will mean and also we are coping so well down here.

I shall just have to keep a fairly sharp lookout and if I start to see ice or growlers then head north a bit more to try and steer clear of them. In some ways I'd quite like to see one but on the other hand I think I can manage without!

7 February (Day 144)

I stayed up all night waiting for the shift to the west and it was a total waste of time and energy. Today when I really need some sleep I have spent the whole day tacking and sail changing. I must have been on deck twenty times or more trying to make sure that at least we were making the best of what there was.

This weather is really really getting me down. I just can't bear to be making such little progress. It's done nothing but rain for ages and the wind is still unpredictable, except that it always seems to have a bit of easterly in it and is jumping up and down from 12 to 40 knots. There is also a large cross swell and enough height in the waves to make almost any progress impossible. All the forecasts and warnings are for gales with westerly sector winds – so *why* am I suffering headwinds?

We've wasted days and days in this awful weather and all the time it's just adding days on at the end. My target of early March for the Horn is starting to look like some pathetic joke.

How ironical. Here I am in the Furious Fifties and going nowhere. I bet if I had stayed up in safer waters nearer 40° I would be winging along at 6 knots. How very unfair life can be – I could almost scream with frustration.

8 February (Day 145)

The weather's really improved. It stopped raining and I have opened the hatches to try and dry everything out.

There has been a succession of rapid wind shifts all day but at least they have all been favourable. The sun even came out for an hour, which was lovely. Everything looks so beautiful with the light on it – what a difference to the bleak grey world I'd been living in. I actually sat in the cockpit for a while all wrapped up in my heavy-weather gear, and to feel the sun on my face was like a dream.

I managed to get one of the cameras working again, so I did a bit of filming. Not so cleverly I left the cap out of the heater exhaust, and the sea came pouring in, so once again I was without heat. How careless can you get? I've now blown a fuse trying to restart it.

The large 56 winch packed up, which was a thorough nuisance, and although I tried to take it apart the important bit was seized. I've tried WD40 and a hammer but still no luck so I just sprayed loads of releaser on it and put it all back, in the hope that a day or so of soaking will free it. I can't imagine having to manage the sails without it.

9 February (Day 146)

Last night was drop-dead gorgeous. *Spirit* and I were under a perfect canopy of princely twinkling stars. Because the air was so clear it was biting cold,

(**above**) My little visitor

(**left**) Up, up and up

(**below**) Don't think I'll go swimming

(**left**) BBC getting a few words. Anchored off Cape Town (*Cedric Robertson*)

(**below left**) Nearly home (*University of Birmingham*)

(**below**) Heading for home at last (*University of Birmingham*)

(**above**) Finishing line (*Pip Chorley*)

(**below**) What a turn out! (*Terry Walker*)

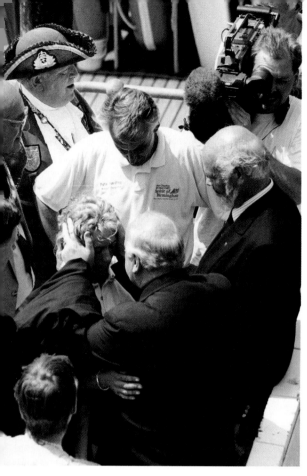

(**left**) Very Reverend Peter Berry, Provost of Birmingham, says a prayer to thank God for my safe return (*Nick Quick*)

(**below**) With Mum and Dad (*University of Birmingham*)

(**above**) With Peter (*University of Birmingham*)

(**below**) 'Well done old girl!' Church of England College for Girls (my old school) come to greet me back (*University of Birmingham*)

(**left**) Signing session (*David Rose*)

(**below**) Press conference in Birmingham – one and a half hours after stepping on shore (*University of Birmingham*)

(**bottom**) Civic Reception. Peter, Dad, Paul, Mum, me and Theresa

(**above**) Doctorate of Science
Congregation with Sir Michael
Thompson, Vice Chancellor,
University of Birmingham
(*University of Birmingham*)

(**right**) Super Diamond Award for
Bravery presented by Princess
Michael of Kent
(*Birmingham Evening Mail*)

(**above**) *Spirit* returns rusty but triumphant to Victoria Square, Birmingham
(*Howard Nelson*)

(**below**) 'I don't believe it!' (*Thames TV/BBCTV*)

but *Spirit* looked resplendent, the frost on her deck glistening like a sequinned gown. I kept nipping down below to make a hot cup of soup and then coming back up to marvel at the wondrous sight. I was still there when the sun came up, and felt full of wonder at this awe-inspiring planet that we inhabit.

Even though I hadn't slept all night I felt wonderful. The sun stayed out till the afternoon, and whilst the wind was biting, the sun was very warm. I found a spot in the cockpit that was sheltered from the wind and even stripped off all my clothes for about fifteen minutes to air my body, but it was bloody freezing and I soon got dressed again! I also gave myself a pedicure – the first time in my life!

I had all the hatches open, and took everything on deck to air out. There were cushions hanging from the rigging, and sleeping bags and clothes draped everywhere – she looked like a Chinese junk.

The wind was fickle and we kept losing course, but you can't have everything!

I felt quite guilty that I had given myself a bit of a holiday when Peter was working so hard in Birmingham, so I spent the rest of the day liaising with him about his potential clients, discussing ways forward.

10 February (Day 147)

I slept right through the alarm during the night – I'd been zonked out for hours. When I finally woke up I jumped out of bed worrying that I might have spent the night travelling the wrong way, but we were on course and I suddenly felt great.

I'd been trying to work out if I could use the gas alarm to give me a very very loud wake-up call. It certainly makes an horrendous din, which is probably what I need in case I fall into a deep sleep again. I suppose that really I should have reconnected the gas alarm system as well. I cut the wires last time it went off because I couldn't find the problem and it was the only way to stop the ear-piercing noise. I decided I wouldn't let anyone know about this as I knew it would only worry them and then I would be hassled until I reconnected it.

It's remained cold all day, and there are now grey layers of cloud blocking out the sun. I am wearing gloves constantly now. Even typing is impossible without, and even through gloves anything metal is painfully cold to touch. Gales are forecast for later.

11 February (Day 148)

....

11 FEB   **FROM: BT INMARSAT-C FAX**   **TO: PETER HARDING**

....

Don't know what happened to those gales, the wind has practically died and I am just drifting along very slowly. In fact the forecasts don't mention any strong winds at all.

I crossed the International Dateline today – another milestone! I feel great today, a bit tired but very positive.

I've managed to sort out the rigging too. I took the main down and furled the foresails, then slackened all the leading stays off. Somehow I managed to disconnect the forestay completely but I eventually got it back in. That gave me a bit more leeway to tighten the backstays and then I tensioned the other stays and it looks and feels much better. The mast looks a bit like a catapult raked back so far but I think it will be OK. I am sure it is better to be steady and looking so strange than to be under stress from the jolting of a loose stay.

Hope all is going as well for you as it is for me, you deserve the very best!

Take care,
Lisa.

....

12 February (Day 149)

It's another gorgeous sunny day, quite a bit of cloud but super when the sun is shining. Still jolly cold though. Can't think what I have done today, apart from my usual deck check and enjoying lunch in the cockpit (all dressed in my heavy-weather gear this time!). No, the day just seems to have disappeared.

13 February (Day 150)

The sea has really picked up a lot, although the wind isn't yet strong enough to justify it, so I guess it must be on the way. It's funny how often the sea arrives before the wind – you would think it would be the other way.

Boy, am I glad I am down here in the Fifties. Just a couple of degrees further north they have still got 35 knots from the east-south-east. I'd be tearing my hair out.

I fixed up my deep-sleep alarm and then decided to open a tin of salmon for lunch. Unfortunately we rolled a bit and it shot off the side and across the cabin creating a most disgusting mess. I sent a fax to my sister Sara in Los Angeles telling her I should be south of LA in about three weeks with any luck. I still aim to be rounding the Horn about 21 March.

14 February (Day 151)

Valentine's Day but no cards. At least not for me, I found one for my stuffed dog Bernard though – what a cheek!

I went on deck and discovered everywhere is dismally murky outside. The heavy fog seems to penetrate through my many layers of clothes and I can feel its clammy fingers on my skin. Surprisingly the wind has got up but the fog has stayed. I always associate fog with stillness. We are having the most fantastic sail but I might as well be blindfolded. It feels like we are racing into obscurity.

15 February (Day 152)

15 FEB   FROM: BT INMARSAT-C FAX   TO: PETER HARDING

Superb sailing. It's a force 9 from the north and the seas are really building up. The visibility is better so I was going to do some filming but the camera is damp again.

I am 50°S 165°W travelling east at 6–7 knots. I am living in my heavy-weather gear ready to go on deck at a moment's notice. I am tired but still enjoying myself, although sometimes taking these seas at right angles on the beam is frightening. I know really that I should do the sensible thing and take them at a better angle further aft on the quarter but progress is so good I don't want to waste it. Crazy I know, but that's how I feel.

Just as crazy is this desire for a crispy bacon sandwich which has been dogging me for the last two days!!

Could you please send some air mail for me???? If not, how about just sending one of your nice messages instead – let me know how you are and what you are doing!

....

It wasn't long though before I had to start being sensible. I had been catnapping at the chart table when I sensed something was wrong. Two waves in succession really knocked us on to our side and I realised how foolhardy I was being. I rushed on deck aware that I needed to change course quickly before we went over again. I grabbed the wheel and started to alter our heading before I realised I hadn't got my boots on. My feet were sopping wet and freezing cold, what an idiot.

I returned below to try and dig out a dryer pair of socks and made myself a steaming mug of chocolate. Was the weather going to get worse? Should I take down the remaining bit of sail? No, I decided I'd wait and see. The seas were higher than I had ever seen them and I felt we had a better chance if we kept some way on. I am not sure where my logic came from, it was more like intuition.

16 February (Day 153)

Well, the weather has returned to its typical form, although this bit further south does seem to mean much more violent shifts in wind and strength and the seas running faster and higher. I was really in my element earlier on today. I wasn't worried that I hadn't slept for two nights, although I was feeling tired. The sailing was sensational and the sea breathtaking, it was the most exhilarating sight to see *Spirit* hurtling along in such conditions. The seas seemed to tower up behind us and all you could see was a vast solid wall of water. It didn't seem possible that we could keep out of its way. But instead of crushing us it picked us up, and as the crest tumbled away we would tear along at breakneck speed on a roaring mass of water, totally out of control and entirely at its mercy.

However, by mid-morning the wind was becoming erratic and often dropping as low as 20 knots and then gusting up to 40. I couldn't make up my mind whether to put up more sail to make the best of the lighter winds as well. The sea was still high and running fast – sometimes it felt we needed more sail to keep up the speed and remain in control. Being tired is not a good time to make any decision of consequence. I knew that, but my tiredness was also turning to impatience – I could put a little more out and make another knot, and then I would make a concerted effort to have a bit of a rest as the forecast was showing very disturbed weather patterns.

I felt much more settled when I had let out a bit more sail, and we were creaming along at 7 knots. I came back down below and realising I hadn't eaten for about fourteen hours, had another Mars bar.

Whether this perked me up mentally I don't know, but I quickly returned to the cockpit to reduce the sail area to what it had been before. God, I was so tired. As I was coming below I saw some very ominous-looking clouds approaching and patted myself on the back for being so sensible. Now I could relax and get some rest.

Within minutes I was back on deck. *Spirit* had come up into the wind. She was now facing right into it and had lost all way. There was the most almighty racket. To my dismay I saw that the sail had backed and half a torn-apart spinnaker pole was crashing wildly around in the wind.

It was a job to bring it all under control. The wind had suddenly got up to over 55 knots, and every time I tried to grab the pole it was wrenched from my hands. I was petrified of being knocked over the side but eventually I managed to get everything under control. I was totally worn out, disheartened and cross with myself. Half of me knew I shouldn't have had the pole in at 40 knots but the stubborn half of me argued that it was sometimes only 20 knots and therefore acceptable. I lashed it all to the deck and went back below cursing myself. How bloody stupid. Now I only had one pole for the rest of my downwind sailing which I expected not only in the Southern Ocean but also in the south-east trade winds up to the Equator.

17 February (Day 154)

Hi Peter,
Still haven't managed to get much decent sleep although I have already got some ideas of what to do with the pole. I think I shall turn it into a smaller pole to use with the staysail. *But*, not today, not when I am still so tired. I don't want to mess it up and will save it for a day when I am feeling more refreshed.

Everything I have touched today seems to have another problem attached so I am just adding to my ever-growing list of outstanding jobs.

The wind is still up and down between 20 and 40 knots. I'd never experienced this sort of weather before I set off on this voyage and yet now it seems to be erratic much of the time. How I hate it.

Oh well, I hope you are having a good day. I will be in touch later. Did you manage to order Mum's flowers for me??? I will send her poem tomorrow.

I've finished composing Mum's poem of which I like the last verse best . . .

> But seriously Mum, you've always been great
> And many a time you've been a great mate
> But during last summer when you helped to the end
> You became not just my mum but my very best friend

Throughout the day conditions have got worse and worse.

17 FEB   FROM: SENTOSA C LES   TO: PETER HARDING

Hi Peter,
Conditions here not good to say the least. The wind is over 65 knots (I was only expecting 40 per the forecast!) and the seas are very steep and tumbling. Not surprisingly we found ourselves slewed off course and beam on to the seas. I still had a tiny bit of canvas up as I hadn't decided how to tackle this storm. Should we go hove to? If so I needed to keep

the sails up. Should we lie a hull? If so I needed to bring them down. Or should we try to keep moving and run downwind, with just a tiny bit of foresail sheeted flat to help nudge the bow and keep her facing the right way? The height of the seas was enough to frighten me into trying anything but just sitting there. I decided to try and run downwind for a while and helm myself.

I don't know what I was thinking really, but as soon as I took control of the wheel and tried to run downwind we were out of control. The speed was frightening and we were totally vulnerable to the waves as they picked us up and surged beneath us carrying us along and totally over-powering the rudder. Within minutes we were once again back where we had started – beam on to the seas. We have now gone hove to but I am wondering whether I shouldn't take everything down, not that there is much up. Oh, I don't know, I just don't know. It's never been this bad before, it's almost unreal. I'm scared to death but there's a strange tingling inside me – I guess it must be adrenalin.

If this were a crewed boat I am sure it would be safer to take all sail down and helm downwind but in reality I couldn't manage that for long on my own.

Anyway, everything on deck is secure and none of the rope can get under the propeller even if we do get knocked down. Hopefully we won't but it's rather difficult to believe when you can see waves towering right over you. They are magnificent but daunting. I feel like a sitting duck – let's hope I float like one!!

Anyway I am fine. I have secured the hatches and strapped myself into my navigator's chair. I felt quite tense at first, anticipating when the next wave would pick us up and send us spilling down the other side. Some of the seas are actually breaking on us and burying us in a cauldron of bubbling foam, but an hour has gone past and we are still surviving so we might be OK. The noise of everything is horrendous and it's obviously impossible to sleep so I am pretending to read and keep myself occupied – I think it's called escapism!

Don't wait up worrying, there's nothing you can do and if I need you I will get in touch.

P.S. *Don't* mention this to my parents!!
Thanks for being there for me.
Lisa.

18 February (Day 155)

Mum's birthday!! Thank goodness I have sent her poem and Peter has ordered some flowers for me. I feel I won't be able to do her justice today.

The storm eventually blew itself out and apart from once going almost gently on our side we survived OK. It took a few hours to clear up the mess both on deck and below but considering what we had been through we were in jolly good nick. What a fantastic boat she has turned out to be – I wouldn't swap her for anything.

I then made myself a hearty meal of chunky chicken, and had a glass of sherry. The sherry was part of a surprise hamper I had been kindly given, and definitely not something I would have chosen myself, but it tasted like nectar!

The wind continued to drop and I was able to let the foresail out and climb about eight feet up the mast to replace the chafed ropes. I can't say I enjoyed that much – some of the waves were still so big and the whoppers broke against the boat leaving us submerged in bubbling white foam – but I was glad that I had done it. It's strange, I can't imagine ever having had the guts, but I just did it. I suppose it was slightly crazy, and I feel extremely pleased with myself for getting everything into reasonable order.

....

18 FEB   FAX TO LISA   FROM: PETER HARDING

....

Hi Lisa,
Glad to hear conditions are better. Have you managed to make any water yet, and top up the batteries?
    Let me know a list of outstanding things as soon as possible.

    Speak soon, take great care,

    Peter.

....

Peter,

It is up to gale force again already and I am busy sailing the boat!

I don't know when you think I have had a chance to fix the prop gen and watermaker since yesterday!!!

As soon as I had sent it I realised what an ungrateful urchin I was. Peter was just trying to be constructive and I'd bitten his head off for his trouble. He must have moments when he wonders why the hell he ever got involved in this horrendous project. I bet he's bloody furious! Or more likely upset. What a horrid person I can be.

The wind was soon back up to force 9–10. It was bitterly cold and we were being lambasted by hail storms. I was starting to feel on edge and a little too worn out from the last one to cope with anything else so soon.

The seas were enormous after the effect of the last few days and I was seriously considering going hove to again. I was so tired and my nerves didn't feel that they could stand the tension of once again sitting sideways on and totally exposed to the colossal force of the sea. So I decided instead to try running downwind with just the storm jib up, but we were going way too fast so I took it down and tried to remain calm whilst I decided what to do.

I was desperately tired and it was taking everything I had to think at all, but I couldn't face lying a hull with no sail up and once again went down the deck and raised the storm jib and sheeted it flat down the centre of the boat. I was hoping that this would help to nudge *Spirit*'s bow back downwind should she start to veer up into the wind. We were still going along at 3–4 knots and in the direction I wanted to go. So it was more like a middle option really. I'd never done this before and didn't know how we would ride it but we seemed to be doing OK so I left her like that and said a quick prayer that we wouldn't pitchpole with the stern gambolling over the bow.

19 February (Day 155)

The wind dropped to gale force again but I didn't expect it to last for long. It all looked pretty ominous and the warning was for force 10 just behind me, but obviously coming my way.

....

19 FEB   **FROM: SENTOSA C LES**   **TO: PETER HARDING**

....

Hi Peter,
Thanks for your nice fax, and once again I am really sorry about yesterday. Something just snapped!

You'll be pleased to know that after just over two hours' sleep I am feeling great. Wind here is very light at the moment – given me a bit of a break, only force 6. And I feel very positive. I was so horribly tired before. Am going to try and get some more sleep in before it gets really grim.

There's driving rain at the moment which is the front coming through. Position is 49.57°S 151.42°E travelling east at 6 knots.

I'm in half a mind to look at the spinnaker pole, the alternator, the sink (which is not draining) or the heater but first will do another deck check.

Isn't it amazing that even with the calms and headwinds I suffered a couple of weeks ago, and with being laid up during the storm, I have still managed to catch up a bit on Naomi's time! I was sixteen days behind her datewise (but seven or eight of those are because she started before me) – now I am only nine days behind. Of course we will lose time on the last 9,000 miles up from the Horn because *Spirit* is smaller, heavier and won't sail so close to the wind, but if I continue like this down here I might be back for your birthday on 8 June.

Anyway, do write, would love to hear from you – I promise I'll send a nice reply!

Lovely Lisa!!!

....

Suddenly it was back up to force 9 and I rushed on deck without time to put on my waterproof trousers. Having once again gone back to the storm jib only I came below soaking and ice cold. Then it backed to the south-east and I brought the sail over.

When I looked at the latest forecast I was seriously beginning to wish I had stayed much further north. The next few days were due to be much the same. However, unexpectedly the weather started to improve a bit, so I went and had a wash and tried to catnap at the chart table. I knew I had to get some rest, especially with the knowledge that it would soon be bad again.

21 February (Day 158)

I feel horribly overtired today. The wind has dropped right down but it's made the sea feel even more uncomfortable. Still, the sea will either die down a bit in time or the wind will pick up again.

I'm trying to keep myself busy by writing down a new list of every job that has to be done and how I am going to tackle it. I must try and get some sleep but at the moment I don't trust the weather. I should eat too, although I can't really face the thought.

To make myself feel better I have marked some more days off the calendar. I should be home in just over three months – surely now I have got this far I will make it.

22 February (Day 159)

Weather is still weird, anything from 12 to 40 knots. It's so bloody tiring. To find the energy to do just the mere essentials is calling on resources I feel I don't have but somehow seem to find. Not that I am being any less vigilant, because in fact I am being more so. My mind seems to be alert when I need it and I surprisingly don't feel clumsy once I've started working on anything hazardous. But as soon as the danger is over I am almost dead on my feet. Feeling drained has taken on a totally new meaning to me, and I realise I have never really felt drained before in my life.

It's coping with fairly mundane things that makes me realise the depth of my weariness. Eating is something I can't be bothered with, but today I knew I would have to have something hot just to give me a bit of energy to keep going. I stood at the cooker for ages, dripping wet in my oilskins and flicking the lighter over and over again. I don't know how long I was there just repeating the performance before it dawned on me that I hadn't switched the gas on. Having heated my gourmet meal (straight from the tin!) I turned the gas knob, but realising it wasn't quite out, instead of turning it a bit further I started trying to blow the gas out. Luckily I didn't have enough puff to do so and frustration made me think to turn the knob. Having eaten most of what I had cooked I had to wash up. I knew I was still wearing my inner gloves but my brain didn't tell me to take them off, although it still surprised me to feel the water seeping through them. Even then it didn't occur to me to remove them.

1830 hours: I managed to get a couple of hours' sleep and feel on top of the world again. It's remarkable how quickly one can recover.

I noticed the batteries were right down, and on investigating why found I had lost the towgen. I replaced it with my spare one but the instructions told me to secure the turbine with a fisherman's knot – I didn't know how to do one! Anyway it looked a bit like the picture and seemed pretty strong so I just said a quick prayer as I threw it out over the stern.

The loo also seems to have filled up, which is probably an air lock, but I can't face the thought of working on it yet.

23 February (Day 160)

I feel much better today and a lot happier. I've spent the day trying to fix the problem on the loo but haven't solved it. I also looked at the wiring of the instruments as everything suddenly cut out though I couldn't identify why.

I found that the towgen still wasn't producing any power but did diagnose that it had blown a fuse. It must have had a surge of power some time during the storm so I just replaced that with a larger fuse in the hope it doesn't happen again.

23 FEB   FROM: SENTOSA C LES   TO: GWEN AND DAN CLAYTON

Hi Mum and Dad,
Hope all is well with you. As you have probably gathered I have been through a pretty rough and nerve-racking time with bad storms, but all is well again now, thank goodness! I must say that *Spirit* has surpassed

herself – she is going to drive me crazy on the leg back up because she is so heavy, but down here she has been excellent (fingers crossed!).

Felt really horrid after not sleeping for so long and living in my oilies for three days – literally never took them off and even when I had one hour lying down I didn't remove anything, not even my boots. When I eventually took them off they were wet on the inside – disgusting. Still, I am fine and progress on this leg is really quite good.

I know it is your ruby wedding anniversary on Sunday so hope you do something special. I am writing yet another awful ode which I will send nearer the time.

Anyway, I had better go on deck and do the nightly check, so love to you all – can't wait to see you again.

All my love.
xxxxxxxxxxxxxxxxxxxxxxxxx

---

24 February (Day 161)

The wind was still fluctuating, now only between 12 and 20 knots, so I decided to tackle the wreckage of the spinnaker pole which was in two pieces. I had originally thought that my workshop on *Spirit* was perhaps on the large side, but when it came to repairing a spinnaker pole (even though each piece was now only eight inches long) I was struggling to find a good place to work on it. I was not helped by the fact that the sea was still surprisingly big, and rolling from side to side and up and down like a see-saw.

Both broken edges were completely mangled and twisted so I knew that I would lose quite a lot of length. The options were to try and make one half into a smaller pole which would be useful in heavy weather, or try and rebuild it into a longer one for lighter conditions. In the end I decided to try and adapt it so I could do both. Not wanting to rush anything I spent the day cutting down one half of the old pole, marrying up the holes and fittings and rebuilding it – it's brilliant! Because of its reduced length it's now stronger than the original and it looks like a professional job. I feel really chuffed with myself and am looking forward to the opportunity of trying it out. Perhaps tomorrow I shall cut down the other half and make some sort of sleeve so I can join the two halves together if I want to.

The only slight hiccough was that I did manage to bust the electric drill and had to finish it off with a hand drill. So I've now got something else to fix. It seems to me that as fast as I can fix one thing, other things jump into line for attention. Oh well, *c'est la vie, n'est ce pas?*

25 February (Day 162)

Feeling fine today but I do hate waiting for this next storm to arrive. I was thinking of running north a bit although I don't suppose I have time to do anything effective and anyway the centre of the low seems to be travelling north-east so I'm stuck. I am finding it difficult to relax just knowing it will soon be here. In many ways it is worse than going to the dentist. I'm trying to keep myself occupied but all the time I keep listening for the rise in wind.

26 February (Day 163)

Mum and Dad's wedding anniversary. I would love to be with them today. I am really missing them. The wind is back up to force 9 and we are once again under storm jib alone. I seem to have developed a split personality. Half of me loves this crazy life but the other half badly needs a rest and is hating it. I am already halfway between New Zealand and the Horn.

27 February (Day 164)

Still force 9–10 but incredibly we are still sailing. The wind is from the north-north-west. It's a funny sensation: the waves are coming from just aft of the beam and whilst you can feel *Spirit* rolling from one side to the other as she climbs and then comes off the waves the other side, you can't feel the forward motion. A couple of times even though I could hear the wind howling in the rigging I went up on deck to check that we were in fact still sailing – which of course we were.

There has also been a handful of occasions when *Spirit* has seemed to have passed her point of positive stability. She feels as though she is in mid-air and about to fall flat on her side, and then she seems to do a very defined flick back to become upright again. It does make me wonder if she is a little stiff. Perhaps the ballast is too far down in the keel, or perhaps there is too much of it? However, the calculations were right. Mind you, if there is too much ballast in her at least it is keeping us upright! I just hope it doesn't put too much strain on the mast and rigging.

I felt more relaxed at one point so put on the 'Three Tenors' CD to drown out the howling sound of the wind, and made tons of spaghetti to keep me going over the next few days.

All this had just been a comfortable patch, and we were soon hit by walls of water. I don't understand how you can seemingly move through different types of seas, but I undoubtedly was. Walls of water were coming out of the blue. No indication of anything, just an almighty smash, then *Spirit* would suddenly stop dead in the water with the impact. She was certainly taking quite a battering and I knew exactly how she felt!

Amazingly the wind started to drop, and the sun came out. The sea was majestic and the colours in the breaking waves made me feel I wanted to try and capture it on film, but there was too much else to do first.

I started by tidying up and restoring some sort of order down below before going on deck to rescue the spraydodgers which were just attached by the top. I didn't want to have to manage without these protective strips down each side of the cockpit. They're really only designed to try and keep you a bit dryer but they have a great psychological effect too, as they make the sea seem further away and give you a false sense of safety. All the eyes along the bottom had been ripped out and I knew I had to take the dodgers off and get them below whilst I still had them. Also one of the stanchions has been bent over with the force of the seas.

I must say I have had enough of being down here on my own. I think I could be enjoying it more if I had someone else to give me a break.

28 February (Day 165)

Weather mostly force 8–10 so we're under storm jib, but I actually feel quite happy. *Spirit* seems to be enjoying it and the motion below is not too bad.

I have been wondering whether to ask Peter for details of how to contact the guys from the BOC single-handed race but I don't think I really want to. They go so much faster than me, I bet they are almost at Rio by now. No, I think it will just depress me. Some of their boats surf at 25 knots and average 16 – I don't think I am quite in their league somehow. However, I would like to meet them one day. We must have something in common, us single-handers.

Peter has sent all the available information on icebergs, which gives details of some near to the Islas Diego Ramirez south of the Horn and also some by the Falklands, but they can't give details of anything smaller. Still, not long to go now till I shall be by the Horn – YIPPEE!

1 March (Day 166)

The weather hasn't so far turned out as bad as forecast and in fact at times has been quite pleasant.

After getting some decent sleep last night I felt relaxed this morning and decided that since there was nothing to worry about with the weather I would spoil myself and have a lazyish sort of day. Having had coffee and checked everything on deck I decided to take my book *Wheelbarrow Across the Sahara* and read for a while in bed, which felt all the nicer for that little tinge of guilt that I wasn't really tired and didn't need to be there. Or so I thought! I woke up five hours later still with the book in my hand. All was OK though, and the wind had dropped even more so I put some more sail out and did nothing for the rest of the day. I feel much better for it and am now very keen to get some more sleep in. It's made me realise just how tired I was. I feel very chirpy and very very content with everything.

I am also excited that I am now heading further south to round the Horn. Apparently there aren't any icebergs around till I get to the Falklands so unless there is some floating ice it shouldn't be a bad run down. I don't know why it suddenly seems as though I am now on my way home – maybe it is because I am at last making this final leg south before I go north again – but it's a lovely feeling. I feel really great at the moment. Still, I am not going to relax my vigilance. I'm growing rather superstitious about feeling too good, it seems to have been the portent to things going horribly wrong – so fingers crossed!

2 March (Day 167)

....

02 MAR   FROM: BT INMARSAT-C FAX   TO: PETER HARDING
....

Good morning,
Just a quickie as I have only this minute come down off deck and am not yet happy with things.
   Speak soon.

....

....

02 MAR   FROM: BT INMARSAT-C FAX   TO: PETER HARDING
....

Hi,
Well, I suppose I should have let you sleep on – I wasn't quite sure what to do.
   Things here are bad: force 10–11, just the storm jib up – couldn't haul the boom in even with all the sail down! Impossible to stand up on deck. Not quite sure what is the best thing. Still sort of sailing at the moment but not happy with it.
   Anyway, I am OK but not likely to get too much sleep though I will try once I feel relatively happy – which isn't just yet!

....

....

02 MAR 08:47 FROM: BT INMARSAT-C FAX   TO: SARA SIMPSON
....

Hi Sara,
Happy birthday!
   You must think yourself quite lucky, as I started a poem to you, but yesterday we hit a bad storm and conditions here are horrendous. Although I have tried I can't quite find the right words to finish it off!
   In fact to type at all is a minor form of torture. The only place to be is

in bed so I hope you won't mind that this is a short fax but the wishes to you are full of love and I hope today is a really great day for you.

All my love, Sara.
xxxxxxxxxxxxxxxxx

....

....

02 MAR 15:30 FAX TO LISA   FROM: PETER HARDING

....

Hi Lisa,
Sorry things are not good. If I can do anything or if you just want to talk let me know. To be honest I am shattered so am going home but please know I am there for you if you need me.

Take great care,
Peter.

....

....

02 MAR 16:58 FROM: BT INMARSAT-C FAX   TO: PETER HARDING

....

Hi Peter,
Thanks for your two messages.

Conditions here are horrendous – the wind is even stronger now. I eventually managed to get warm but only by getting up and heating a hot-water bottle and snuggling up inside two sleeping bags. Luckily I was facing the hull, as all the books which were so tightly jammed on the shelves (and are held in by curtain wire) flew out and landed heavily on me – I was buried in them. Unless it is screwed or strapped down nothing is staying in its place.

It is quite simply bloody awful and to write this is taking an age. The only sensible thing I can do is go back to bed. I could try and sheet the storm jib flat or take it down but I think it would be more dangerous and to be honest if I get caught out with one of those waves I don't suppose that even my safety harness would be of much use – so basically I am hiding down here. At least here I have the best chance of staying with the boat! Anyway, can't write any more but we are OK.

....

02 MAR 17:55 FROM: BT INMARSAT-C FAX   TO: PETER HARDING

I need to talk to you – please tell me you are there.

02 MAR 18:11 FROM: BT INMARSAT-C FAX   TO: PETER HARDING

No, I'm not OK – well, I am still alive, but only just. God, I am so scared. I went on deck to try and sheet the storm jib flat but saw that all hell was let loose. The big sail that is strapped to the deck was over the side and dragging through the water so I went forward to bring it in. I tied my long safety line to the stay. The next thing I knew I was through the guard rails and in the sea. I felt myself totally submerged, couldn't breathe and really thought I had seen the end. I just remember thinking 'Crikey, just like that, it's all over. I thought I was meant to make it.' Then somehow I got yanked back.

I came below and then the boat screamed forward and now the sail is backed, the self steering has snapped in two and I know I have to go back up – but I am too scared.

02 MAR 18:15 FAX TO LISA   FROM: PETER HARDING

Lisa,
Thank God you are OK. Are you safe down below? Is there anything I can do? Talk to me, I am here and going nowhere.

BE CAREFUL!

02 MAR 18:19 FROM: BT INMARSAT-C FAX   TO: PETER HARDING

God, I hope I make it – it doesn't seem possible at the moment.

02 MAR 18:23 FROM: BT INMARSAT-C FAX   TO: PETER HARDING

had just decided to go on deck to tkae the storm jib down. Thank goodness I saw your message coming through – we have just capszied, I woudl have been ovr the side.IT was jst like being in a violent car crashh, the impact was tremmensous. I've still got to go up but I am nto sure it is safe. I wish i felt sure about what is hte best thing to do
I wish I wasn't so scared

02 MAR 18:32 FROM: BT INMARSAT-C FAX   TO: PETER HARDING

no there is not point alerting anybody – no one can do aything – apart from the fact it would take days it would endanger other lives as well. No the only thing to do is sit tight. I have just been on deck and managed to lash the rudder so hopefully that will be saved. The spraydodgers were pracitically off – I have tied them as best I can but won't be surprised if we lose them and I have managed to get all the ropes back in. I as going to get the sial down but I couldn't as it suddenly got worse. Might try again in a minute – capsize again since we last spoke Thanks again but nono point in alertin gnayboyd – nothing nayone could do – believe me I know

02 MAR 19:03 FROM: BT INMARSAT-C FAX   TO: PETER HARDING

Just to let you know I have got the storm jib down

02 MAR 19:10 FROM: BT INMARSAT-C FAX   TO: PETER HARDING

Just capsized again God this is frightening

02 MAR 19:25 FROM: BT INMARSAT-C FAX   TO: PETER HARDING

and again

02 MAR 19:30 FAX TO LISA   FROM: PETER HARDING

Lisa,
Do you want me to get help?

02 MAR 19:40 FROM: BT INMARSAT-C FAX   TO: PETER HARDING

No I am not considreing giving up yet. I will obviously wait until thiings have got a little better and then try and see the state of things.

If everything is reaonsable then I shall be able to continue – but I dont know for now – obviously I have to just keep my fingers crossed that I survive this and then sial on – stopping for repairs if necessary. It's not as if there is any decision to make about abandoning hsip – I couldn't even if there wer helicopters and ships around – it would be pracitcally impossible.

No I have to just hope that it pass es soon – though if anything it feels as htough it is getting worse not better.

I think I will lay my head down here at the chart table and then see hwo I feel.

Thanks for everything.

No need for you to not go to bedd – f I need you y ou wil hear the phone.

02 MAR 19:45 FAX TO LISA   FROM: PETER HARDING

Lisa,
Of course I am not going to go to bed. I shan't sleep till I know you are

OK and sailing again. Talk to me all you want. I'm here for you.

Peter.

....

....

02 MAR 19:59 FROM: BT INMARSAT-C FAX   TO: PETER HARDING
....

Please will you do me a favour. If you kow Peter Berry's number phone him and ask him to say a prayer for me or else phone Peter Chippendale at Lickey Vicarage and ask him to – I don't think I am going to make htis.
   God I am so sorry

....

....

02 MAR 20:20 FROM: BT INMARSAT-C FAX   TO: PETER HARDING
....

Hi t hannks – it's good to know.
We must have juust done a compllete 360. I was waitting for the flick back up but we jjust keept goiing rouund. Everything endd up on the ceiiling. Thank God I ws strappped in my chair. My hair was hannging up and I felt he blood rushhing to my head.
   All everything is everyjwerer iif it weren't so tragic it would be funny. Even the floor board accesses have ended up stuck to the roof and the bilge pumps are oout of action but I dont think that is too bad as we haven't taken on too much water. I have just triied to clear all the saucepans and everything round the corner. I have a few cuts but nothing serious but he boat is a disaster – no way am I going on edeck = If Ihad been up there then I would have been derowned. Please just keep talking – I am sorryi you are tired by I need you desperately.
   If i get htrough this I shan't care about carring on I shall just be glad to e alive.
   Please keep talking al the time – don't stop.

....

....

02 MAR 22:45 FROM: BT INMARSAT-C FAX   TO: PETER HARDING
....

Yes I am cold but I don't thnk I can go to bed – at least i my chair I amheld in place – all the cushions are all over the palce. ther are broken pots all over the palce saucepans stuck everywhre, there is blood and =god knows what else spalttered over te h computer hte ceiling everyhing nad yet I don't seem to be bleeding muhc. No I think I will have to stay here. I don't knowo hwere the wind is anymre because the mast head unit is obviously broken.

....

....

02 MAR 23:34 FAX TO LISA   FROM: DAN AND GWEN CLAYTON
....

Hello sweetheart,
We hear you are in trouble. Everybody is praying for you.

All our love, Mum and Dad.
xxxxxxxxxxxxxxxxxxxxxxxxxxx

....

3 March (Day 168)
_____

....

03 MAR 00:33 FROM: BT INMARSAT-C FAX   TO: PETER HARDING
....

Peter
Its amzing but we are stll OK. Gow wlliing we'll beO K.

....

....

03 MAR 03:20 FROM: BT INMARSAT-C FAX   TO: PETER HARDING
....

sTill capszing but still heeere.

....

---

03 MAR 10:15 FAX TO LISA   **FROM: PETER HARDING**

LISA, PLEASE LET ME KNOW YOU ARE OK. HAVE SENT OVER TWENTY FAXES BUT HAVE NOT HEARD FROM YOU SINCE 0405 HRS – OVER SIX HOURS AGO. PLEASE PLEASE PLEASE GET BACK TO ME.

PETER.

---

03 MAR 13:10 FAX TO LISA   **FROM: PETER HARDING**

LISA – PLEASE PLEASE TELL ME YOU ARE ALIVE! GOD, LISA, PLEASE BE OK – HAVEN'T HEARD ANYTHING FOR OVER NINE HOURS!

---

03 MAR 13:45 TO: YACHT *SPIRIT OF BIRMINGHAM*

FAX to Lisa Clayton from Falmouth MRCC
Dear Lisa
Your Project Director Peter Harding informs me that he has received no response from you for nine and a half hours. Could you please advise this office if you are OK. Do you require assistance?

Mike Collier,
Falmouth Marine Rescue Co-ordination Centre.

---

03 MAR 13:36 FROM: BT INMARSAT-C FAX   **TO: PETER HARDING**

Peter, I am OK – sending to office and flat. Will speak again immediately when sent message to MRCC Falmouth.

....

03 MAR 14:45 FROM: BT INMARSAT-C FAX   TO: PETER HARDING

....

Yes I am OK – I remember being jolted with the capszie then hitting the ceiling and having all the tins and everything come up to hit me. I reckon I knocked my head and it put me out. I've gt the most cracking headache. Sorry about that, I really thought it was only a few minutes since I last wrote. I have notified MRCC at Falmouth.

the boat looks a wreck but I t hink it is mostly superificial. Impossible to walk below becaue of teh debris and I can't get anywehre near the engine room to check anything in there. I have just pulled all the ropes back in again.

I am so sorry to have caused all this wrorry – do I need to contact my parents?

Yes I am happy tooo – I prayed to God last night to let m e live guess he must have heard!

God what a mess, everywehre is complete chaos.

....

....

03 MAR 15:00 TO: YACHT *SPIRIT OF BIRMINGHAM*

....

FAX to Lisa Clayton from Falmouth MRCC
Lisa,
Glad to hear you are OK. Could you please advise us of your condition and exact position. We have received a distress signal from a BOC boat *Henry Hornblower,* and have been unable to make contact with the skipper Harry Mitchell. Also distress messages have been received from the Japanese contender of the race. The Chilean Navy are co-ordinating the rescue. We think you are approximately 300 miles from *Henry Hornblower* and 200 from the Japanese yacht. Please give an idea of the weather conditions, sea state, etc. and possibilities of assisting.

Mike Collier,
Falmouth Marine Rescue Co-ordination Centre.

....

03 MAR 15:45 FROM: BT INMARSAT-C FAX   TO: PETER HARDING

I must say my nerves are hsot to peices but apart from total chaso I think we can sail eventually though conditions are still bad.

About the BOC guys I need to know where they are and what there problems are – ASAP, will stand by for that – I also need to know fi they have inmarsat. If so how do I contact them direct – if not details of the frequencies on SSB if they can communicate.

I need details urgently

will wait to hear

03 MAR 16:30 FROM: BT INMARSAT-C FAX   TO: PETER HARDING

OK got your message about *Hornblower* – will wait for more ino. What about the Japanese yacht?

So sorry for all of this – bet you've been to hell and back. Let's just hope the wind doesn't keep rising as I am nto sure we have seen the end of it yet. I am just concentrating on tidying up – too much wind to sail yet and anyway I dont' know hwich way I am supposed to be headed.

I remember seven capsizes and two rollovers – so very glad to be alive.

03 MAR 16:50 FROM: BT INMARSAT-C FAX   TO: PETER HARDING

I am OK – obviously badly shaken but OK. I am trying to clear up some of the debris whist I wait to hear about the BOC boats. weather is stil not good – I am not sure it isn't getting up again – got about 45–50 knots at the moment

03 MAR   FROM: BT INMARSAT-C FAX   TO: PETER HARDING

Got your message – but I can't possibly sail off in the opposite direction if he might still be alive. I couldn't bear to do that.

Is someone polling me ont he inmarsat? I can see by the lights that something iss sending or retreiving signals on a regular basis.

Will wait to hear back from you. Have managed Have managed to clear th eengine room – nothing too dreastic and I ahve the engine running now to top up the batteris as they were flat – so at least hat is working.

....

....

03 MAR 17:01 FROM: BT INMARSAT-C FAX   TO: PETER HARDING

....

Peter

Yes Falmouth have suggetsed that I am not in the bst position to help and so carry on BUT I CAN'T unless I am sure someone else is better placed. I know it's not waht you want to hear but hope you understand. The record means nothing now and I might be Harry's only chance

Lisa

....

....

03 MAR 17:19
FROM: BT INMARSAT-C FAX   TO: GWEN AND DAN CLAYTON

....

Hi Mum and Dad

I know you know I am OK = this is just to say Hi. Things still aren't good but at least whilst there is absolute chaos everywhere what I can see appears to be superficial damage rather than anything else. Feel rather shaken up but so glad to be alive and thankful that *Spirit* is so strong.

I am still not sailing – is still a force 9 or so, which is nothing compared to what it was but it will take some time to organise things enough to get going, and I shall obviously wait to hear about the two boats in trouble in case I can help there. Anyway, thanks for your two messages yesterday – it helped a lot – I was so scared.

I love you both very much – send my love to everyone else too
xxxxxxxxxxxxxxxxxxxxxxxxxxxxxxxxxxxxxx

....

03 MAR 23:45 FROM: BT INMARSAT-C FAX   TO: PETER HARDING

Hi Peter

No nothing more than cuts and bruises. My head is the worst but is better for the Nurofen – must have really cracked it!

Yes I am continuing to tidy up bit by bit,t he weathaer is squally, lots of violent hailstorms but I am hoping that it is generally getting better – I am not sure.

Barometer has risen a lot but the wind is still very strong. Feeling rather knackered to be completely honest but I guess that isn't surprising.

I will do a bit more tidying up and then see what the situation is. God I really feel for poor Harry Mitchell – I wonder if he is still alive. How luck I am.

4 March (Day 169)

04 MAR 03:30 FROM: BT INMARSAT-C FAX   TO: PETER HARDING

the bloddy rudder is bent on the self steering but no way I can fix in this will try and sail anyway

04 MAR 05:44 FROM: BT INMARSAT-C FAX   TO: PETER HARDING

No I am not heading for Harry. Yes I am trying to get sialing but I've got a few more problems than I realised

04 MAR 11:45 FAX TO LISA   **FROM: DAN CLAYTON**

Hi sweetheart,

So so relieved to learn you were still there. I'm sure things are pretty horrendous but both you and *Spirit* have proved you can survive.

I know you must be scared and frightened but if you can come through something like this then you have the ability to make it.

We are both just glad that you are still there to talk to, and hope and pray that whatever problems you have to face, you will come through in the end. Our thoughts are with you all the time and we look forward to seeing you safely back home.

All our love, Sweetie,
Mum, Dad et al.

04 MAR   FAX TO LISA   **FROM: SARA SIMPSON**

Lisa darling,

Thank goodness you are alive and OK.

I had a feeling there was something wrong when I woke up this morning and it was confirmed when you signed yourself using my name! But I believe you will be OK now. I can't tell you how I just know it inside. You're going to make it, Lisa.

I am sure conditions must be pretty horrendous and I am sure you are frightened but you have come through the worst. Just remain calm and have faith in yourself.

We all pray for you every day.
We love you, Lisa.
Sara, Anthony, James, Adrian and Richard.

04 MAR 15:00 FROM: BT INMARSAT-C FAX   TO: PETER HARDING

Peter
I am sailing slowly becuase I am nervous but I am sailing and heading for the Horn

04 MAR   FROM: BT INMARSAT-C FAX   TO: PETER HARDING

Yes I am fine – still shaky and a bit unsure of yself but we are sailing, though finding it difficult to keep course. I'm not even sure what course e are making at presentas I can't get the compass to agree with the GPS satellite fax.

I have backed the staysail to try and help us steer against the bent rudder but it is all rather nerve-racking.

I have managed to find the top of the cooker, and all the gas lines appear to be OK so have been able to make a hot drink, in the only mug I can seem to find at the moment.

I have responded to MRCC Falmouth and told them I am carrying on as suggested.

I have salvaged what I could from the First Aid kit and managed to disinfect my cuts etc and bandage myself up – not very well but at least I can use my hands without bleeding all over the place.

04 MAR   FROM: BT INMARSAT-C FAX   TO: PETER HARDING

Peter if that is you sending it didn't come through

04 MAR   FROM: BT INMARSAT-C FAX   TO: PETER HARDING

Peter are you trying to contact me

....

04 MAR   FROM: BT INMARSAT-C FAX   TO: PETER HARDING

....

I am not receiving any text, leave it a while and try again later.

....

Ironically, although terribly tired I'm unable to sleep for long. There's too much going through my mind. I get a surge of panic with every wave that surfs us along or breaks on the boat. It might be my imagination but the wind seems to howl in the rigging in a particularly eerie way.

Every time I shut my eyes all I can think of is Harry Mitchell and his boat *Henry Hornblower*. Are they still there or are they smashed to pieces? Tears keep welling up inside and I've got a lump in my throat. Oh please God let him be alive.

Since I can't sleep I've tried to keep myself busy tidying up more. It's pathetic really, being so tired I seem to be working in slow motion, but anything achieved is better than nothing. One of the worst things is that everything is horribly wet, even my chair won't dry out. There's water constantly dripping from the roof lining and running on to the computer and all the other instruments. All the cushions are sopping wet, and my sleeping bag's soggy.

I'm really worried about the self steering but know I can't fix it till conditions are calmer. I can't attempt to switch to the autopilot as the charging system for the batteries isn't working and the batteries are practically flat. I'm having to manage without instruments. I know the windvane must have gone from up the mast along with the aerials for the VHF but hopefully the SSB radio will still work.

On deck both the life raft and EPIRB distress beacon were dislodged and almost out. Carefully I managed to untangle the ropes around them and get them both resecured.

Some of the stanchions had been bent right over and were preventing easy use of the winches. I managed to straighten them a bit but will replace them when I get the opportunity. The sprayhood's completely flattened and distorted. I'd found that out the first time I tried to go on deck – I couldn't shift it. It would have been easier to take it off altogether but instead I managed to bend it back a little so that it would give a bit of protection although it did mean that it was difficult to use all the rope controls and winches beneath it.

I can't do any more, I just have no energy left. It's so terribly depressing looking at the mess, that it's making me feel even more drained. I know I ought to get something to eat to give me some much-needed energy but I don't know where to start digging around for all the necessary things to make an easy meal. So I've settled for a couple of Mars bars and a large glucose drink.

Oh God, what a horrible mess.

5 March (Day 170)

Managed to get a couple of hours' sleep cuddling Edward, my teddy bear, and felt a little better. I spent a couple more hours sorting through the heap of things shored up in the heads where I had thrown them in a bid to clear some space in the rest of the boat.

Conditions are not good and once again the storm jib is sheeted flat.

I've managed to clear out the collection of things in the bilges and found some useful bits of kit like a tin opener, some tools and a few bits of clothing. The bilge water was very milky but I couldn't see why. The bilge pump still wasn't working but that's probably to do with the electrics.

The water coming through the lining is a real problem. It's still dripping straight on to all my equipment, including the computer screen and some of the keys aren't functioning. The screen's also worse.

....

05 MAR   FROM: BT INMARSAT-C FAX   TO: PETER HARDING

....

Dear Peter

Not receiving your files at the moment, could you please try and resend.

Hardly made any progress in the night – it's very unsettled here.

There is no point giving you a total list of all the damage – I just wouldn't know where to start, and anyway apart from the fact I am too tired to think I am having problems with the computer. I can only see the few lines I am working on and not go back to see what I have already written.

I have faxed Portishead to ask them not to allow any more messages to come through. I can only read the preamble and not the message, which is just infuriating me. Please keep all your faxes to just six lines. Portishead are being wonderful though and I have promised to keep them updated on my progress and condition until I have rounded the Horn.

I am not at all happy at present – in fact I feel horrid. I seem to feel constantly nervous and am even less confident today than yesterday. But I am so tired and there are so many problems. I am just hating it and having to dig really deep. It's a good job I have no option but to just carry on as otherwise I would get off and say enough. But I can't, which is probably a good thing. I have no choice but to keep going and hopefully as time goes by I will regain some sense of balance about everything.

....

6 March (Day 171)

I spent some time trying to fix the heater but then I realised that the batteries were flat again so there was no point in pursuing the heating till I had remedied power. The towgen was trailing but not turning, so I pulled that in. The prop gen was not turning, so I was getting no power from that. I switched the engine on but nothing. Not a flicker. I couldn't believe it. It had worked the other day. WHY NOT NOW?

I checked all the wiring, the starter motor, everything, but nothing would get it going. Peter got in touch with Nick Nutt who had done the electrics and we worked through everything till it was fixed. I was like a child working on instructions, incapable of thinking for myself and needing step by step instructions. I just felt dead on my feet.

The engine fixed, we started on the heater, and Peter worked with me for hours trying to find out what the problem was, and in the end we had to give up.

It might have helped if I could have found the manuals but they are still missing.

I've written PLUS EST EN VOUS in large letters and stuck it up in the cabin. Every time I feel beaten I shall look at it in the hope it will give me the extra boost that I need and instil in my mind ... THERE IS MORE IN YOU.

7 March (Day 172)

Overnight I wrapped the computer up in my driest fleece and put a water bottle inside that. It didn't seem to do much good apart from the fact it wasn't any worse.

The wind was lighter so I put some of the foresail out but it wasn't long before it ripped and I had to bring it in. I went to pole out the staysail with my new small pole only to find it wasn't there – it must have been washed over the side in the storm, so I was forced to revert back to the storm jib. The seas still seem to be racing by, the barometer's dropping again, and I'm constantly scared we're going to broach. It's like living a nightmare. It seems incredible that I so recently felt confident about everything. Instead of enjoying that surging when a wave picks us up, now it fills me with terror. I seem to spend my life holding my breath, shutting my eyes and saying, 'Please God . . .'

Nothing's working properly, in fact everything's getting worse. I spent ages on the heater again and finally put it to one side with disgust. I went to have a wash to try and freshen myself up but found that I was right down on water. I went to make some, only to find I couldn't get the pressure I needed, and to cap it all the engine spluttered and died.

But I'm still alive – all I have to do is keep going. It doesn't matter how slowly, just as long as I gradually get closer to the Horn and out of the Southern Ocean. But I'm worn down, and so tired. I feel faint with hunger and know I should eat properly but all I can seem to manage is dry biscuits and Mars bars.

8 March (Day 173)

My hands are in a terrible state. It's impossible to keep the cuts clean and they're all swollen and very very sore. Doing anything with them is almost unbearable. I'm also finding it difficult to walk. My feet are horrendously painful and swollen. I don't dare take my boots off as I know I would never get them on again. I just want to be somewhere else, where I am safe, and warm and dry. But I'm not. I've just got to cope with the situation as it is. I'm alive, with a boat that still sails. I've been lucky and I'm not going to waste that luck. I will survive and get home.

However scared I am, however pathetic I feel, I *will* get back. I WILL!

I'll do more tidying up, the sort of thing that requires no mental effort, like cleaning the roof lining that's covered in a mixture of what looks like golden syrup and disinfectant splattered with now bloated raisins. Looking round I can see many things I haven't noticed before. A saucepan jammed between the roof and the top of the electrics control panel, broken pieces of something now unidentifiable stuck everywhere.

1800 hours: I decided that regardless of how tired I was I couldn't leave the problem of the engine any longer. If I don't top up the batteries soon they will be completely dead and I'll lose all contact with the outside world, as well as lights and instruments. I also need to make water. If I'm careful I might have enough to see me round the Horn but then I will be without. Without water I'll be unable to continue. All my spare containers were damaged in the storm and leaked.

I checked the fuel filter on the engine and saw it was completely full of dirt. I managed to get it off and back on again but when I went to prime it again I couldn't bring any fuel through. Volvo and Nick Nutt have been on standby for sixteen hours as I've frantically worked on it, liaising step by step with Peter.

....

08 MAR   FROM: BT INMARSAT-C FAX   TO: PETER HARDING

....

Peter,

Listen, if we lose touch don't panic. The batteries are now dreadfully low and unless I manage to fix the engine soon they will not give enough power to send messages. Please send me details of how I can switch the batteries around in case I have to use the engine starter batteries for emergency domestic power. God, I am so glad they welded them in place – I dread to think what might have happened otherwise!

Anyway, you can be sure that I will be so so careful. I shall take it slowly and not take any risks. Think of the positive side: at least after that fright I shan't be tempted to do anything crazy. Someone is polling me and I think it is the Chilean Navy, so they should be able to keep you up to date on whereabouts I am.

Main thing is not to worry.

In the meantime, yes, let's just keep working on the engine, but I am now having to work by torchlight so it is a little more complicated.

....

9 March (Day 174)

I couldn't bring any fuel up to the filter and we decided that the fuel line must be full of dirt. It was in a very difficult place to work and impossible to try and clear the pipe unless I bent it up.

Praying that I wouldn't do more damage, I lay flat on the floor, angled the pipe towards my mouth and started to suck and blow down the pipe. It was obviously blocked, as I could do neither to any effect. I tried and tried but eventually gave up feeling dizzy and lightheaded. I flopped down on the bunk feeling defeated. I couldn't think of any other way to do it. And there wasn't. So I got up again and kept trying. Eventually I heard bubbles and knew I must have cleared it. Great, all I had to do was to suck some fuel through. I swallowed quite a bit in my enthusiasm but soon had the filter full and then I bled it through the system.

09 MAR   FROM: BT INMARSAT-C FAX   TO: PETER HARDING

Brumm brummm!

We had been working solidly for fourteen hours, and it had all been worth it until I heard the rise and fall in revs. Air had to be getting in somewhere and I wearily went back to look at it all again. The problem was pretty easy to find: the bleed screw on the mail filter was leaking fuel. I tried wrapping it in PTFE tape but no good. So then I put more on. Still no good. I dried it off, screwed it in and covered it in Wrigley's chewing-gum. Whether I didn't wait long enough or whether I hadn't completely got all the diesel off I don't know, but that didn't work either.

Peter was busy liaising with the specialists about what else could be tried. I got a little tired of waiting and sent him what I thought was an amusing fax.

09 MAR   FROM: BT INMARSAT-C FAX   TO: PETER HARDING

Don't worry, I have fixed it with super glue!

Peter wrote back half an hour later to say OK but please don't do anything in future unless you have checked first, you might well have got it into the injectors.

I was giggling to myself as I typed:

---

09 MAR   **FROM: BT INMARSAT-C FAX**   **TO: PETER HARDING**

Ha ha!!! Only joking!!!!!

---

09 MAR   **FAX TO LISA**   **FROM: PETER HARDING**

Lisa,
Well, I'm glad you think it was funny – personally I don't. I have been rushing around trying to get you the best advice and this sort of prank is not appreciated. I am tired and can well do without further worries!

Suddenly my patience snapped. Who the bloody hell did he think he was, speaking to me like that? Well, sod it, I had had enough. I'd been working on the engine solidly for sixteen hours and I was tired too, and if he couldn't appreciate a bit of humour he could keep his tantrum to himself. I sent him an equally stinky fax back.

---

09 MAR   **FROM: BT INMARSAT-C FAX**   **TO: PETER HARDING**

I hope you feel better for your outburst, because you have certainly ruined my day. Don't bother to try and contact me over the weekend as I am switching the computer off in the hope that by Monday you will have overcome your tiredness and tetchiness, and regained at least a modicum of reasonableness.

Peter got back to me immediately and we both agreed that we were overtired; he added that ironically enough the only way to make it airtight *was* to epoxy round the top of the screw.

I was just about to get some sleep when I realised something was banging on deck. The spinnaker pole was flailing around. It had fallen off the mast and the end had sheared off. Great, now I don't have one at all.

10 March (Day 175)

For the first time in nine days the wind dropped, in fact it practically died during the hours of darkness, so at the first light of day I went on deck to have a look at the rudder on the self steering. Everything was shrouded in thick fog and eerily silent. I was still not feeling decisive. If I managed to take it off would I be able to fix it and put it back or would I be left with nothing and even worse off?

I ummed and aahed. Yes I would; no I'd leave it. But when would I have the chance again? No, I'd go for it. I'd do it.

The sea was still very lumpy and the whole thing was nerve-racking. I had just managed to disconnect the rudder when I got the fright of my life. Within a few feet of the boat a huge whale loomed up out of the water and blew through his airhole. How I didn't drop everything I don't know. At one time I would have been quite excited but now I was just nervous. I wished to God he would go away, but he just kept lazily circling the boat as though he were courting us.

I went below to try and replace the damaged parts. I had trouble taking it apart but eventually had it all back together. Brilliant, everything was perfectly lined up and I went back on deck to start the complicated task of putting it back. The wind had risen again already but at least I couldn't see my whale anywhere. I put the rudder back on and really studied it for the first time. Funny, really one would have expected that paddle to be facing the other way. I tightened everything up extra tight so there was no chance of it slipping round or slipping off. When it was all back I sat up on deck and felt pleased with myself. I'd done it, I'd fixed the steering, the wind was now strong again but at least we would be much safer and surer for the rest of the run to the Horn. It felt so good, then my smile died on my face. Of course it looked strange, the whole bloody thing was on back to front.

I didn't know whether to laugh or cry. What a silly silly stupid thing to do. Well, I couldn't leave it, regardless of the weather. Trying to remain calm in the strengthening winds, I started to strip it all again, took it back below, rebuilt it correctly and went back on deck to fit again. It seemed to take for ever to fit it all on deck but finally it was there.

To cap it all the engine went again, and this time it was a different problem: it had blown a fuse on the engine itself. I don't know why, but it didn't matter. It will be easy enough to find out where and then replace it. What's more, there are plenty of spares so I don't have to worry for the time being.

The weather continues to deteriorate and warnings are coming through for storm force 10 due to last two days.

11 March (Day 176)

The engine's now fine and despite the forecasts the weather has improved a lot although it's still foggy. I've repaired the watermaker, which had got an airlock in it from being upside down, and also the high pressure pipe had blown again. I needed to make water so just stuck at it till it was working.

We are now down at 56.23°S 84.29°N.

I've had a message to try and keep a special look-out for Harry. An extensive search has been carried out but no trace found. He isn't yet given up for lost but I'm the only other boat down here. Poor Harry, I can't get him out of my head. I keep thinking how lucky I am to have survived – I'm praying that somehow Harry has been lucky too, I can't seem to accept that he's not alive.

12 March (Day 177)

I'm feeling much more my old self, which is great. This is probably due to the fact that I fell asleep for an incredible five hours! We're sailing along in thick thick fog. It's very eerie and I got a strange premonition that I am either going to hit ice or come across a ghost ship, which I've put down to a desire to find Harry, but the ice is something different. I know that ice and fog often go hand in hand so got out the *Mariner's Handbook* to read up on it.

They say ignorance is bliss and I really wished I hadn't bothered. It's really got my imagination going and I spent ages comparing what I could see on deck to what it said in the book. Yes, there was no doubt about it, I was positive I could see ice blink in the fog. This is a much lighter patch of fog that is a reflection of ice. But I had no idea how close it was. Still, it was enough to make me panic and I asked Peter to check again for any report of ice.

I'm desperate now to try and repair the radar. I've managed to fix the fuse by wrapping it in silver paper (I'd never have thought of that myself). The radar started up and then stopped and gave out warning messages. Everything in the dome is useless, so I can't use it to check for ice or ships rounding the Horn, and more importantly I can't watch out for Harry Mitchell who might be hobbling along dismasted.

I'm sailing blind and I don't much care for it.

13 March (Day 178)

....

13 MAR   FROM: BT INMARSAT-C FAX   TO: PETER HARDING
....

Hi,

Very nasty conditions here – all sail is down apart from storm jib which is sheeted flat and we are running downwind. Hope it doesn't get much worse.

I am down at 56° south, the wind has shifted from south-west to north and now it's coming back again. It has caused a nasty cross sea and I shall be glad to be out of here – it's not the wind so much as the seas which are frightening and running so fast.

Thanks for the info from Bracknell. Yes, it does help – at least I know it is going to remain much the same. God, how I hate the seas down here – I wish I had stayed further north.

Anyway, I am fine. I hope this turns out to be a good week for you.
....

....

13 MAR   FROM: BT INMARSAT-C FAX   TO: PETER HARDING
....

Peter, I have just received your messages on East Atlantic – can't get

through on West Atlantic. My log shows none of my messages received. Please confirm if you are picking them up – I have tried nearly thirty times.
  Sending to both office and home.

....

I was still having no luck and spent two hours trying to get through on the radio via Portishead and Chile Radio, but no success there either.

The push rod on the self steering broke off the gears and I have lashed it with elastic and blobbed some fibreglass on it. I'm keeping my fingers crossed it will hold. The thought of being without it is just too much.

14 March (Day 179)

The wind has shifted rapidly from south-west to north-west then north and now it's coming back again. It's bitterly cold and wet with the spray. My hands are in desperate need of some tender loving care but they're unlikely to get it. The best I can do is to try and clean them a bit better, soak them in TCP, and continue taking the anti-inflammatory tablets. They're badly swollen and weeping but with all the jobs I have to do and the seawater they're not clearing up as easily as normal.

Peter wants something live for the TV but I don't feel up to spending all that time trying to get through to Portishead to link up, and conditions are again so bad that I feel I just have to put all my concentration into looking after the boat. The barometer's still falling, and we're slowly running downwind.

I've managed to get the heater working, which is a treat.

15 March (Day 180)

Unbelievably the wind's from the south-east which is really bad news, and also unusual. I'm feeling a bit of a wreck. My chilblains are worse than ever and although Peter has got some advice as to how to look after them it doesn't really help. I don't have plenty of water to wash them in, I don't have clean dry socks to put on, and I can't keep them in my sleeping bag all day. Mum's sent a message to say that if I can bear the thought I should wrap my feet in rags soaked in urine! At first I thought it was some sort of sick joke so I looked it up in my *Yachtsman's Emergency Handbook* and sure enough it is a jolly good antiseptic. But no way! They might be bad but so are my living conditions. I'm already cold and sleeping in wet sleeping bags and I'm certainly not going to add to the discomfort by wrapping my feet in disgusting rags. I'd rather be jolly uncomfortable and wait for the warmer weather when I can go round in bare feet. I'm sure they'll soon clear up then! After all, I'm only 210 miles from the Horn. Soon the weather should be lovely and I'll be sunbathing on deck and out of these layers of thermals. I can hardly wait.

I decided to treat myself to a little warmth and put my feet in the hot locker. I went on deck, took out the bung I had so carefully put in the exhaust, went back below and switched the heater on. It was lovely. Until, that is, a bloody wave shipped us, and once again the heater was sabotaged. Well, that's it. I'm not going to go through the rigmarole of stripping it again – I'll jolly well manage without!

The rest of the day's gone by in a swirl of hailstorms.

16 March (Day 181)

Copy for Lisa's Log in Birmingham *Evening Mail*.
Looking back since I entered the Furious Fifties, I can't help but think that I would have made a safe and quicker passage by staying further north until much nearer the coast of Chile. The same winds down here create much steeper and faster running seas and have forced me to spend much of my time running downwind without sails in order to reduce speed.

My faith in *Spirit* as a seaworthy vessel knows no bounds but since the storm I have been made very aware of man's vulnerability in this lonely and forbidding ocean. The memory and horror of it all comes flooding back every time the wind reaches force 10 or more and I hear the propeller shaft screaming as we are picked up by the seas and surfed along. The intense heavy weather has obviously taken its toll and I am now having to be much more cautious if I want to make it back home without having to stop for essential repairs. Still, the rate of progress is not bad and whilst I would dearly love to tick off more miles quicker, the priority now is just to get around, and timing has been very much reduced to second place.

Since the storm I have been counting the days until at last I am free of this Southern Ocean. I can't say I have gained any pleasure from this recent sailing – it has purely been a matter of survival in worse than average weather for the time of year. I am sure that some day I will look back on this voyage with a great deal of satisfaction – but I'm not sure whether I shall also feel it was an enjoyable experience.

17 March (Day 182)

....

17 MAR   **FROM: BT INMARSAT-C FAX**   **TO: PETER HARDING**

....

Passed the Islas Diego Ramirez at 0530 – picked up the light eight miles off. The moon came out briefly and I could see the island as well. YIPPEE, now it all seems real – it's the first thing I have seen apart from sea since Cape Town and now I feel great!!!!!

....

I'm just hoping the weather will settle down. It's still pretty horrendous, one hailstorm after another and force 9. The barometer's right down. It certainly doesn't look as though it's about to improve. We've been running downwind and earlier I was steering in the cockpit when a wave pooped us and I found myself standing in a bubbling cauldron of water.

....

17 MAR   **FROM: BT INMARSAT-C FAX**   **TO: PETER HARDING**

....

I can see it!

....

The weather is like April showers: there was a snowstorm like you couldn't believe, then the clouds momentarily parted, the sun broke through and just for a couple of minutes the seas were sparkling and magnificent – then I saw Cape Horn. I quickly snapped some pictures but knew they wouldn't be any good because it was partially shrouded in cloud.

As I stood there on the deck I suddenly felt tears running down my face. I'd made it; God, I'd made it.

I didn't feel like celebrating with champagne, it didn't seem appropriate somehow and I was frozen right through as it was. Then I suddenly remembered I had a present from Ken to be opened on rounding the Horn so I dug it out. Inside was a miniature bottle of brandy, some shortcake, a congratulations banner and a CD. Well, I couldn't play the CD as the player was no longer working, and I didn't feel tempted to put the banner up and add to the existing mess, but I could enjoy a tiny sip of brandy and gorge myself on shortcake – delicious!

I stayed on deck though, as in the short time that visibility had cleared, I had also glimpsed a freighter somewhere not too far off. I lost sight of it again behind the seas but I knew it was there somewhere, and if I couldn't see it, it definitely wouldn't see me. I need to be more vigilant now than ever.

----

17 MAR **FAX TO LISA** **FROM: GWEN AND DAN CLAYTON**

Hi there,
YIPPEE, well done. Proud of you.

All our love,
Mum, Dad et al.

----

17 MAR **FAX TO LISA** **FROM: PETER HARDING**

Well done. Congratulations. You've done it!

Love, Peter.

----

18 March (Day 183)

Portishead Radio sent me a lovely congratulations fax – what a friend they have turned out to be. I've never met any of them and yet they have been there for me. We haven't always been able to make a good link-up but I know it hasn't been for lack of trying. They have quite simply been tremendous, and it has been a great comfort to me. I know I will one day have to meet these people so that I can say 'thank you' personally.

I've been feeling much better today. The wind's still strong and because it's from the south-west we are still straight in its path. I can't wait till I get a bit further north and am sheltered by land.

19 March (Day 184)

Spent the day helming. Gosh, I am feeling so much more like me today. I've decided I'm OK. For all my faults – of which there are few (!) – I have finally accepted myself for what I am. Definitely not perfect, just as vulnerable as everyone else. I need to do things on my own but admit that I am always shored up by the love of others. I am very lucky. I care for other people deeply and am loved in return. I don't find life easy but at least I try. I don't always get things right but then who does? I'm OK – I am happy with who I am.

Peter's checked with *Ocean Routes* and the Met Office, and having given them my intended route up to 40°S they advised me that I would be safer to go quite a bit more to the west. The last reports on the icebergs place them right in my path.

20 March (Day 185)

Got a message this morning from Peter to say that my sister Sara and her family are coming over for my return – how wonderful.

The weather is still not good but it's improved a bit, and we are sailing – what's more, it's nice sailing. It's a little bit fickle but comfortable and not frightening. I'd forgotten that I ever enjoyed sailing!

1930 hours: The wind is now heading me, so I'm left with the awful decision of either heading for the Falkland Islands or risking the icebergs – what a choice!

21 March (Day 186)

Woke up muggy headed but obviously feeling in better spirits. As I drank my coffee on the cold deck I sang a hearty 'good morning' to the world and did my pirate act of one hand shielding the nonexistent sun from my eyes. Surveying the horizon, I announced to the birds, 'I see no bergy bits.'

The weather's still bitterly cold and very wet and I'm just waiting for the day that it'll be warm and dry and I can start to dry the boat out. Even if it doesn't feel it I know it must be a little warmer as I've managed to get my boots off and back on again. When they were off, my feet jerked around with a severe case of pins and needles.

22 March (Day 187)

We got becalmed halfway through the night so at first light I decided to have a jolly good bent at clearing up. I put a tape of Elton John on really loud and sang as I worked. I decided to leave the job of sorting out the cupboard doors which seemed to have swollen and were jammed. Maybe when the weather improves they'll shrink again, but in the meantime it's frustrating.

I went on deck and was still singing to the music as I walked when suddenly I felt strange. My head went muzzy, my legs went funny and I had to sit down on the deck. I felt so incredibly weak and it took all my effort to get up and make my way below. I seemed to be walking and moving in slow motion. I decided I must be hungry, even though I didn't feel it, and went to get something hot to give me some energy. But I couldn't co-ordinate the tin opener. I couldn't understand it and tried for ages to get it attached then found I hadn't the energy to turn it. I finally managed to eat something but I still didn't feel right.

There was still no wind and even though I felt strange I felt I couldn't afford to waste any opportunities so I unfurled the foresail and partially lowered it so that I could sit on deck and try and repair it. It was a pretty lousy repair which seemed to take for ever and I found I was instructing myself – needle through, pull needle out; needle through, pull needle out – but at least it wasn't wasted time.

I think in hindsight it's a great reflection of that sick quip, 'As soon as I get time I shall stop and have a nervous breakdown.' I guess I've been living on nervous energy since the storm and now the pressure has gone it's like releasing a stretched elastic band. I'm wobbly, unsure, not thinking clearly and ready to collapse with exhaustion.

2200 hours: The wind whipped up from nothing to force 9 and I kept wondering whether to put the storm jib up. I had been thinking about it for two hours before sense pointed out that if I had been thinking about it I should have done it – what is the matter with me?

23 March (Day 188)

The wind didn't last long and soon we were back with nothing. I wanted to move, get closer to home, and kept willing the wind to arrive, but it didn't. I tried to pass the time by resting and slowly working on the vast amount of things that needed to be done. I spent three hours making what I consider an in depth and marvellous repair to the car on the mainsheet track which had come right off and was swinging around.

It's worn me out and so I've decided that I need to get more sleep and take better care of myself – three or four hours a day aren't enough to bring me back into good form, and I need to be. Just because I've rounded the Horn doesn't mean I'm home. I can't afford to be careless. I have over 9,000 miles still to go.

24 March (Day 189)

Still no real wind. Even so, my fantastic repair of yesterday didn't last the night. I felt quite amazed that I had spent so long making a totally ineffectual repair and set down to it again with a much clearer mind. Within an hour it was fixed properly and I couldn't help but squirm when I saw the effort and botch of the day before.

I got out the spare windvane and decided to replace it whilst I could. I climbed to the top of the mast and checked to make sure that the clamp was still there. It took me three trips up to get it all fixed but it was worth it when I went below and switched it on – yes, we were registering 0.6 knots of wind which was about right!

The sea has been like glass, not a ripple. I hadn't expected this so close to the Falklands and am now wishing I hadn't discarded the idea of the BBC coming out and getting a helicopter with a range of 200 miles to find me. However, I don't know when the wind will pick up so there's really no point in reversing that decision. Still, I have made the most of the fine weather and put everything up on deck to dry out. How wonderful it will be to have dry clothes and a dry sleeping bag.

The engine filter was full of dirt again and I came up with some weird and wonderful ways to remove the broken bung from underneath, but I shan't embarrass myself by revealing those.

The steering is still a concern, although all I can do is take the compass off every day and pour oil down it to lubricate it. The problem is that the bearing rusted after we turned over and is no longer held properly *in situ*. However, to strip it all is a major job and even then I might not be able to fix it. I will just have to keep my fingers crossed that it'll last. Certainly the rest of the steering is in good shape – surely one little bearing won't bring it all down.

Just to be on the safe side I decided to look at the emergency tiller. This had nicely rusted up, so I cleaned it as I knew the two parts wouldn't screw together. I was horribly tired and couldn't remember if I needed to do anything to keep it in place if I had to use it, so asked Peter's advice.

24 MAR   FAX TO LISA   FROM: PETER HARDING

No, Lisa, I've checked with both Carl and John Pinder. All you need to do is screw it together and tweak it with the stilsons.

24 MAR   FROM: BT INMARSAT-C FAX   TO: PETER HARDING

What the hell's the stilsons?

God, I've really had it. I feel totally worn down so have treated myself to half of the half bottle of champagne that Richard Uridge gave me for rounding the Horn. I've put a spoon in the top of the bottle, put it in a safe place and am saving the rest for another day.

I've wrapped the computer up with a hot-water bottle and am taking it to bed.

25 March (Day 190)

There's been no wind during the day and I've had a marvellous sleep in my dry sleeping bag. It's still cold and having peeked in the mirror I'm rather shocked to see myself looking so pasty and frail. I can't wait to be up nearer 40°S where the weather will be warmer and I can start to get a bit of colour in my cheeks.

I received a file from Peter named 'Alive' and my heart leapt as I automatically thought it was a message to say Harry Mitchell was OK. But it was actually to say that MRCC Falmouth had said that it wasn't unknown for people to be found three months after they had first gone missing. I felt unreasonably cross that Peter had been so insensitive, but of course he hadn't really, which is a clear indication of how horribly tired I am.

We've got a little wind now so I've made sure we're on course and I'm going to crawl back into my sleeping bag to try and warm up again.

26 March (Day 191)

The wind's arrived with a vengeance. Within half an hour it went from nothing to force 9 then started gusting force 10. I can't believe it. It's all or bloody nothing. I feel really fed up. Oh, for some decent sailing.

27 March (Day 192)

Weather is still horrible and we are surrounded by thunder and lightning. It's freezing cold and I am sick of getting so wet. The only place to keep warm is in my sleeping bag but that means taking off my wet gear and sometimes it is too much effort. I've really upset myself by reading Naomi's account of this part of her voyage. She was here exactly the same time as me and was making great progress and already in jeans and a T-shirt. So why aren't I?

227

28 March (Day 193)

The wind is between 20 and 40 knots and heading me. I just can't believe it. It's been a horrible day today: the weather is lousy, the waves are breaking against the boat and I have spent all day unsuccessfully trying to repair the bearing on the towgen. Batteries are low again, I am not getting any power to them and am having problems starting the engine which I guess is because of the amount of dirt in the filter. What a simply awful awful day.

29 March (Day 194)

I woke up this morning feeling rather out of sorts and to cap it all saw that we were heading west instead of north-east. It was blowing force 9 from the south-west so I sheeted the storm jib flat and started to run downwind. The batteries are in the red as I haven't yet found a way to put any power into them, and everything seems to be getting very worn from the hard usage of this voyage. I am getting horribly fed up with this heavy-weather sailing that is not made any easier by the constant stream of things breaking down. I keep working away at everything because I have to, but to be quite honest I feel totally fed up with everything. If it's really true that you are supposed to be rewarded by the effort you put into things, then surely I should be having rather better luck than this. Oh well, I guess things will improve, in fact I feel better for my gripe!

30 March (Day 195)

....

30 MAR   FROM: BT INMARSAT-C FAX   TO: PETER HARDING
....

Hi there,
Well, up until this morning I was beginning to feel like an ideal contender for the Hamlet cigar commercial. But today things are starting to feel different. When I went on deck this morning the sun was just rising and on my left the sky was picturesquely shaded with pinks, blues and purples.

Where the sun was rising the bright yellow of its rays was penetrating the clouds like gold. There was the most amazing rainbow – you often see a full rainbow at sea, but this one filled most of the horizon and was a perfect semi-circle. It was beautiful. There also seemed to be hundreds of tiny birds swooping and flitting across the tops of the waves and altogether it feels like a different world. Tomorrow I hope to cross the 40th parallel where I shall consider myself in safer waters and nearer to warmer climes.

Even the maintenance and repair work is going well today. I think I shall have a shower when I have fixed the watermaker. Roll on the sunshine!

....

I feel a little guilty that now I am in good spirits Peter is having even more concerns at home. His mother has suffered a stroke and is very poorly. He's worried sick about her.

31 March (Day 196)

I sent a fax to Peter's mum today. I've never met her but hope it will help to perk her up a bit. I also sent a fax to everyone in Birmingham. Thousands of letters have been sent to the local paper encouraging me and I feel quite overwhelmed by the tremendous support of all these kindhearted people of my home city.

I spent the rest of the day once again taking the towgen apart and trying to fix it. Hours of effort have gone in already but nothing's lasted more than half an hour before it stops again.

1 April (Day 197)

There's still no wind. We are at 35.3°S 39.1°W and going nowhere! My feet and hands are in a terrible state. My hands are badly infected and I've had to slit them with a Stanley knife so that I could clean the gunge out. Ugh!

Battery power is low and I'm unable to top it up. Neither of the pieces of equipment that produce power from movement through the water is working and the solar panels aren't getting much sun. To save what power

I have left I am having to switch the computer off during the day and just transmit once.

I decided to have one final look at the towgen to see if I could replace the ballbearing and get it working again. I'd already been through all the little puzzles I had been given for Christmas to see if any of those little balls were the right size, but none were. I was lying on the bunk with my head resting on my hands thinking. Surely there must be something else. Surely there were ballbearings inside pressurised containers. What else had ballbearings? I needed something with a range of sizes really. My pearl necklace! Of course! They might not be strong enough in the end, I didn't know, but it was worth a try. Sure enough the pearls gradated in size and there were four the same that were exactly the right size. What a crazy crazy idea – what a brilliant idea!

I spent an hour and a half rebuilding the towgen with the replacement pearl ballbearings by which time there was some wind. So fingers crossed I threw the turbine over the stern and watched in amazement as it started to spin. I didn't actually expect it to last very long, so when fifteen minutes later it seized again I wasn't surprised. But it was important. I had got it working, and psychologically I feel better. I also know that there is simply nothing else I can do to make it work. It needs a new bearing which I don't have. I can now disconnect it permanently and put it out of sight without wondering if I might have got it working if I had tried just a little harder.

1800 hours: The wind's suddenly whipped up to a force 9. Oh God, this is unbearable! The wind is from the north-east and so strong that we are not really making any headway, but I've got no option. If I run downwind I shall be going south-west and back over area I have already covered.

Still, it can't go on for ever – things have to improve some time and it is just a matter of hanging in there until the wind direction changes. Surely I can't be dogged with bad luck all the way back.

2345 hours: The barometer's still dropping, and just after darkness had fallen the steering went. I rushed on deck to find that the locking pin connecting the self steering to the main steering wheel had simply sheared off. We went hove to and I went below to try and think of how to repair it. The only option was to try and rebuild it. After two and a half hours of sorting for pieces I might be able to use to make a repair, drilling, shaping and fitting it back together, I had it reconnected and working. However, I've used up valuable power again on the lighting over the workbench.

2 April (Day 198)

Still force 8 and barometer still dropping. Dropped 16 since yesterday evening – should be going up as I go north.

My repair on the steering is as good as new, which is a great comfort, but I am concerned that everything is showing signs of extreme wear and tear. It all seems to need constant maintenance now just to keep it ticking over.

3 April (Day 199)

It's much warmer and the wind has all but died. We're struggling to make one knot!

At least the sun came out so I could shed some layers of clothing and get a tiny bit of power by setting up the solar panels on deck.

I've been hearing vibration noises and keep dashing on deck thinking there must be a ship about but I haven't seen anything else, just the sea.

....

03 APR   FAX TO LISA   FROM: PETER HARDING

....

Hi Lisa,
Hope things are going OK. Thought you would like to know that some kindhearted person has sent an anonymous donation of £800 to the office – I just wish I knew who it is, so I could say thank you. Bet that will cheer you up!

I will stand by for your transmission.

Keep going, you're doing great!
Peter.

....

There seem to be people sending in bits of money all the time – I can hardly believe the interest and helpfulness of so many people I have never even met. Peter is being inundated with letters sending good wishes, prayers, and any bit of money they can spare – some senior citizens save 50p every week to send to help the costs of the project. So many people are willing me on – how will I ever be able to thank everyone? This project has now involved hundreds and hundreds of people.

I'm starting to get worried about the main steering, which seems to be getting a bit stiff and is squeaking badly. I'm still pouring oil down which is turning into a thick brown sludge and running out all over the prop gen below it. The bearing must be totally disintegrated, it's the only explanation. If only we hadn't turned upside down there wouldn't be half the problems. I really can't imagine having to cope with using that unwieldy emergency tiller.

4 April (Day 200)

I am now parallel with Buenos Aires and slowly working my way closer to home. But slowly is the word. Since rounding the Horn I have only had about fourteen hours of decent sailing. I have had five days of absolutely no wind and otherwise it has been force 9 or 10, sometimes coming from the direction I am trying to go in.

I had really expected to be there at least five days ago, so it is pretty dismal. There's hardly any wind and even the sun isn't out today, but Spirit is gently inching along and any progress is better than none.

Had an invitation from Prince Charles to go to Highgrove in July which has really perked me up.

5 April (Day 201)

Can't be bothered to write a log today.

6 April (Day 202)

....

06 APR   FROM: BT INMARSAT-C FAX   TO: PETER HARDING
....

Hi Peter,
I am heading for Ilha da Trinidade – which I passed on the way down and

ST. JAMES'S PALACE
LONDON SWIA IBS

From: The Assistant Private Secretary to The Prince of Wales

4 April 1995

Dear Peter,

The Prince of Wales has asked me to write and thank you for your fax of 30 March to my colleague Stephen Lamport.

His Royal Highness was delighted to learn that Lisa Clayton has now covered 21,000 miles. He is enormously impressed by this achievement and sends his very best wishes for the remainder of her journey.

Lisa is an outstanding example of what determination and single-mindedness can achieve. His Royal Highness has therefore asked me to send your letter on to Tom Shebbeare, Director of The Prince's Trust, to see if there are ways in which, on her return, Lisa'a example can be used to inspire other young people.

He also hopes - assuming she has returned by then - that Lisa and a partner may care to join him at a Garden Party at Highgrove on 11 July. Perhaps I could send you an invitation to this in due course?

Yours sincerely,

Matthew Butler

Matthew Butler

Peter Harding Esq
Project Director
Spirit of Birmingham
33 Lionel Street
Birmingham B3 1AP

will effectively mean I have made a circumnavigation! Should be there in nine days.

With no navigation lights I am not getting much sleep at night. I am feeling quite jaded during the day so am just pottering and not being too energetic.

Really can't wait to be home.

Hope all is well with you.

Ciao.

....

Looking over the side at *Spirit*'s hull I was disgusted to see a green beard of weed that she's wearing like a skirt. But even worse are the most horrid-looking gooseneck barnacles. Many of them over half an inch thick and about five inches long have literally suckered themselves to the hull. What creepy-looking things they are – huge and black and presumably full of muscle. The water momentarily sways them to one side, then they stiffen themselves out again. I can't even think how to get off the ones I can see, let alone the ones on the underside of the hull which must be causing a lot of drag and slowing us down even more. Last time I had a go I used a paintscraper but I lost it when it slipped from my hand. It looks like I'll be returning home with a full-blown garden and aquarium as a memento of my voyage around the world.

This probably explains why my other source of power isn't working. The prop gen can only work when the prop shaft is freely spinning in the water, and normally at about 3 knots this is excellent. However, we're currently doing 5–6 knots and the prop shaft is not turning at all, so presumably the barnacles have embedded themselves in there. Producing power for the batteries is becoming a real bloody headache.

7 April (Day 203)

Still just a breeze – not even making 2 knots. Trying to fix prop gen or anything to get power into batteries.

1930 hours: Still no wind – it's almost unbelievable. Today has been a gentle breeze of around 7 knots which isn't enough to move us very far and neither is it enough to keep me cool. The transition from freezing cold to this baking heat has happened so quickly that I am finding it rather difficult to adapt. Not that I should be complaining – I've been dreaming of warmer weather for ages but I would like some wind as well.

I was nearly tempted to go for a swim today but just as I was about to dive into the inviting blue of the sea I saw a dark shape which turned out to be a shark – that's put paid to any further mad inclinations I may have to go swimming, but also to going over the side to try and clean the barnacles and weed off the hull. I shall just have to be content with getting too hot and cooling off with a bucket of seawater. I shall also have to accept going more slowly with the effect of the drag on the hull.

I might be prepared to have a go at most things but taking on sharks is something else!

8 April (Day 204)

Peter sent me a booster fax, but with just a gentle breeze progress is awful and I am not in good spirits. I'm trying my best to relax but find that after an hour or so I get uptight.

9 April (Day 205)

Just sixty miles in two days.

Repaired the spraydodgers and started to clean the rust marks off the deck and hull so we look smart when I get back.

10 April (Day 206)

....

10 APR   FROM: BT INMARSAT-C FAX   TO: PETER HARDING
....

Hi Peter,
It's very muggy but at least I'm getting a bit of a tan. Wind at last! Not much but better than nothing. I'm not even too depressed that

it's from the wrong direction – at least we are moving. My fingers are crossed that the wind will now shift a bit further round and give me a bit of a good run before it inevitably dies again. Still, with any luck we will knock forty-five miles off by the end of this twenty-four period, which is by no means brilliant (my poorest estimate for this leg was ninety-six miles per day) but it's a vast improvement on the five I achieved yesterday. I think I have just got to accept that this is going to be a frustrating leg.

I'm trying to restrain myself from looking at the fabulous progress Naomi had up here at exactly this time of year. I feel really envious and though it is like rubbing salt into the wound I can't help but keep comparing and thinking how unlucky I am.

I am really looking forward to the south-east trades which should give me some wonderful sailing but am dreading the doldrums – Naomi got stuck there for just two hours – I wonder how many *days* I'll be drifting around!

Really looking forward to seeing you when I get back.

....

11 April (Day 207)

The last week has been frustrating in the extreme. I've hardly made any progress and have now entered an area where there is unlikely to be much wind at all.

With no battery power for lighting, the long dark nights mean sleeping or thinking. Last night my mind was too restless to sleep – I seemed obsessed with the fact I am getting nowhere. Visions of being stuck here for months and never having enough wind to sail out of it were plaguing my mind. My stomach uptight, I got up and went on deck to spend the night looking at the sky and willing the wind to arrive. I felt lonely up there so grabbed Bernard my stuffed dog and took him up to watch the dawn.

The rising of the sun didn't bring a rise in my spirits, it was obviously going to be another almost windless day and those ridiculous fears haven't been erased from my mind. Today has been sheer hell, just a gentle breeze coming from the direction I am trying to get to meaning a pitiful twenty-four-hour run of eight miles, and only five of those in the right direction.

The next 600–1,000 miles could conceivably be as bad – I hope they aren't but as each day passes I feel fated to stay here for an eternity. I can't bear the thought – I am desperate to be home.

12 April (Day 208)

Today has been disappointing to say the least. I find it impossible to enjoy anything because this feeling of total helplessness and utter despair that we are making no progress has totally engulfed everything else.

In a bid to break myself out of it I have tried to keep busy but my soul isn't in it and all too quickly I find I don't have the energy or willpower to do any more.

I haven't taken up Mum's suggestion to 'make the most of the nice calm weather and paint my toe nails' but at least it made me laugh.

13 April (Day 209)

The wind's really picked up and I'm once again fighting into 35 to 40 knot winds. WHEN WILL I GET SOME DECENT WEATHER!

14 April (Day 210)

YES YES YES! Peter Berry, Provost of Birmingham, said a prayer for me to get better winds, and it's shifted to the west. How wonderful. Oh thank you, God.

15 April (Day 211)

I'm regretting that I have been so open about my feelings of the moment in the faxes I send to Peter. It makes me feel better to say how I think but it leaves him worrying.

Sometimes I am lonely, sometimes frustrated, but others I am happy and feel great; my mood easily changes. It isn't all doom and gloom, but it might well seem like that from my messages, and it is obviously taking a toll on Peter's health – he is apparently suffering from shingles with all the worry he's been through.

16 April (Day 212)

Wind is light and variable.

17 April (Day 213)

Totally becalmed. The only movement anywhere was a whale circling the boat. It was about the same place I saw one on the way down, and I felt sure it was the same one so I sat on deck and talked to him about where I'd been since I saw him last. I've always been envious of Dr Doolittle!

18 April (Day 214)

If it wasn't for the fact that I want to make this trip in a reasonable time, if I didn't have Naomi's book to keep reminding me how badly I feel I am doing, *and* if I didn't know I should be enjoying the beautiful and constant trade winds, I might find life a bit easier to swallow. After all, the days are quite pleasant. I've seen whales, sharks and all manner of things. But when the most predictable winds of the voyage are not here I feel I want to scream. The unprecedented lack of wind must surely mean better odds tomorrow but I am beginning to find it difficult to convince myself. I should have been at Ilha da Trinidade a week ago. If the wind got up now I could be there tomorrow but at my current rate of progress it will take anywhere between a week and ten days.

I keep the sails up just in case I get a light breeze but the noise of the boom going clink clank callankkkk clinkclinck and the sails lazily chanting flaaap flaaaaaaap flapppok fallaaaap is slowly getting on my nerves.

Whatever happens now I shall have to live with a bad overall time and it's depressing.

The computer has finally stopped working altogether. Somehow water came pouring through the hatch – it was strange as there really wasn't any wind and no waves but the computer got soaked and although I've tried I can't repair it.

19 April (Day 215)

I can't get through to the UK on the radio and although I have once again stripped the computer I can't make it work.

20 April (Day 216)

Caught ten gallons of water in a squall so now I have plenty if I'm careful.

I wonder what they are thinking at home? I'm sure they will know I am OK. Won't they?

21 April (Day 217)

Yet another day of northerly winds – how unlucky I feel. To make matters worse they are very light – we're only able to make a course of either east or west so basically we are getting nowhere.

The computer is definitely kaput. I've reset it and put in the spare hard disk but I think it's the LCD display that has had it. Still no luck with the single side-band radio. Shall try again during the night – may have more luck as atmospherics should be better and there will be less traffic on the air.

The sun is out today which makes a change at least – it's been very overcast the last few days.

How much better I shall feel when we are headed in the right direction and making some decent progress. This is no good for my morale at present.

22 April (Day 218)

Tried the SSB Radio for two hours at 2330 GMT and then again this morning at 0530 GMT but no luck. I'm beginning to get worried. I ran the engine for hours to boost my signal but all it's achieved is to use up valuable fuel. I don't know how much is left but it must be near the bottom as the fuel filter is full up to the top with gunge, and I'm worried that if I take it off to clean it I won't have enough fuel to rebleed the system.

Basically no wind at all today – just 2.6–5 knots from the north. I did have an hour and a half of south-westerly 25 knots but then it died again.

I was determined to try everything to get the SSB working so rigged a block and tackle and hoisted myself up the backstay to the insulator for the aerial. However, it wasn't as I thought. I thought it was just holding the wire to the stay and I was intending to cut off the end and make a new connection but in fact the wire was coiled round and round. It looks dreadfully corroded but I couldn't replace it so instead I just sprayed it with WD40.

As soon as I had done so I started to regret it; something in the back of my mind was telling me that oil might reduce conductivity rather than enhance it. But it was too late, I'd done it. I hated being up there; even with a retainer I was swinging around a lot and when I went to come down I found I couldn't very easily, but eventually I was once again on the deck. I then came below deck to get underneath the back stay, cleaned up and reconnected the grounds for the tuner unit, and made a new connection between the tuner and the aerial. Then I thoroughly checked the SSB unit. There's nothing else left to do but wait till nightfall and try again. If I can't get through I will probably have to be sensible and wait a week and hope that I will be closer and in a better position.

One thing I've forgotten to bring is a set of code flags so that I can raise them in the rigging and get messages to other ships. I only need three but it's three more than I have, so I spent the rest of the day making up the three letters I need – ZD2. I haven't made up flags, I've just taped them out on to the back of the spraydodgers. I don't suppose I'll see any ships, but if I do they should be able to read them and hopefully understand my message: 'Please report me to Lloyd's of London.' Then Lloyd's will let someone at home know I am OK.

1600 hours: If I don't get through tonight what do I do? Leave everybody wondering and worrying for one week? Two weeks? Eight weeks? There is no guarantee that I shall see any ship or be able to report I am OK. I've done everything I can on the radio but am not at all convinced I shall get through. I can hear Portishead fine but they don't appear to hear me. The theory is if I can hear them then they should be able to hear me so perhaps I am still transmitting.

The other option if I don't get through is to head for Rio when the wind comes and hope that as I get nearer to the coast I can get a message to someone.

If there is such a thing as telepathy, they will sense that I am OK. I keep willing them to know that all is well.

2300 hours: YIPPEE!!! Got through to Mum and Dad and they are very relieved. Sounded as though they had been under a lot of strain – a search was due to start tomorrow. Thank goodness I averted that. Also spoke to Peter who must have been relieved but didn't sound relaxed – I guess he has been too uptight for too long to feel abruptly better. But for me, it's wonderful. I feel as though a weight has been lifted off my shoulders. It's dreadful thinking that people might be worrying about you, especially when you know yourself that you are OK. I can well imagine the anguish they have been going through. I feel I've really put my parents and Peter through hell on this voyage.

God, I'm looking forward to being back. Arranged to contact them again a week on Tuesday at 0700 or late in the evening. Portishead were great and gave me some simplex frequencies to try if the others are busy and I get short on power. They have been so fantastic, they just can't do enough to help. It's funny but when I'm talking to them I'm visualising what they look like and where they are working, which is ridiculous because I haven't got a clue about either!

23 April (Day 219)

Becalmed overnight. Lovely starlit night but I would rather have been sailing. The sunrise heralded another day without wind so I decided to clean some of the rust off *Spirit* and spruce her up for her triumphant return. I also made a replacement flagstaff from my broom handle. It looks quite impressive, I have to say, so I have flown the ensign and felt extraordinarily proud to be British. I feel good today despite the lack of progress and I guess that is because I no longer have to worry about people thinking something has gone wrong.

24 April (Day 220)

There were some beautiful fish around the boat today and just a light breeze. I was really enjoying myself but the wind has now died. I just can't believe it – where is the wind? I could cry with frustration.

25 April (Day 221)

I couldn't sleep during the night. Every time I lay down I kept thinking it can't be, it just can't be – the wind must be nearly here. I kept going on deck but the sea was like glass.

I feel totally demoralised today. How can I be getting so little wind? I am in the right place, but nothing. How can that be? I feel totally sick at heart, dispirited and although I am trying to keep myself busy I can't ignore the fact that I could be doing all these things just as easily under way. I am hating it so much at the moment that my throat feels constricted with the effort not to break down in tears.

I really feel God has deserted me and I feel very alone and out of luck.

I had a screaming fit on deck today. It really frightens me that I can react in such a wild way. In a normal environment one couldn't do it – it just wouldn't be acceptable. I don't know how I am going to retain my sanity, but in a way I felt a sort of release after this crazy behaviour. I was quite calm again, until I stood on the deck and shouted, 'Wind, please come, *please ...*'

26 April (Day 222)

I made up my mind during the night to give up. Not that it makes any difference. I don't have fuel to motor anywhere but I feel I have taken as much as I can. I'm starting to look how I feel – desperate.

I was already ashamed of my slow time, but now I am weeks behind. My parents and Peter say it doesn't matter, but it matters to me! It's like some sick joke.

I tried to get through to Portishead today but I couldn't, so instead I lay on my bunk trying to read anything to keep my mind calm. I've gone past doing any jobs.

God, it's so horribly muggy everywhere.

27 April (Day 223)

We are sailing very slowly. There is just a slight breeze from the north-east but at least we are moving. Anything is better than nothing.

Feeling tired after a horrible night, I just couldn't sleep.

I've tried to boost myself by making some bread and washing some clothes in seawater.

28 April (Day 224)

Sailing quite well at last and in the right direction!!! What a difference it makes. I feel totally at peace with myself. Sitting on deck just watching *Spirit* sail through the water, with the breeze on my face, the dolphins to keep me company again and the knowledge that I am getting closer to home.

I tried fixing the computer today. Didn't really think I would be able to but just had to give it another try. It all looked very interesting inside but everything seemed OK. The hinge is broken though, so that might be the problem as this does activate the screen. Every time I looked at it I kept switching it on in the hope that it would suddenly start working, so I've now locked it out of sight in a cupboard – out of sight, out of mind.

29 April (Day 225)

Tried again to get the prop shaft generator working but it only seems to work spasmodically when we are making over 6 knots. Do I take it apart again?

It's definitely not the connection, which I wish I hadn't touched, but it looked so horribly corroded. Now I have to make new ones each time I take it off and I am running out of anything sturdy enough to make them with.

Done a lot more work on deck today – she's looking really good but I am worried about the rigging. Some of the toggles seem stiff and I couldn't unscrew more than two of the bottle screws so have sprayed the rest with releasing agent and will try again in a day or so. I hope there's no metal fatigue – I don't fancy the thought of anything shearing off.

243

30 April (Day 226)

Spent the day reorganising below. Unfortunately I haven't quite finished anything. As soon as I start one job I get sidetracked by another, and everything is looking a bit disorganised at present.

Managed to get the camera working again so have done some filming.

I wonder whether I will be able to read any of this tomorrow – it is almost total darkness as I can't afford to use any power or lights at night. All I can see is my hand, and the blue where the pen meets the paper.

Gosh, it's horribly muggy – oh for a shower.

1 May (Day 227)

Up most of the night – very humid and uncomfortable. At 0700 hours listened to the SSB radio but couldn't pick up traffic lists. Feeling full of good intentions, at 0720 I started to take the starboard 56 winch apart but inside is jammed solid. After two and a half hours I managed to clean and strip half of it but the rest of it won't shift. I've sprayed it with lighter fuel, which I hope will help, and put it back together for now.

How I hate that. I felt so positive about things. I'm not feeling like tackling anything else that is complicated now as I don't feel a winner. Guess I'll stick to things I know I can achieve – like cleaning!

I am using the sextant now as a back-up since I am using no electricity at all.

I'm staying out of the sun so I don't suffer effects from the heat but it's still awful. I wish the wind would come.

2 May (Day 228)

After several attempts I managed to get through to Peter via Portishead on a simplex frequency. My parents are in good spirits and they have organised a house for twelve in Kingswear for my return.

I definitely feel more settled now that I am not in touch every day. I am able to get on with my little world and just do the best I can. I love not having that feeling that I 'should be doing better' when I can't do anything to improve my progress. Goodness knows why I kept feeling I should be making excuses for my slow time. I know the problem is within my head, nobody else has commented on it at all, but if nobody knew I was out here it wouldn't matter how long it took. My time is slow, there's nothing I can do about it.

3 May (Day 229)

No wind all night – the sails are just clattering and the noise is driving me crazy. How can I be becalmed again in the trades where the wind rarely drops below force 4 and the direction is constant? I seem to attract these windless days. The only puff of breeze is from the north-east when it should be from the south-east. Still, I feel quite happy in a way and resigned to it. I'm determined to enjoy the rest of the trip as much as I can. Flying the ensign and the burgee of the RDYC today – well, it's not actually 'flying', more like hanging really.

4 May (Day 230)

I just can't believe it. The wind came from the east for a while but now it's back from the north-east and force 2. This should have been lovely sail and a part of the trip that I could rely on for good constant progress. It's unbearable. Oh, what the hell!

I can see a waterspout a few miles to the west. It just looks like a grey funnel-shaped column going from the sea up to the cloud and quite innocent. But it's far from that. It's formed when a whirlwind draws up a whirling mass of water, so I'm glad I'm not over there!

5 May (Day 231)

Part of last night was magic. I put my Walkman on so I couldn't hear the sails clattering about. It was a beautiful night and I happily spent hours just singing along to the stars.

6 May (Day 232)

The wind was mixed till lunchtime. I was just ready to take the midday sight when it started to get very black on the windward horizon. Twenty minutes later it was gale force 8 which lasted for two hours. It dropped to force 5 but I didn't care – I was sailing. The only worry was that it might be foretelling of a worse crossing of the Equator.

The wind continued to go up and down around force 5 and even reached 48 knots at one point. Then it settled from the north and died.

It was a beautiful night – spectacular in fact. There were two ships very close by so I stayed on deck during darkness and kept watch. I am glad I did. I saw seven shooting starts between 0515 and 0700 hours and lots of smaller streaks of light. Fantastic.

7 May (Day 233)

Still no wind – I've hardly moved for days. What can I say about how I'm feeling, apart from desperate? I used to think I was one of the lucky people, but at the moment I feel victimised. I can't imagine ever laughing or smiling again.

WHY WHY WHY do I keep getting these calms? I only ever seem to move in a squall. I really feel at the moment that I am not meant to get back – perhaps God is telling me to give up.

I just spend my time sitting on deck, or lying down below. Waiting, waiting, waiting for something to happen. I am totally incapable of doing anything else. Only one thing matters – wind. All I want is a bit of WIND!

9 May (Day 235)

No log yesterday – nothing to write. All I did today was drop my lighter over the side. I've got only 60 matches to last for hot food and drink till I get back.

1200 hours: So depressing. Wind via a squall at 1000 hours, first time we've made any progress – YIPPEE!

1600 hours: God, what is the matter with me? The only charted danger in the area is a submerged rock. And what do I do? I sail right over it!

I set my clearing line to avoid it. The wind shifted, I didn't adjust for it and suddenly realised I must be over the top of it. I can only presume that the question mark against it is right – it can't be there. Thank God! How bloody stupid. It doesn't matter what the excuse is, or however tired I am, it simply isn't good enough.

The wind died again whilst I was just off Sao Pedro and Sao Paulo rocks – they were above water so I saw those! And then it rained like billy-o for six hours.

10 May (Day 236)

I feel sick with a lousy feeling of foreboding today and I don't know why. Perhaps I am too tired. I only managed to sleep for about an hour and then I had bad dreams. I feel quite stressed from being becalmed so much of the time. I am horribly tired, almost to the point of being ill, but I'm too uptight to relax. I am homesick today and really miss Mum and Dad. Cried my heart out for a while. I *must* try and rest!

11 May (Day 237)

Wind force 2 from north-north-west which quickly moved through north to north-east and then died. It's been raining all day but my face is burning up. It can't be from the weather, as I haven't seen the sun for days. I guess it is self-induced from being so tired and fractious. I feel totally broken today.

12 May (Day 238)

Today has been a nightmare. An occasional light variable wind from the north but strong gusts of wind from the south and it's impossible to make any way. The odd violent gusts are really shaking the rigging and the noise is horrendous. I'm scared this is doing more damage to the rig than anything else, everything is being blasted and left trembling. There's a horrible swell of about two metres which means there must be strong winds around somewhere.

13 May (Day 239)

A horrible swell coming from the south-west. It's like riding one of those roller-coasters at the fairground. But why am I getting nothing more than the occasional gust? If only the wind would settle and become constant, but when it's like this I get a gust that shakes the boat and then nothing. It's driving me *mad*!!

14 May (Day 240)

Had a serious debate again with 'him up there'. Well, it was rather one-sided really and most unsatisfactory. All I want to know is WHY WHY WHY is he doing this to me? What have I done to get so much bad luck!!!!

15 May (Day 241)

Spent the day screaming at the top of my voice. 'WHERE IS THE WIND, WHERE IS THE BLOODY WIND? YOU CAN'T HIDE FOR EVER, YOU CAN'T CHANGE THE RUN OF NATURE LIKE THIS AND GET AWAY WITH IT, SO WHY NOT GIVE IN GRACEFULLY AND STOP PICKING ON ME! ALL I WANT IS A BIT OF WIND FOR GOODNESS' SAKE – I'M NOT ASKING FOR MUCH!'

I felt quite frightened by myself after I had calmed down. I have never lost my temper like this before. Then I started to think that I must consider myself someone rather special if God was spending all of his days making my life unbearable. So it must just be bad luck after all. I popped my head through the hatch and said a rather meek 'Sorry' to the world and tried to get some rest.

16 May (Day 242)

YES YES YES – the wind has arrived from the north-north-east and I am sure it is here to stay. Now all I would like is for it to go a little bit more round to the north-east, or even better east-north-east, then I could make a better course.

17 May (Day 243)

Still sailing!!!!

18 May (Day 244)

Finding it difficult now to wait until I am back, but I'm also feeling apprehensive. The last few years have been so focused on what I wanted to achieve, and once I get home it will all be over. I shall have another piece of blank paper before me and it's a little difficult to imagine what life is going to be like. I am slightly scared of falling into a humdrum existence. Although initially this is what I would like, I don't want it to last for ever. I know now that I need something to be working towards. I don't just want to slip into whatever and find life has passed me by.

19 May (Day 245)

I've decided I'm quite a complicated character in that I willingly let other people do things for me, but then I don't find out what I am capable of. It is only really when I am on my own that I push myself and become more confident and competent. I know we all do it – it's rather a human failing really. It's so easy to let others do things for us that we are quite capable of doing ourselves. We don't do things because we don't need to.

I am scared that I will slither down the slope and become a nothingness. I must have some direction, autonomy and independence if I want to stay me.

I am also concerned about the money I owe. Well, I guess that can be my first task, to pay it off – that should keep me busy for ages!

20 May (Day 246)

Wind still north-north-east – when will it move round, or won't it? Oh well, I am making reasonable progress and even though I am not actually headed directly towards home I am getting nearer. Soon I will be close to the Azores and then I know there are only a few frustrating days before I pick up those lovely reliable westerlies to take me home. Home – I can hardly imagine what it will be like to be able to go to bed at night and sleep a deep sleep and wake up with nothing to worry about except how I shall spend the day.

21 May (Day 247)

Still from the north and now over 30 knots. This is pathetic pathetic pathetic!!!!!

22 May (Day 248)

Perhaps I should head for America instead with this wind. I could soon get there and I could see my sister. How nice that would be. God, I am tired of my bad luck.

23 May (Day 249)

Wind shifted to south-east and is now back to north-east. Surely I can't have lost the trade winds already, I am only on 20°N.

24 May (Day 250)

Seas are really flatter today which is not surprising as we are only getting the odd bit of wind from the north-east. Oh roll on the Azores – I am so looking forward to those westerlies.

25 May (Day 251)

Squally during the night, but that's the only time we moved. Otherwise it's just dead everywhere. Fingers crossed it picks up soon.

26 May (Day 252)

Just a slight breeze from the north-east. We are barely making one knot.

27 May (Day 253)

Super sailing. YIPPEE, wind from the east – not strong but a much better point of sail.

28 May (Day 254)

Variable nothing. Spent the day sprucing the boat up again.

29 May (Day 255)

Wind picked up from the south-west towards the evening. Was tempted to put in a bit of easting but decided to stick to the recommendations per *Ocean Routes* to get the better weather later.

30 May (Day 256)

Great, just *great*!!!! The wind died overnight and when it did come up again it was from the north. God, I'm hating it.

31 May (Day 257)

Making a nice course for Greenland!

1 June (Day 258)

Still sailing, and still not towards home. I want to go home!!!

2 June (Day 259)

May Day relay from Falmouth Coastguard. Nimrod Rescue being effected to EPIRB distress beacon signals at 49.35°N 29.22°W and 50.31°N 29.53°W. God, it's frightening, I shall be up there myself soon.

3 June (Day 260)

Nothing to write about today.

4 June (Day 261)

Wind from the south-west – only force 3 but fingers crossed it keeps with us.

Felt very close to my Nana today – don't know why.

5 June (Day 262)

Spent the day trying to get a nice tan. I have packed my overnight case for when I return as I don't suppose I shall have time when I get sailing again. Washed some clothes in seawater so I shall have something clean to wear when I step off. I've also chosen what meals I want for the remaining two weeks before I am back. I've thrown much of the rest off but there's still quite a bit. The biggest problem is that I have been a bit reckless with the fresh water. I am now right down and unable to make any. Stupid idiot. I'm trying to steam the rice and pasta over seawater but it's bloody useless.

6 June (Day 263)

Sailed well for a few hours but then got becalmed again. Saw two huge whales, what a surprise to see them this far north. Loads of dolphins and porpoises around, it's like sitting in a circus ring.

Broke the wide-angled lens on the camera today, damn it.

7 June (Day 264)

Well, we've moved but not very far. Cut my hair today after washing it in seawater and rinsing it with a cupful of fresh water. Starting to get a bit brittle on the ends, but it feels tons better now, all silky.

8 June (Day 265)

Peter's birthday! Really thought I would be back for this. I've managed to give him a call but it's not the same – why aren't I back to say it in person?

Via Portishead returned regards to Tony Bullimore who is having poor wind conditions in the Med. He is on a race so is very frustrated. I know how he feels. Felt a great camaraderie with Tony – he's from Birmingham too, and he *is* well known in the yachting world!

9 June (Day 266)

Winds cyclonic or becalmed. I just can't win.

10 June (Day 267)

Spoke to Bracknell weather station today. I'm in a no-win situation. The high over the UK means I need strong winds to get near the Channel whichever way I try and approach it. We agreed I would be better to keep going north and hope that conditions will improve. Unbelievable. Bet they are having a wonderful unexpected bout of good weather at home. God, I am missing everyone. I've had enough.

11 June (Day 268)

I really wish I wasn't having to approach the Channel from so far north. I am following advice and heading up to 50° but I am worried about the amount of shipping up here, especially with no power for navigation lights.

Please, please, God, send me some decent weather. I'm tired and don't seem to have the energy to carry on.

12 June (Day 269)

Weather stations advise to try and go south now. This is utterly depressing.

13 June (Day 270)

Been advised to go north today. Oh God, I can't take much more of this.

14 June (Day 271)

Oh scary. One minute it was a dot on the horizon and only ten to fifteen minutes later a ship passed us within a quarter of a mile. It was broad daylight, but no indication that he had seen us at all. What good are half-hour checks when it happens so quickly? Oh God, please let me make it back. All I keep thinking about is that May Day alert last week that was about here. Oh I wish I wasn't on such a busy shipping route. I daren't sleep at all for fear we'll get run down. And who would know? I have no navigation lights at night, but if they are not seeing me in the day what good would they be anyway?

I know that Portishead and Falmouth are asking shipping to be on the alert but I just don't feel lucky – and I'm going to need lots of luck.

15 June (Day 272)

Seem to be a lot of ships around today. I am in heavy shipping lanes now, the UK–New York route. I don't feel safe if I come down below. I'm up and down like a yo-yo. It's like playing chicken on the M6. God, I'm so bloody tired.

16 June (Day 273)

Don't seem to have any energy left. I can't seem to find the drive to continue. I feel I have nothing left to give, as though I have used up every ounce in my body. I just want to give up.

17 June (Day 274)

The wind dropped right down and I felt slow, sluggish and defeated all day.

18 June (Day 275)

Oh God, I don't believe it. Everyone was sure I would have westerly winds until the weekend, which would have been enough to see me home. I've just checked with them, because we were becalmed for a few hours, and before that the winds were stronger than I expected. But now a new low has zipped over from Newfoundland and I can expect to have light and variable winds (which is basically no wind) for a further two to three days at least. And then? Then I can expect easterlies. I'm never going to get home!

19 June (Day 276)

The only exciting thing today was hearing the *baboom* of Concorde breaking the sound barrier.

Spent ages discussing crazy things with Bracknell – the only option to get any wind is to go north round Ireland! That would be mad!

Managed to speak to Peter – told him I rather liked the idea of drifting to Ireland. The thought of trying to hang on in here for what could be weeks just to sail the last little bit is unbearable.

20 June (Day 277)

Becalmed. So near yet so far. So many people are willing me on. It's the only thing that gives me any incentive. Eight matches left.

21 June (Day 278)

Heading for Ireland.

22 June (Day 279)

Now heading for France – will be in the shipping lanes round Ushant unless I tack again soon.

23 June (Day 280)

Five pigeons came to stay today. Made them a home and then left them to it. I couldn't face the thought of them coming down below but they obviously needed a rest. I guess like me they are trying to make progress against these beastly easterlies. Can't remember when I last slept or ate properly.

24 June (Day 281)

OH GOD, I'M HATING THIS! Only 120 miles away – just one day's decent sail. But it's taking me for ever.

25 June (Day 282)

Self steering connection to main steering sheared during the night. Luckily there was only 15 knots of wind, as this time I cannot fix it, it is totally kaput. I've spent hours trying to make up a good jury system but at the end of the day it's a little pathetic. It needs to be redone every few hours now until I am back – if I ever get back. I've still got winds heading me instead of helping me.

26 June (Day 283)

Spoke to Peter. Everyone has been in Dartmouth for days. Some have already gone back home. The BBC are there, and it seems that every journalist and media correspondent imaginable is there as well. I can't bear the thought of them coming out to meet me and being alongside when I am making such lousy progress. I get the impression that Peter is under pressure to let people know where I am, but I am adamant about them staying away, and luckily he seems to understand how I feel.

The thought of watching them all eating nice things and drinking beer and wine whilst I am having to cope with what little I have left is unbearable. I don't want to see anybody at all. I don't want to have to chat charmingly to people I have never seen before, I just don't feel I have it in me. I'm really having to draw on all my reserves to do what little needs to be done on the boat. I want to be left in peace and quiet, and in my own little world. I don't want to share it. I'm just too damned tired. Eighty miles to go.

I was buzzed by a fisheries patrol plane. I saw them swoop down and thought they were checking on a fishing boat not far off but they turned back and buzzed me, dipping their wings in salute as they passed. They sent details back. I hadn't realised that everyone was worried and that a search was under way. I can't really imagine what prompted that, except, I guess, that I am zigzagging along and doing so so slowly that they might have been trying to locate me and can't.

27 June (Day 284)

Saw land today. YES YES YES, the English coast! I'm sure that I should feel something about this momentous part of my voyage but I don't, I just feel tired. God, I am just forty miles away – so close but still ages away. With the right wind I could be there in a few hours but I just don't seem to be getting much closer. *Spirit* is sailing like a pig. I've ripped the sails again trying to make some headway although I guess the problem might be those blasted barnacles. We hardly seem to be moving, however much wind or canvas.

We were accompanied by about fourteen pilot whales earlier but I think they got bored with my slow progress as after an hour they got into gear and easily passed me.

28 June (Day 285)

The batteries were right down but I managed to speak to Peter on the VHF radio.

The BBC have been out in a helicopter for the last two days looking for me and want to film. I agreed to listen out for them on Channel 16.

At lunchtime I heard them call me up – they couldn't find me, but as soon as I confirmed my position they were there within a minute. It was wonderful to see a familiar face: Ian from the BBC. They circled and swooped, coming very close to the mast, and blocking all the wind so that the sails fluttered. I didn't care, it just hit me that I really was nearly home. I got out my present to be opened the day before I got back. A quarter bottle of champagne which I took back on deck and celebrated whilst the helicopter continued to circle and film. They stayed for ages and when they eventually left I cried my heart out. Oh God, I can hardly believe it – I'm nearly home! Soon I'll be able to see my parents.

1900 hours: I still don't know when I will arrive but can't imagine I will make it for the agreed ETA of 1000 hours.

Peter's being very understanding. I think he realises that I have reached the very bottom of my endurance. He's agreed that whatever time I arrive at Dartmouth I should either come straight in or otherwise he'll send a boat out to keep an eye on me so that I can make a better timed entrance the following morning.

I can understand in one way that it would be nice for me to arrive at a convenient time but I don't think I will be there till late in the day and all I want is to be home. I don't want to have to wait about till the following morning. I know that mediawise it will be better if it is daylight when I come in but at the moment that doesn't seem to matter. God, I know it's selfish but I don't remember when I last got some sleep and I'm not sure I can bear to wait another day.

29 June (Day 286)

At 0500 hours it seemed I would be all day trying to make those last few pitiful miles to Dartmouth but at 0745 the wind shifted just enough for me now to head straight there. In a rush of excitement I radioed Peter to say I would be there early. Not surprisingly, Peter was horrified. Having thought I would be hours I was now ready to come in. The BBC had gone off on a launch to find me, with Mum and Dad on board. There was no way I was going to cross the finishing line after all this without my parents present so ironically I had to slow down. I actually went hove to for a couple of minutes then realised it was ridiculous -- what if the wind died? It would be just about my luck to be becalmed just off the finishing line. No, I would be much safer to carry on slowly. I went below to have a wash and change but it seemed the minute I was down below I heard a hooter and shouting – they were there already. It was so so lovely to see them as they carouselled round us.

My parents were in high spirits and relieved it was all over. Dad shouted across, 'I've told you before about staying out late!' They rushed back to land, so that the BBC could relay their filming, and promised to return shortly. The wind had gone lighter and I was starting to wonder whether I would still arrive on time. The sun was out and it was simply a perfect day for sailing. I could see the entrance to the Dart in the distance and a few boats coming out to make the most of the day. There seemed to be a growing number of boats and suddenly I realised they were all headed for me. Surely there couldn't be this much interest when there had been so much uncertainty over my ETA?

The Lord Mayor of Birmingham was one of the first out with the Provost on board, the Navy were soon alongside and saluting me, then the helicopters. I was surrounded in a sea of vessels. I was high with excitement, so grateful to see the harbour authorities there, trying to keep boats out of my path and leading me in. I was nearly there!! So many people; every time I looked there were more – some faces I did recognise, some family, many faces I didn't, but every one of them was beaming from ear to ear. I couldn't believe it when I saw the Canadian ensign, but yes it was true, *Northern Fantasy* was there right alongside – and my close friends, John and Caroline, had come to see me safely home, and their boat was full of many of my closest friends. The only faces missing were Peter and Richard. Richard was apparently filming from some point on the hills above the Dart. Peter – Peter was where we had agreed. He was waiting on the finishing line, so that he could be the first to step aboard. He'd always said he'd see me 'to the line and back'.

I jokingly asked someone if I was heading the right way for Dartmouth. I don't know quite what they thought but they advised me to head for the Mew Stone on the hill. I couldn't help but laugh – did he think I was serious?

The jollity went on and then suddenly everyone was going crazy, champagne corks whipped through the air, the noise of the hooters, claxons and shouting and cheering was incredible. I'd done it, I was home! Peter jumped up on board with a huge bouquet of flowers, champagne, glasses and a ton of bacon and sausage sandwiches. Simon and his crew jumped on to relieve me of the helm and Peter Lucas took a line and started to tow us in. It was simply crazy, everyone was going barmy. Peter had brought me some new clothes and I dashed below to change. The clothes seemed far too big and I felt crestfallen as I said to Peter, 'They're the wrong size.'

Peter looked at me and said, 'No, Lisa, it's you, you've lost a lot of weight.'

So in rather baggy garb I picked up a bacon sandwich and a glass of champagne and we went back on deck where all the excitement was. On the hillside and by the castle people were waving flags and cheering. We entered the Dart to a seven gun salute. Then I gazed in stunned silence. There were tens of thousands of people lining the quayside. Every window and balcony was crowded with people welcoming me home. I couldn't believe it, it was mind shattering. I knew that many people had had to return home as my ETA was more and more delayed and many others wouldn't have had enough notice to come down, so where had all these people come from? It was unbelievably glorious. I was aware of all the simple things that normally one takes for granted: the wonderful splash of colours, the beautiful music of excited chatter and laughter, the smells. So many different aromas: flowers, trees.

It really was the best day of my life. Peter and I stood on the bow drinking champagne as we were paraded up the river to wave to the cheering masses. Gary Glitter was in his boat waving and shouting. It was tremendous. Then we turned to head for the Royal Dart Yacht Club where all my friends, family and supporters were now waiting.

Peter tried to tell me to be careful when I got off. He could see I was excited and likely to leap ashore but having discussed it with several other friends they decided I would have a problem walking once I was back on steady ground. Peter got off, I took his hand, and totally forgetting his words leapt off. I gave him a hug then picked Mum up and swung her round. Then I hugged Dad, Sara and Paul. Quite a few photos were taken then we went to the steps to climb up. At the top was the town cryer who introduced people to me, John, the Commodore of the Royal Dart Yacht Club, all the official party. Lord Mayors, Provost of Birmingham. I was also notified that I had been awarded a Doctorate of Science by Birmingham University.

It was a hectic day, totally taken over by the press conference and interviews for TV and media, but they were all so patient and nice that I didn't mind a bit. By the time I had finished with the media it was almost early evening and everyone had gone. The only break I'd had all day was to have a look at my sponsored Volvo car – she was lovely!

It was sad not to have had time to chat to family, friends and supporters – I didn't really know who had been there. There was just the immediate family left. Someone switched on the television to watch the coverage. We were all rather hyped up but the jabbering fell silent as our piece came on. The rules of the trip meant that nothing could be stated as fact until it had all been ratified, but respectful hush turned to stunned silence as we heard a slight question in Sir Peter Johnson's voice about the fact it had been strange I hadn't seen any ships. How odd. Especially since both Peter and I had spoken to Sir Peter himself on the telephone not long after I had docked when he had congratulated me and told us just to send off the declaration form when we were ready. Oh well, it was probably taken out of context, and was soon forgotten as we all started to catch up on each others' news.

There were some welcome-home parties for me that evening but I knew I was too tired. For weeks now I hadn't slept properly. To go to a party I would need to drink along with everyone else and I decided it was exactly what I didn't need. I'd had enough excitement for one day so settled instead for an early meal and a relaxing evening. Leaving everyone behind I crept away to my hideaway that Peter had organised. Peaceful and secluded, it was like walking back in time. It was perfect.

Professor Sir Michael Thompson DSc FInstP
Vice-Chancellor and Principal

THE UNIVERSITY
OF BIRMINGHAM

Edgbaston
Birmingham B15 2TT
United Kingdom
Telephone 0121 414 4536
Fax 0121 414 4534

23 June 1995

Dear Lisa

Many, many congratulations from Lady Thompson and me and on behalf of the University.

Your achievement is a magnificent one. The courage, determination and strength you have demonstrated will be an example and inspiration to students at the University and we are proud to be associated with your venture. No-one but yourself will ever fully understand what you have been through and the reserves upon which you have had to draw, but please be assured that we do have some appreciation of coping with the sea and thereby can respond to what at times must have been a massive ordeal.

All that is now behind you and you can enjoy the richly deserved accolades which will surely come your way. One of the first will be that referred to in the enclosed formal letter. I am delighted that the Senate of the University have wholeheartedly accepted my recommendation that you should be awarded the Honorary degree of Doctor of Science of the University in recognition of what you have done and the close and friendly relationship between you and the University.

Yours Sincerely

Michael Thompson

Ms Lisa Clayton
Spirit of Birmingham
33 Lionel Street
Birmingham
B3 1AP

MWT/FCA/mm/EF4/S8/179-34

BUCKINGHAM PALACE

26th June, 1995.

Dear Alderman Barwell,

    Thank you for your letter of 26th June to Sir Robert
Fellowes. I have shown your letter, with its message of loyal
greetings, to The Queen who has asked me to pass on her
thanks. The Queen would be grateful if you would wish Lisa
Clayton welcome home on Her Majesty's behalf, and offer her
warm congratulations on her achievement.

Yours sincerely,

Kenneth Scott.

(KENNETH SCOTT)

Alderman Peter J.P. Barwell, MBE.

BUCKINGHAM PALACE

29 June 1995

Dear Lisa,

The Duke of York has asked me to write to you and to say how delighted he was to hear of your outstanding achievement in completing your round the world voyage today. Having just spoken to Peter Betts at the Royal Dart I can imagine the scene as you proceed up river on this glorious summer's day. It will not only be unforgettable for you but for all those who are lucky enough to be at Dartmouth and Kingsweir to welcome you and Spirit of Birmingham home.

Prince Andrew has the following message for you:-

"I was simply delighted to be informed this morning of your outstanding achievement in circumnavigating the world in a single handed voyage which demanded the greatest courage and determination. It will be an unforgettable day for you as you return to the Dart and I offer you my very warmest congratulations.

     signed: ANDREW"

May I join everyone in offering you my congratulations on your return home. Every good wish for the future.

Yours sincerely,

Neil Blair

Captain Neil Blair, Royal Navy
Private Secretary

Miss Lisa Clayton

Home Again

The following day we returned to see that *Spirit* had already been lifted out of the water and was standing on the hard at the marina. She was covered in the most disgusting carpet of gooseneck barnacles. She looked awful and I could now see why progress had finally been so slow. The BBC did some more filming and said that to clear up the suggestion that I might not have gone round would I allow Craig Rich from BBC Plymouth to examine my log? He had been involved in exposing Donald Crowhurst's false attempt during the Golden Globe Race in 1966. I have to admit I was rather peeved that a comment of the day before had provoked things to this extent but was convinced in the end that it would quickly clear things up, which was what I wanted.

Having checked my log and route, Craig Rich went on television to say that he had no doubt I had done what I claimed and then said he would notify Sir Peter as well. It was a great relief that it was all cleared.

The rest of the day was enjoyably passed with my family as we chatted non-stop in a bid to discuss ten months in a few hours. Someone told me that a school of dolphins had followed me into the River Dart – the first time they've been seen there for ten years.

The next day all the family went to the beach for the day. I hadn't been able to find a bikini or shorts that would fit so I purchased a sundress. I felt great although admittedly skinny. Mum reckoned I weighed no more than five stone but I think I was nearer six. I was like a walking skeleton and to my amusement Mum wouldn't even let the youngest of the children touch me in case they unwittingly hurt me!

Most of the following day was spent with *Hello* magazine, doing my first really in-depth interview.

All too soon it was time to return to Birmingham. I think we had been thinking that once I was back we could all relax and have a bit of a holiday, but we couldn't have been more wrong. The office was simply overflowing with post and messages and straight away we were thrown into the frenzy of trying to restore some sort of order.

One thing that needed to be done was to complete the declaration to get the record for my voyage ratified. We were surprised to see just a simple form asking only for the basic details of my name, boat name, attempt made, departure date and number of days taken. We quickly completed it and sent an accompanying letter saying that since a question mark had initially been put against my attempt we would obviously be very happy to supply any additional information they may require, and sent it off.

About ten days later we returned to the office to find we were once again inundated with mail. Amongst it was a letter from the IYRU requesting a vast amount of detail about the attempt. It would take weeks to sort it out. Well, it would have to wait till I had time to sit down for a few days and start to go through it.

Meanwhile it was back down to Dartmouth to get the boat ready to appear on show and be brought back up to Birmingham. We had worked non-stop since our return, and really could have done with a team of people, but since we couldn't afford to pay for any help we ended up doing most of the work on our own, helped out by volunteers as and when they could make it.

In the meantime we were getting the boat prepared for its triumphant return. The Lord Mayor held a Civic Reception in my honour which was a great accolade.

Since I had been back I had been busy but Peter wanted to keep many things to himself and I was getting just a little tired of it. Still I would sort it out after I had made my official return to Birmingham to meet the people.

We turned up dead on time and it was wonderful to see so many people there. I made a short speech and then for the first time since I had been back I was speechless.

Michael Aspel suddenly appeared and I couldn't believe my eyes – yes, he was carrying the much-coveted red book. As he said to me, 'Lisa Clayton, this is your life,' I was momentarily struck dumb. But it was really happening and before I knew it I was whisked away in a car to the studios in London.

It was one of the nicest surprises in my life and I was delighted. In fact it was an evening of surprises with messages and appearances from many people – Gary Glitter, Nigel Mansell, Chay Blyth, Toyah Wilcox, and other schoolfriends. The evening was made perfect by the last person to come on stage. I finally met the lady who had inspired me to go off on my crazy venture – Dame Naomi James.

It was a wonderful evening, and something I'll never forget. It explained also why everyone had been a bit strange. Michael Aspel has a policy not to go through with *This is Your Life* if the surprise is found out before he turns up.

No sooner had we arrived back in Birmingham than we received two phone calls, one from the *Telegraph* and one from *The Times*. Their yachting correspondents had been at Cowes Week, but as there was no wind there was no racing and the only news to report was the gossip in the bars. Rumours were going round about the validity of my trip. I was astounded but quite happily chatted to the reporters.

The next day the office was inundated with journalists and photographers from every national newspaper and TV interviewers with their camera crews. Our poor little two-man office was crammed full. We had nothing to hide, so that was not a worry, but I was also determined not to add fuel to the fire and get cross.

It all seemed to go well, but what we really needed to do was speak to Sir Peter. However, all efforts to reach him were in vain. He was yachting, and not contactable. Over the next few days things got worse but eventually we spoke to John Reed at the WSSRC office and discussed what information would be most useful.

We put it all together and hand delivered it to John Reed, offering to provide any further information that might be required to ratify the record. We liked him and felt sure he would check everything out and come back to us if he needed verification on anything. Neither side was enjoying the situation and we just wanted it cleared up. We would just have to hope that justice would prevail.

Inevitably it cast a shadow over everything. I was after all being accused of cheating, and whilst I knew I was innocent I was sure that even after I had proved it, the smudge would always be there.

Fortunately life was too busy to worry about it. Peter and I had agreed that we made a brilliant team and so set up our own marketing, promotions and sponsorship company in Birmingham – Clayton Harding Associates. I rushed around the country making appearances, opening things, doing television and radio interviews.

Then one day we received a fax from South Africa to say it was in the newspapers – I was now officially in the history books. Peter phoned the WSSRC but they said that an announcement would be made in the next week or two and they could say no more. More and more people sent congratulations.

I went off to London to do my interview for the *Selina Scott Show* and then I got a message from Peter. It was ratified. I was elated. Thank goodness it was all over. The really nice thing was that the media covered it well, when they could have just given it a couple of lines. Now everyone knew. It was a good feeling.

I'm really surprised that I feel exactly the same, maybe a little more confident in myself, but I have retained my slightly zany sense of humour. I have loved being with people since I returned, especially my family and those who helped in some way. And I'll always remember Peter's contribution towards my achievement – he was simply fantastic.

I'm certainly glad that I have done it, as it has proved to me that what I believed before is right – if you want to do something and you want to do it enough, you can probably achieve it, whatever the odds.

I'm not sure where life will lead me next but I shall hold on to my conviction: if you have a dream – Go for it!

I wonder what it's like to walk to the South Pole?